The First Amerasians

The First Amerasians

*Mixed Race Koreans
from Camptowns to America*

Yuri W. Doolan

OXFORD
UNIVERSITY PRESS

Oxford University Press is a department of the University of Oxford. It furthers the University's objective of excellence in research, scholarship, and education by publishing worldwide. Oxford is a registered trade mark of Oxford University Press in the UK and certain other countries.

Published in the United States of America by Oxford University Press
198 Madison Avenue, New York, NY 10016, United States of America.

© Oxford University Press 2024

All rights reserved. No part of this publication may be reproduced, stored in a retrieval system, or transmitted, in any form or by any means, without the prior permission in writing of Oxford University Press, or as expressly permitted by law, by license, or under terms agreed with the appropriate reproduction rights organization. Inquiries concerning reproduction outside the scope of the above should be sent to the Rights Department, Oxford University Press, at the address above.

Chapter 4 draws on research previously published as "The Camptown Origins of International Adoption and the Hypersexualization of Korean Children," *Journal of Asian American Studies*, Volume 24, Number 3, October 2021. Copyright © 2021 Johns Hopkins University Press. Published with permission by Johns Hopkins University Press.

Chapter 5 draws on research previously published as "The Cold War Construction of the Amerasian, 1950-1982," *Diplomatic History* 46, no. 4 (September 2022). © The Author(s) 2022. Published by Oxford University Press on behalf of the Society for Historians of American Foreign Relations. All rights reserved.

You must not circulate this work in any other form and you must impose this same condition on any acquirer.

Library of Congress Cataloging-in-Publication Data
Names: Doolan, Yuri W., author.
Title: The first Amerasians : mixed race Koreans from camptowns to America / Yuri W. Doolan.
Description: New York, NY : Oxford University Press, [2024] |
Includes bibliographical references and index. |
Identifiers: LCCN 2023049336 (print) | LCCN 2023049337 (ebook) |
ISBN 9780197534380 (hardback) | ISBN 9780197534397 (paperback) |
ISBN 9780197534410 (epub) | ISBN 9780197534427
Subjects: LCSH: Intercountry adoption—United States—History—20th century. |
Intercountry adoption—Korea (South)—History—20th century. |
Korean American adoptees. | Racially mixed children—Korea (South) |
Korean War, 1950–1953—Children.
Classification: LCC HV875.5 .D665 2024 (print) | LCC HV875.5 (ebook) |
DDC 362.734089/957073—dc23/eng/20231212
LC record available at https://lccn.loc.gov/2023049336
LC ebook record available at https://lccn.loc.gov/2023049337

DOI: 10.1093/oso/9780197534380.001.0001

For all Korean children and their mothers

CONTENTS

Acknowledgments   *ix*
Note on Language   *xv*
Prologue   *xvii*

Introduction: The First Amerasians   *1*
1. Managing Cold War Intimacy   *16*
2. "The Problem of the Mixed Blood Child"   *44*
3. "Confucius' Outcasts"   *77*
4. Becoming American   *109*
5. The Second Rescue   *136*
Epilogue: Beyond Amerasian   *157*

Appendix   *171*
Notes   *175*
Bibliography   *221*
Index   *233*

ACKNOWLEDGMENTS

As a student, I remember reading the acknowledgments section of numerous books written by scholars whose work I admired and who I aspired to be like one day. I would try to imagine myself in the author's place, thinking about what it would feel like to finish a manuscript of my own or what words I might put together at the culmination of almost a decade's worth of research and writing. In this moment, I am overwhelmed with gratitude. There are so many individuals who believed in this project and whose support helped usher it to completion along the way. From trusted mentors, colleagues, friends, and family—the lines between so blurred and overlapping—I thank you. This acknowledgments section will never do justice to all the feelings I hold deep inside my heart, but I will give it my best try.

This book began as a doctoral dissertation at Northwestern University. However, the spirit of this project was born several years prior, during my undergraduate Asian American history course. It was in that class that my then professor, Judy Tzu-Chun Wu, handed me her personal copy of Ji-Yeon Yuh's *Beyond the Shadow of Camptown*—a book about Korean military brides like my own mother. As I read stories of migrant women who longed for greater understanding from their families, especially their children, I felt I heard my mother's voice for the first time in language so clear and so compelling that it was able to reach me and touch the very core of my being. Then, I knew what history was and what this discipline could be. And it became my life's goal to one day write a book that would speak to real people looking for answers to questions about their own lives. I would pursue that ambition under the guidance of the very author whose work changed my life's trajectory. I cannot overstate how much I owe to Ji-Yeon who chaired my doctoral studies and shepherded me through all of the ups and downs of graduate school as a first-generation college student. She was graciously joined by Bruce Cumings, Nitasha Sharma, and Judy Tzu-Chun Wu. Over all these years, I have benefited tremendously from the generosity and *(x)*   *Acknowledgments*

continued support of these four brilliant scholars. I hope this book will make them proud.

In addition to my trusted mentors, I am indebted to scholarly communities at the institutions of which I have been part. At Northwestern, individuals including Kate Masur, Leigh Soares, Myisha Eatmon, Amanda Kleintop, Jessica Biddlestone, Michael Allen, the members of Northwestern Anubhav, Daniel Immerwahr, Laura Hein, Soo Ryon Yoon, Asako Masobuchi, Joy Sales, Jinah Kim, Kelly Chung, Sarah Maza, Elzbieta Foeller-Pituch, Haydon Cherry, Andrea Christmas, Michelle Bezark, Andrea Rosengarten, Melody Shum, Norman Joshua, Lois Hao, Matthew Foreman, and Alvita Akiboh provided the intellectual and personal sustenance necessary to get through the marathon that is graduate school. In 2019, I was hired as the first assistant professor of Asian American and Pacific Islander studies at Brandeis University. My position was the end result of many years of student activism. I am honored and thankful to be at an institution where the students and faculty both value and understand the importance of my field of study. It is, in many ways, a dream job and Brandeis has been an ideal place to finish this project. I am especially grateful for the support and collegiality of Harleen Singh, ChaeRan Freeze, Aida Wong, Faith Smith, Govind Srinivasan, Michael Willrich, Xing Hang, Dorothy Hodgson, Elaine Wong, Naghmeh Sohrabi, Hannah Muller, Abigail Cooper, Jill Greenlee, John Plotz, Matthew Fraleigh, Sarah Lamb, Ulka Anjaria, Carina Ray, Alice Kelikien, Amy Singer, David Katz, Shoniqua Roach, V Varun Chaudhry, Brian Horton, Wangui Muigai, Gowri Vijayakumar, Wendy Cage, Sue Lanser, Chen Chen, Grace Talusan, Karen Hansen, Gregory Freeze, Gregory Childs, Joel Christensen, Jon Anjaria, Chad Williams, Anita Hill, Toni Shapiro-Phim, Howie Tam, Emilie Connolly, AJ Murphy, Brandon Callender, and Mitsu Salmon. The administrative work of Alexandra Brandon and Kristen Mullin has been crucial to the publication of this book—thank you all for all you do behind the scenes.

Over the course of conducting this research, I have had the great pleasure of collaborating and sharing meaningful intellectual space with a number of scholars in the fields of critical race and ethnic studies, Korean studies, Asian American studies, critical adoption studies, women's studies, and history, as well as artists, activists, and organizers working around important issues like US militarism and empire, and gendered and sexualized violence. For delivering critical feedback, facilitating venues where I could present my research at its various stages, or for simply being a good person to be in community with, I would like to thank Byul Yoon, Juwon Lee, Kimberly McKee, Monica Trieu, Yaejoon Kwon, Katie Botto, Winston Hamel, Yejoo Kim, Taylor Sutton, Eric Yoon, Joyce Kim, Esther Im, Ngoc

Pham, Dan Kim, Dahye Yim, Jongsik Yi, Dong Hyun Woo, Youngoh Jung, Sophie Bowman, Inga Deiderich, Anat Schwartz, Nataly Han, Na-Young Lee, Youn Mee Hyang, Hae Yeon Choo, Yoonkyung Lee, Kyu Hyun Kim, Theodore Jun Yoo, Carolyn Choi, Sina Lee, Hye Eun Choi, Nora Hauk, Hajin Jun, Sohoon Lee, Soon Seok Park, Michael Prentice, David Pomfret, Robert Kramm, Sarah McNamara, Cecilia Marquez, Eugenia Kim, Sandy Chang, Jack Neubauer, Lynn Hollen Lees, John Cheng, Rachel Nolan, Dohye Kim, Minjung Kim, Jung-mee Hwang, Kyonghee Moon, Hyunhee Kim, Ji-Young Lee, Stephen Suh, Lily Kim, Ryan Gustafsson, Angie Chung, Evgenia An, Jee-Eun Regina Song, Boram Yi, Nicole Constable, Jeong-Mi Park, Deann Borshay Liem, Arissa Oh, Yeojin Park, Sangwon Yun, Ji-Eun Lee, Ann Choi, Angelica Allen, Do-Hyun Kim, Sony Coráñez Bolton, Kareem Khubchandani, Tom Sarmiento, Ian Shin, James Zarsadiaz, Elena Shih, Sumi Pendakur, Christopher B. Patterson, Christine Hong, Crystal Mun-hye Baik, Eleana Kim, Kim Park Nelson, Grace M. Cho, Mia Charlene White, Hj Lee, Jessica Park, Janice Park, Kimberly Young Sun, Minyoung Kim, Becky White, Cedric Stout, Chris Eng, Kelly Mee Rich, Catherine Nguyen, Kelly Condit-Shrestha, Hosu Kim, Kori Graves, Kit Myers, Marina Fedosik, Emily Hipchen, Hannah Youngeun Park, the late Soo-Je Lee Gage, and many others. I have learned so much from each of you.

Of course, as historians and scholars of the past, we cannot do our important work without archivists and community leaders committed to those whose voices are often absent from traditional records. At the Social Welfare History Archives, Linnea Anderson welcomed me with open arms and spent so much time sharing with me her amazing collection on Korean adoption during my numerous visits. At the National Archives in College Park, Eric Van Slander guided me through a vast collection of military documents and helped me scour for critical materials on camptowns. During my Fulbright fellowship in 2016, I had the good fortune of meeting Joyce Kim of *Durebang* (My Sister's Place), a camptown NGO in Uijeongbu. Joyce spent a considerable amount of time talking with me, showing me around the camptown, introducing me to the *ŏnnidŭl* at her center, and patiently answering my many questions. In Pyeongtaek, Soon Duk Woo, the director of the Sunlit Sister's Center supporting elderly camptown women, provided me with collections of oral histories conducted by the organization's research team. Without these sources, this book would have never fully realized its goal to recover birth mother perspectives. During my fieldwork, a number of individuals helped me to recruit mixed race adoptees for oral history interviews. In fact, it was very common after finishing one interview to leave with the contact information of several other potential narrators. However, one individual went above and beyond in her *(xii)*   *Acknowledgments*

efforts to support this project. Thank you, Katherine Kim, for all you do for so many of us. The primary sources on which this study is based also include a number of important Korean language sources. Over the years I have been fortunate to have supportive friends like Jongsik Yi, Dong Hyun Woo, and Dahye Yim who have helped me to locate and translate many of these materials. I have also benefited immensely from working closely with several talented undergraduate students on translations including Jung Hyun Lee, Yoo Ra Sung, and Erin Choi. The Women's Studies Research Center at Brandeis University has supported much of this collaboration through their Student-Scholar Partnership Program.

I cannot take credit for the historical images that appear in this study. The cover of this book and a number of interior photographs are from Joo Myung Duck's collection titled *The Mixed Names*. These amazing images of mixed race Korean children and their mothers were taken at the Harry Holt Memorial Orphanage in Ilsan in 1965. I enlisted many individuals to help me get in touch with Joo Myung Duck but only Miyako Yoshinga and Mihyun Kang of the Miyako Yoshinga Gallery in New York proved successful. Sy Kim at Holt International gave me permission to use the organization's archival photos that provide rich visual record of Korean adoption in its earliest years. Richard Bridges's personal collection handed down from his tour of duty in South Korea during the 1950s give us a snapshot into what daily life was like for an American GI in US-occupied Korea. Blair Naujok is an incredible photo archivist and his collection at the Korean Image Archive has been an invaluable resource. This book also contains images drawn from the Amerasian Program Collection in the Gonzaga University Archives, courtesy of special collections librarian Stephanie Plowman. Tricia Gesner at the Associated Press helped me to identify historical newspaper prints of mixed race children. Many adoptees also offered pictures handed down to them by their Korean mothers, GI fathers, or adoptive parents, or found in their adoption files and family photo albums. I regret that I could not include all of what they shared with me in this book, but I am moved that so many of these individuals trusted me with these precious artifacts from their past. This book would not be complete without all of these amazing visual sources.

As a first-time author, I am fortunate that this book has found its home with Oxford University Press. Susan Ferber discovered this project when it was in its early stages, believed in the story it was telling, and recruited me as one of her authors. I knew I was lucky to have Susan as my editor because time and time again I would hear from colleagues about how she was the best in our field. Indeed, Susan's influence on US historiography is undeniable and it has been an honor to work with her on this undertaking.

Acknowledgments *(xiii)*

I learned so much about how to write from her incredible line-by-line editing and I know this manuscript has benefited immensely from her important suggestions. I thank the anonymous peer reviewers whose constructive and generous comments helped to make this book the best possible version of itself. The production team at Newgen, headed by Stuart Allison, was a pleasure to work with. I am grateful for their attentive labor, including the meticulous copyediting of Patterson Lamb.

Between 2016 and 2024, this project was supported by generous grants from the Fulbright Program, the Social Science Research Council, the Korea Foundation, the Northeast Asia Council of the Association for Asian Studies, the American Council of Learned Societies, as well as internal sources at my graduate and current institutions including the Nicholas D. Chabraja Center for Historical Studies, Tomberg Research Funds, the Theodore and Jane Norman Fund for Faculty Scholarship, and the Mandel Center for the Humanities Faculty Grants. Without this support, I would not have had the time and resources for archival research, oral history interviews, fieldwork, translation, writing, and revising.

It would be wholly remiss of me if I did not give special thanks to my family and to my partner. I began graduate school in 2012 when my paternal grandmother, Kathleen Aleshire, was fighting a long battle against cancer. During my first semester of doctoral studies, the stipend I was provided by Northwestern was hardly enough to pay rent and groceries, in addition to my course materials for that fall. It was a fortune to her—a person who had never attended college herself and experienced much of her life as a working-class woman out of wedlock—but she sent me five hundred dollars so I could buy the books I needed. She would not survive the spring, let alone see the culmination of all the work I began in those first graduate seminars, but I know she would have been the first to read this book if she had any say in it. My older brother, Anthem Doolan, has always taken a keen interest in my studies despite our vastly different life trajectories. His encouragement over the years has meant so much to me. Jesse Yoon is the life partner I always dreamed of finding, but never thought I actually would. In addition to his primary duties of supporting and loving me, he has spent countless hours reading draft chapters, providing copyedits, and being a sounding board for my ideas. I do not deserve him, but I will surely keep him.

This book tells the powerful story of how Americans created and used the concept of the Amerasian to remove thousands of mixed race children from their Korean mothers in US-occupied South Korea to adoptive homes in the United States during the 1950s and 1960s. Although I was not born in the immediate postwar years, did not immigrate to the United States

(xiv) Acknowledgments

under the legal category of Amerasian, and was never adopted myself, I came to write this story while searching for my own origins.

During the 1980s, my Korean mother married my American father after meeting him in a camptown neighborhood near Osan Air Base. Like the vast majority of military bride marriages, theirs ended in divorce. Growing up, my mother rarely spoke of her past life in South Korea or how it was that she came to be in the company of US soldiers. Yet her struggles as an immigrant woman of color outside the boundaries of national belonging and also a social pariah—assumed to have been a former military prostitute who found her way out of the camptowns through marriage to a GI— shaped the ways our small family was treated and perceived by Koreans and Americans alike.

I became a historian by thinking critically about my mother's life: the shame, the secrecy, the gaps and blank spaces in her narrative. For over a decade now, I have tried to fill in those missing parts through studying the historical processes that have, since 1945, enabled a massive and prolonged US troop presence in Korea, the intimate contact between millions of Koreans and Americans, the formation of new kinds of interracial families, and the transpacific movements and migrations of hundreds of thousands of people. Indeed, these are the very issues at the heart of *The First Amerasians*—a book that is not just the culmination of much of what I have learned while searching for the circumstances surrounding my own existence in this world, but also a book about so many other lives shaped by US militarism and war.

Before that story unfolds, however, I would like to make one final acknowledgment and thank the many mixed race Koreans and adoptees from all over the world whom I met in the process of writing this book. To Ella Purkiss, Zak McGrath, Bella Siegel-Dalton, Shirley Chung, Katherine Kim, Susie Whitford Hankinson, Kathy Authurstein, Sarah Pak, Linda Papi Rounds, Tia Legoski, Cerissa Kim, Joel L. A. Peterson, Meeky Woo Flippen, Nancy Blackman, Paul Cannon, Rochelle Kaye, Victoria Namkung, Blair Adams, Frankie Legoski, Ruth Keller, Eileen Thompson, Maria Leister, Estelle Cooke-Sampson, Albertine Hughes, Jacky Lee, Milton Washington, Nancy Cho-Auvil, Kim Einhorn, Vance Allen, Sarah Harris, Lily Lu, Richard Ricardo Reese, Colleen Piparo, Alexandra Bauer, Jan Landis, Yoon-mi Butler, Jennifer Shin, Don Gordon Bell, Georgia Burns, Margaret Fitch-Hauser, Nena Adams Benhoff, Shelly Balke Reddish, Susan Lee Stewart, Diann Rowland, Peggy Sue Goldsmith, Kimberly Haga, Sybil Brickley, and so many others I cannot name: I hope that you will find some part of your own personal journey represented in these pages. This book is for you.

NOTE ON LANGUAGE

In this book, Korean names and terms have been romanized using the McCune-Reischauer system. Exceptions are made for places (e.g., Seoul), names commonly recognized under different transliterations (e.g., Syngman Rhee), and direct citations from primary and secondary source documents.

Problematic terms such as "mixed blood," "pure blood," "full Korean," and "half-American" as well as racial pejoratives appear in this study. My intention in using this language is not to conflate blood and parentage with race and nationality or to re-biologize these human-made devaluations that scholars of critical race and ethnic studies have long deconstructed. Rather, these terms are employed to preserve the tone of the historical documents in which they appear, capture the popular language of the era, and demonstrate how mixed race Koreans were viewed by Americans at the time. Additionally, the general term "mixed race Korean" is used when an individual's full parentage is not entirely clear within the source materials. This term is also useful for highlighting experiences common to mixed Korean persons of various racial backgrounds. Thus, while I occasionally note full racial backgrounds (e.g., Korean Black) to show specificity to that particular experience, readers should not assume that "mixed race Korean" is synonymous with Korean white individuals. Similarly, American is not a racial category—it is a legal category of citizenship. Terms like "half-American," thus, do not always imply whiteness and can also mean having half of one's parentage from the United States.

PROLOGUE

On May 10, 1949, US Army Corporal Nicholas Rossow of Headquarters Company, 5th Infantry Regiment, married Mang Chung Hi without the permission of his commanding officer.[1] Had he asked, like the many other US servicemen in Korea who came before him, his request would have been denied. Clear on this matter was the Immigration Act of 1924, which barred "aliens ineligible to citizenship" from entry into the United States and justified such a widespread military ban on marriages to Korean women.[2] Although an amendment to the War Brides Act of 1945 had allowed Asian spouses to temporarily bypass these racial exclusions for a brief period during the summer of 1947, that window of opportunity had long since closed.[3] It was for precisely this reason, then, that military superiors offered their personnel temporary companions in the form of entertainers and dancers brought onto base and prostitutes and hostesses made available just outside US gates in the tightly regulated confines of the camptown. Nicholas Rossow, however, had opted out of such relations and instead married the woman he loved. But, in 1949, formal rule of the US Army Military Government in Korea (USAMGIK, 1945–1948) was quickly ending and the Americans were rapidly withdrawing all but 500 of their high-ranking officers from the peninsula.[4] As a serviceman of enlisted rank, Corporal Rossow would soon have to leave his wife behind. Without a husband, Mang Chung Hi could be regarded by Koreans as a "ruined" woman who had fraternized with a foreign soldier, and her chances for social or economic mobility were severely curtailed.[5] And yet, there was more to this story, for she would not remain in South Korea alone.

A year and a half earlier, Nicholas Rossow and Mang Chung Hi had welcomed the birth of their child. In South Korea, where nationality could only be granted through a paternal surname, their marriage was recognized under local civil law, but the baby fathered by a US soldier was not.[6] On the American side, Rossow would require the US Army to recognize his marriage and work with diplomatic offices to secure his infant's citizenship.[7] If not, the child could remain a stateless nonentity, barred from entry into the United States on grounds of racial inadmissibility and marked in South Korea as a bastard whose racial mixture threatened the purity of a homogenous nation and reminded locals of their subordinated status to yet another foreign military so recently after Japanese colonial rule.[8] For the US military, however, the presence of a half-American child made no difference—Corporal Rossow was in "violation of a standing order" and could not be supported.[9] Confirming this, officials cited a military circular that stated: "Personnel who marry without permission will not be furnished any assistance in securing immigration documentary nor will they be granted any privileges normally accorded married personnel."[10] It was further noted in military records that he had "married without authority."[11] The report on this incident concluded: "Soldier will depart Korea alone."[12] Days later, on June 21, 1949, Nicholas Rossow would leave for Hawai'i on his next tour of duty.[13] From there, his story disappears from the historical record. In 1950, the Korean War would begin. What came of Nicholas Rossow's wife and his mixed race child left behind remains unclear. *The First Amerasians* offers some clues.

The First Amerasians

Introduction

The First Amerasians

This book positions mixed race Koreans as the first Amerasians. Such a chronology may initially appear ahistorical, given the longer trajectory of transnational intimacy and family making between the people of Asia and the people of the Americas since the nineteenth century,[1] the history of formal US empire in the Philippines dating back to 1898,[2] and the occupation of Japan in the immediate aftermath of World War II. All of these encounters preceded US military presence in southern Korea and produced substantial mixed race populations of their own.[3] But in 1982, when the Amerasian Immigration Act was enacted to extend preferential immigration rights to children of US citizens illegitimately fathered in Asia, it defined the Amerasian as an "alien . . . born in Korea, Vietnam, Laos, [Cambodia], or Thailand after 1950 and before the date of enactment."[4] Although earlier drafts of the bill had also included mixed race individuals born in the Philippines, Japan, and Taiwan, and expert testimony urged that the final version of the law include the "broadest geographic base" to increase its humanitarian effectiveness, Congress pushed back, confirming that "all the parties involved now agree that this bill could be limited to fewer countries."[5] To date, the legal definition of Amerasian remains restrictive despite numerous legislative attempts since 1982 to amend the law.[6] No explanation based on solid empirical evidence has ever been provided to justify the very specific boundaries of the Amerasian.

The First Amerasians. Yuri W. Doolan, Oxford University Press. © Oxford University Press 2024.
DOI: 10.1093/oso/9780197534380.003.0001

(2)   *The First Amerasians*

While most observers have critiqued the limited provisions of the Amerasian Immigration Act, calling it an ineffective piece of legislation, this book instead suggests that the strict geographic and temporal boundaries set by the law was a careful and purposeful articulation of something much more meaningful on the part of the US government.[7] Throughout the twentieth century, US military incursions spanning the globe had spawned numerous illegitimate mixed race persons, left behind in Europe, Asia, and elsewhere in the world. But never before had any of these individuals been named, singled out by law, or offered preferential entry into the United States until Congress legislated immigration reform and legally defined the Amerasian in 1982. Thus, the Amerasian, conceived of to achieve expedited closure on the long-standing issue of "certain" mixed race children fathered by US servicemen and left behind in Asia, serves as a reminder that as much as the Cold War was a series of protracted military conflicts, it was also a war in which words had symbolic value and mattered immensely.[8]

This book argues that the Amerasian is not simply a mixed race person fathered by a US serviceman in Asia, nor is it a racial term used to describe individuals with one American and one Asian parent. Rather, the Amerasian is an important figure in US political culture—a Cold War construct—that has helped Americans to explain and promote, both at home and in the world, the dominant ideas undergirding the Cold War.[9] In such a master narrative, the US government was not motivated by imperialistic ambition but embarked on a global crusade to spread democracy and freedom to all those willing to take it.[10] Its self-purported goals were not to produce or exploit colonial subjects but to transform Third World peoples into reformed and advanced citizens of the new free world. Juxtaposed against Soviet ambitions that Americans decried as red imperialism, communism was to be understood as morally bad and democracy as objectively good. Through expanding global military presence and waging wars on foreign soil, Americans claimed they were safeguarding the world from a new form of tyranny resembling that which humankind had only narrowly escaped during World War II. Thus, communist rivalry, defeat, and extended conflict—both military and ideological—produced the conditions through which mixed race Asians were transformed from bastard children of little significance into Amerasians worthy of rescue.

Central tools in this Cold War construction of Amerasians have been to portray their plight as tormented and rejected persons in the racially homogenous societies of Asia and to set their subsequent rescue via US refugee, adoption, and immigration laws. Their plight has worked to position the United States as a nation capable of embracing mixed race children, valorizing US branded democracy by highlighting America's morality, responsibility, and racial pluralism—qualities that justified its position as the world's indispensable leader. Rescue has enabled Americans to further narratives about communist insufficiency and tyranny by casting Amerasians as refugees and liberated persons, thereby redeeming US authority in the absence of outright military victories in Asia.[11]

This was explicitly evident in the aftermath of the Vietnam War, when mixed race children left behind following the fall of Saigon in 1975 were depicted as being ruled over by a communist regime that "cannot feed them and or will not educate them" due to "their failures as a government and system."[12] However, following the Korean War (1950–1953), where stalemate marked not a formal peace treaty but a mere cessation of hostilities, the question of whether democracy might persevere amid continued hostilities with North Korea created a different kind of argument surrounding the Amerasian. Rather than rescuing mixed race Koreans directly from communist rule, Americans were removing Amerasians from the devastation and "widespread human suffering" wreaked by "communist aggression," the indirect threat of another imminent North Korean invasion, and, to a greater extent, the poor treatment of such children by their newest democratic allies.[13] While saving children from the possibility of communism served US Cold War interests, the idea of having to save Amerasians from South Korean tyranny did not. Narratives surrounding the rescue of mixed race Koreans were thus fashioned around the backdrop of war, highlighting postwar poverty and the geopolitical instability of an unending military standoff against the North, so as to not undermine the credibility of the southern regime. "Amerasian" soon became conflated with the "war waif" and "war orphan"—phrases that Americans used interchangeably in advocating their extraction from South Korea and rescue via adoption, even though many of these children had been born before and after the years of military combat and were neither orphans nor abandoned but living with their Korean mothers in the camptown communities surrounding US military bases.

Of course, many Americans were also eager to highlight South Korean racism, homogeneity, and Confucian traditions in their efforts to justify and set the stage for an Amerasian rescue, which involved taking children from their birth mothers and turning them into "orphans" eligible for placement into adoptive American families. But these criticisms never sought to undermine South Korea's fragile sovereignty relative to North Korea. Instead, they were utilized to further a narrative of the United States as a liberating force that would remain to clean up the ruins of communist belligerence and teach the Korean people the ways of American democracy. Thus, comments about South Korean mistreatment of mixed race children highlighted primarily the possibilities of American benevolence. This veneer of humanitarian rescue not only helped Americans to lay claim to South Korea's children and justify the US military's continued presence, but it also aided in constructing sentimental victories amid Cold War setbacks. Indeed, both American wars in Korea and Vietnam had been vastly unpopular due to their deadly costs, the questionable morality of each conflict, and their disappointing endings. Given their proximity to these two wars, mixed race Korean and Southeast Asian children were especially important in helping Americans to understand and support the United States in its broader Cold War standoff against the Soviet Union at times when they most vociferously questioned the supposed good intentions of their government. Therefore, it was these two groups specifically whom Americans made into Amerasians.

Americans imagined their relations with Asians in familial terms during the early Cold War years; women and children, in particular, were especially important to that project.[14] This was related to an emerging internationalism and prevailing racial liberalism mobilized to validate US global expansion amid claims that racism made the United States ill-equipped to lead the free world.[15] It also served to mitigate some of the "anti-Asian violence"[16] and destruction wrought by US misdeeds abroad by replacing images of American soldiers indiscriminately bombing and killing innocent civilians with wholesome and paternal images of GIs caring for war-torn women and children.[17] As Asian waifs, orphans, and refugees became multifaceted prisms through which ordinary US citizens sought to understand the geopolitical importance of Asia in the Cold War, some Americans went one step further and welcomed military brides and adopted children into their families, using these "sentimental pathways" to bring remnants of US military occupations abroad home.[18] All this suggests that kinship between Asians and Americans was positively beneficial to US Cold War imperatives. And while it might be tempting to leave it at just that, this explanation alone is not entirely satisfying with regard to Amerasians.

As individuals fathered and then abandoned by US servicemen in Asia, mixed race Koreans—Americans by flesh and blood—constituted some of the strongest family ties Americans had to Asia in the early Cold War years. But their presence was not immediately beneficial to the United States nor acknowledged by Americans. Having been associated with military prostitution in South Korean camptowns as well as reckless personnel who abandoned these children with cold indifference, Amerasians bore a striking and uncomfortable resemblance to the Eurasians of earlier colonial encounters. Consequently, mixed race children and their mothers became the direct source of communist accusations of US imperialism, immorality,

INTRODUCTION   *(5)*

and irresponsibility in the Third World.[19] At a time when a quarter of the world's population was revolting against colonialism and the United States sought to vie for these allegiances against the Soviet Union and its allies, proximity to European imperial practices posed a major problem for US Cold War ambitions.[20] Americans responded to this crisis by crafting the Amerasian and its rescue. Only through such a discursive amelioration of US imperial practices did familial relations between mixed race children and Americans shift from detrimental to beneficial. Another point of entry, then, is to place the history of Amerasians within a larger tradition of Western colonial expansion in Asia dating back to the seventeenth century and understand Amerasians as part of the experience of children and empire.

European officials initially viewed the conjugal relations and familial bonds formed between colonized and colonizers as advantageous to the development of an enduring colonial state.[21] Such intimate Old World encounters between European men and native women produced large Eurasian populations from the Indos of the Dutch East Indies, to the Anglo-Indians of Colonial India, to the Métis of French Indochina. But soon, the familial relations that were supposed to strengthen the colonial project threatened to destabilize the fragile racial hierarchies on which European imperialism so desperately depended. As Eurasian children sought proximity to whiteness and European fathers began demanding on their behalf equal rights of the metropole, empire was in crisis. The British responded by passing numerous laws outlawing miscegenation, denying legal claims of inheritance to Eurasian children, and bringing British women into colonial societies. Officials argued that mixed race children, having been exposed to the influence of their native mothers and immersed in Indian ways, were part of a degenerate race and not the Britons that its colonies required.[22] By asserting these ideals, colonial bureaucrats believed they were protecting the boundaries of whiteness that would preserve British prestige and, in the long run, protect the empire. French debates about the Métis of Indochina teetered between arguments resembling the British and others that claimed that the stability and authority of their empire depended on rescuing Eurasians and seeing their successful assimilation into Frenchness. In nineteenth-century Indochina, efforts spearheaded by missionary and voluntary aid groups sought to remove mixed race persons from the bad influences of their Vietnamese mothers and native milieus and instead rehabilitate them within Western society as docile imperial subjects.[23] Without state intervention, some warned, Eurasians would become nothing but paupers, prostitutes, and affronts to European prestige, thus contributing to national decay.[24] The Dutch, having legally designated

(6) *The First Amerasians*

their mixed race population as European since the early 1600s, put the Indo problem at the center of colonial and social reform in the nineteenth century, undergoing a "civilizing offensive" to "uplift" those "delinquent" and "neglected" mixed race children and turn them into decent Europeans.[25]

Reformers back home in Cold War America would eventually embark on parallel campaigns to rescue Amerasians. They would build on similar discourses surrounding mixed race children employed by previous colonial powers. Social workers' claims that Korean women were depraved whores unfit to raise their own children and Cold War culturalists' allegations that mixed race persons were affronts to American prestige (destined to become nothing but beggars and prostitutes) fueled demands that these individuals be taken from South Korea and transformed into respectable Americans by adoptive families in the United States. In media reports, mixed race Korean children were painted as abandoned war orphans ready for and in need of adoption. These descriptions echoed earlier references to the Métis of Indochina as abandoned and orphaned despite having been raised by their biological mothers.[26] Colonial officials often accused Vietnamese women of "profiting from the divestment of children into prostitution or slavery," just as Americans would, some years later, publish stories of "half-caste" girls "for sale to US servicemen."[27] These narratives justified coercive measures on the part of both US and European humanitarians "to prise Eurasian children from native mothers" and place them into American homes or French protection societies instead.[28] Similar to how Amerasians are Cold War constructs by Americans, Eurasians were colonial constructs by Europeans. They were problems that needed solving, whose plights threatened to usurp colonial authority and whose rescues ensured empire's endurance.

Colonial government policies toward local Asian women also resembled those of the US military in South Korea some decades later. In the formal years of US Army Military Government in Korea (USAMGIK, 1945–1948), the military adopted a policy condoning regulated prostitution while forbidding longer-term relations between their personnel and Korean women.[29] While this was owed in large part to the racial inadmissibility of Asian women in US immigration law at the time, negative attitudes toward Korean women persisted even as those toward Asian women in other occupation zones changed.[30] For instance, in a post–1952 era when immigration laws had begun to liberalize,[31] American men began to marry Japanese women in large numbers, whereas relations back in Korea continued to resemble Old World forms of colonial concubinage with military commanders discouraging any form of intimacy beyond regulated military prostitution.[32] Like the British in colonial India, who took on local wives

INTRODUCTION (7)

and bore Eurasian children, oftentimes in secret from their families back home, Korean wives and mixed race children of American GIs were imperial subjects not to be brought back to the metropole.[33] As a result, many US servicemen maintained parallel families, unbeknownst to their loved ones both in South Korea and the United States.[34] Such practices expose unsettling continuities between European colonialism and US empire in Asia. Just as conjugal relations, familial bonds, and the construction of the Eurasian were important tools in preserving the authority of colonial powers throughout the eighteenth and nineteenth centuries, policies to manage military prostitution and mixed race children in South Korea were central to the maintenance of US empire during the twentieth century.

The rise and the demise of the Amerasian, then, roughly framed by the decades of the Amerasian Immigration Act (1950–1982), also tells a broader story about the changing contours of Western powers in Asia. While many of the first mixed race children born during US military encounters in Asia were called Eurasian, the term would eventually be replaced with Amerasian as European dominance was eclipsed by US militarism in the East.[35] The term "Amerasian," popularized by Pulitzer and Nobel Prize-winning author Pearl S. Buck in the 1950s and 1960s, would be a metaphor for that transition.[36] By contrast, "Eurasian" was first coined in the early years of the British imperial century (1815-1914) to refer to the Anglo-Indians of the British Raj. [37] The term expanded in its usage throughout the twentieth century, symbolizing the massive geographic expanse of the British empire and the vast reaches of other European powers.[38] In the aftermath of World War II, when the Marshall Plan and Truman Doctrine made clear that the United States had surpassed the great powers of Britain and France,[39] it seemed that the dawn of the so-called American Century, anticipated in 1941 by *Time* publisher Henry Luce, had finally arrived.[40] The naming of the Amerasian not only marked the emergence of mixed race peoples as the result of unprecedented US military incursion into Asia but also signaled a new global order characterized by US political, economic, and cultural dominance in the world. By 1975, however, after two wars that were not quite won against communist revolutionaries in Korea and Vietnam, the last American helicopter would symbolically depart Saigon. In subsequent years, US military commitments would shift from East Asia to the Middle East.[41] By 1982, when the Amerasian Immigration Act was signed into law, it would mark the end of an era in which "Asia seized center stage in the nation's political consciousness."[42] Although a massive US military commitment would continue throughout the region, it would be a relatively smaller presence scaled back by the end of the Cold War—and the Amerasian, frozen in time between the years 1950 and 1982, would be

(8) *The First Amerasians*

no more, even though many mixed race children would continue to be born from the legacies of these military encounters.

But beyond the construction of the Amerasian within US political culture, this book also recovers the on-the-ground realities and lived historical experiences that such a narrative obscures. It is in many ways an attempt to "narrate a history of adoption that pays as much attention to the position of those who lose children in adoption as to those who receive them."[43] Drawing on social welfare professionals' meticulous documentation and studies of the happenings around US military bases in their efforts to understand and advocate for mixed race children, it treats the adoption archive as an archive for camptown women and the camptown more generally. By using these sources, in addition to memoir and oral history, Korean birth mothers become significant figures in this history.[44]

Furthermore, despite widespread acknowledgment that South Korea's intercountry adoption program began with the placements of mixed race children, this is often mentioned only in passing, as mere background context to a larger point.[45] Consequently, the stories of mixed race individuals who were adopted into US homes during the 1950s and 1960s have seldom, if ever, been featured centrally.[46] To foreground their voices, this study draws upon thirty oral history interviews conducted by the author between the years 2016 and 2022. These narratives help to fill gaps within the historical record about what happened to the very first children who were placed in American homes during an era when international adoption did not yet have the regulations in place to safeguard children from unethical and dangerous practices like proxy adoption.[47] Such perspectives expose the deep contradictions and anti-Asian violence at the heart of these transnational encounters and underscore the important role of humanitarianism in strengthening, justifying, and maintaining US empire.[48] Focusing on the camptown and mixed race origins of international adoption also reveals how the narratives Americans created to lay claim on South Korea's children have been so pervasive that they continue to undergird the most critical of scholarship on these topics.[49]

In this dominant narrative, Americans saved mixed race children from a racist and backward South Korean government and society that sought to excise these individuals at all costs. But while Orientalist depictions of South Korea as insular, static, and unwavering in its discrimination toward mixed race individuals help to define the postwar United States as internationalist, progressive, and racially tolerant by contrast,[50] they negate indigenous efforts to assimilate and integrate these children. By the early 1960s, Korean social workers had begun working with international organizations to establish several major programs to assist mixed race Koreans

INTRODUCTION   *(9)*

and their mothers. Some of these programs had even gained the official support and funding of the South Korean government, representing a dramatic and positive shift in state policy toward mixed race persons. But US agencies and advocates working in South Korea at the time privileged their own professional interests and insisted on intercountry placement as the best possible solution for these individuals. As US adoption advocates funneled American dollars into programs directly competing with indigenous agencies, they effectively dismantled the local integrationist movement and retained control over mixed race children's welfare. As a result, adoption became an enduring solution, and many individuals continued to be separated from their Korean mothers even in their late childhood and early teenage years. However, all this is not to suggest that the lives of mixed race children in South Korea were, by any means, uniformly better by the 1960s; among those left behind, some faced extreme hardship and ridicule and others lived with their mothers in the protective confines of the camptown. Rather, this shows the diverse range of experiences among these individuals and how US humanitarians forever altered the position of mixed race people and changed the trajectory of child welfare in South Korean society.

While another group of so-called GI babies suffering similar marginalization existed in Occupied Japan, Americans did not intervene to the same degree in local efforts to absorb such children.[51] Additionally, the conditions of the US military occupation there vastly differed from that of South Korea which has, to this day, remained a designated war zone and therefore a virtual bachelor society. By 1946, the US military had brought "Levittown" to Japan and welcomed military wives and dependents to help support the efforts of the occupiers.[52] Therefore, although some Americans did participate in the adoptions of mixed race Japanese children in the 1940s and 1950s, the family-oriented culture of Occupied Japan meant that 90 percent of those adoptions occurred on Japanese soil by American military and government families stationed there.[53] In the end, these two factors kept the mixed race problem in Japan, more or less contained and out of the immediate reaches of humanitarians in the United States; and the rescues of such children did not culminate in the establishment of a permanent intercountry adoption program as it did in South Korea.

As the number of mixed race children in camptowns slowly dwindled, adoption would expand to include those of full Korean parentage, and eventually South Korea would become a model for other nations that wished to establish intercountry practices. To this day, the laws that allow for international adoption in the United States are those first argued on behalf of mixed race Koreans in the 1950s and 1960s. Additionally, many of the organizations that continue to participate in international adoption in the twenty-first century got their start with mixed race Koreans in the aftermath of the Korean War. Approximately 200,000 Korean children have been sent to Western nations for adoption, with nearly two-thirds going to the United States.[54] Hundreds of thousands of other children from US Cold War battlegrounds around the world have also been adopted by families stateside. This book about Amerasians as exemplars of American exceptionalism, then, is also story about the origins of international adoption as a major practice in US society and culture.

While many have noted how adopting Asian children across national boundaries was evidence of an internationalism and racial liberalism that would come to define American values in the Cold War era, such a narrative should perhaps be reconsidered in the case of mixed race Koreans, whose placements generally preceded those of fully Asian children. As these individuals were sent to all corners of American society in the 1950s and 1960s, they left prejudicial attitudes in South Korea only to encounter a different hostile racial terrain, even within the intimate confines of their new US homes. Overwhelmingly, Amerasians seem to have made desirable adoptable children not because of their Asian heritage but rather for their proximity to Americanness and, to a greater extent, whiteness. White prospective parents asked adoption agencies for any Korean child as long as it was not "Negro."[55] Others requested "Korean-Caucasian" children "so as long as her looks are more Anglo than Oriental," and in at least one case, a set of prospective parents was allowed to adopt even after they admitted their plans to perform plastic surgery on their child's eyelids to help them racially pass as white within their community.[56] In extreme instances, adoptive parents even failed to naturalize mixed race Koreans as citizens of the United States, rendering them undocumented to this day. In many ways, the Amerasian rescue fell short on its promises to rescue these individuals from racism and illegitimacy in South Korea.

When Americans lobbied Congress in the 1980s for Amerasian immigration reform that would eventually culminate in the Amerasian Immigration Act and a subsequent amendment that would allow for the migrations of 23,000 mixed race Vietnamese and 67,000 of their immediate relatives, it was through Korean Amerasians that Americans began to understand the Vietnamese children born from later military encounters in Asia.[57] At that point, US voluntary agencies in South Korea had been facilitating the adoptions of mixed race Koreans and tending to the needs of older children deemed unadoptable for nearly three decades. Such experiences made champions of mixed race Koreans the most relevant subject matter experts to speak on behalf of Vietnamese Amerasians

INTRODUCTION   *(11)*

in congressional hearings. Additionally, following the fall of Saigon in 1975, a severing of diplomatic relations with the communist nations of Southeast Asia meant that Americans lacked access to an older generation of mixed race Vietnamese children. Instead, mixed race Koreans (alongside their adoptive parents) offered Americans curated testimony, both oral and written, and attested to the discrimination they faced back in Asia as well as the colorblind love they received from their new American families and communities. This provided US lawmakers a glimpse into the possibilities of another Amerasian rescue and allowed Americans to imagine Vietnamese children in the United States as well.[58] It was the first Amerasians, then, that provided the human evidence necessary to argue for Amerasian immigration reform and construct a post-Vietnam story of rescue and redemption.

Despite this, the vast majority of the literature on Amerasians has centered on documenting the histories of mixed race Vietnamese.[59] Journalists and academics have investigated the lived experiences and identities of Vietnamese Amerasians, including children adopted into American families during the war years, those left behind following the fall of Saigon, and individuals who came to the United States in the 1980s and 1990s as part of Amerasian immigration laws. But while these works showcase the Amerasian as a particularly sympathetic figure in post-Vietnam America, they have done less to interrogate the Amerasian as a category or concept (instead deploying the term as an objective descriptor for individuals of mixed Asian and American parentage). They have also failed to make meaningful mention of their Korean predecessors. Similarly, in the field of critical refugee studies, where Vietnamese Amerasians often appear, little attention has been paid to mixed race Koreans despite the fact that a large number of these individuals entered the United States in the 1950s, first under the legal category of "refugee orphan."[60]

This disproportionate representation favoring Vietnamese Amerasians is in many ways connected to the social memory of both the Korean War and the Vietnam War. While Korea has been rendered "forgotten," Vietnam is marked by a certain historical awareness within the American psyche.[61] As sociologist Grace M. Cho points out in her discussion of the bridge at No Gun Ri,[62] dubbed "Korea's Mai Lai," the Korean War has been so unknowable to Americans that it is only through referencing Vietnam that we have begun to understand and grapple with its history.[63] Focusing on mixed race Koreans as the first Amerasians, rather than furthering narratives about Vietnamese Amerasians' primacy, inverts this "amnesia mask[ing] a reality in which," as historian Bruce Cumings suggests, "we are all a product of Korea whether we know it or not."[64]

(12)   *The First Amerasians*

Indeed, as the first "hot war" of the Cold War, it was this civil war in a decolonizing country that set into motion a number of dynamics that would come to characterize capitalist alignment under the aegis of US empire.[65] What follows, then, is not simply a story about the Cold War construction of the Amerasian and how this concept has shaped the lives of Korean women and children. What follows is also a broader investigation into the "intimate Cold War"—or how the geopolitics of this era shaped, enabled, and curtailed relations involving US occupier and occupied, and how American institutions like the US military and US immigration system categorized and managed those relationships, first in Korea before expanding to other sites of US Cold War entanglement. The intimate Cold War, it must be said, was inherently violent and anti-Asian insofar as it reflected, produced, and justified the structural devaluation of Asian lives and humanity on which these so-called proxy wars in Asia were initially predicated. Thus, embedded in the book's title, *The First Amerasians*, remains this contention that Korea and the Korean War are origin sites for twentieth-century America—not a "forgotten war" but a watershed moment in US history—and remain central for understanding postwar modernity.[66]

To recover this history, this book draws on a wealth of primary sources. These include military documents such as memoranda, circulars, correspondences, meeting minutes, and reports regarding military prostitution, venereal disease rates, recreation, marriage, and paternity;[67] and congressional hearings on international adoption in the 1950s and 1960s as well as those on Amerasian immigration reform in the 1980s. Correspondence between adoption professionals and field studies conducted by social workers operating in South Korea during the 1950s and 1960s, part of the International Social Service (ISS), document the conditions of camptowns and Americans' understandings of mixed race Koreans and their mothers. ISS adoption case files provide insight into the motivations of adoptive parents, the adoption process, and the adjustment of mixed race Koreans in their new American homes. Meanwhile, press reports highlight how all this was communicated to the American public. Retrospective sources such as oral history and memoir of mixed race Koreans and their birth mothers further complicate the story told within these written documents.

Chapter 1, "Managing Cold War Intimacy," explains how the US military's concerns surrounding rising venereal disease (VD) rates immediately on

INTRODUCTION   (13)

their arrival in southern Korea created two crucial precursors in the making of the Amerasian. First, it spatially mapped out the camptown, a tightly controlled space around US military installations where the sexual activities of troops were strictly curated. Second, the VD control regime encouraged military officials to see all Korean women working in close proximity to US bases as likely prostitutes and therefore VD carriers whose interactions with soldiers needed to be strictly monitored. This stereotyping of Korean women blurred the lines between camptown local, civilian employee, girl-friend, bride, and prostitute and would become very important in denying marriages between US servicemen and Korean women, separating mixed race families, and justifying adoption practices.

By the mid-1950s, thousands of American missionaries and voluntary aid workers had traveled to South Korea to help assist in the humanitarian crisis following an absolutely catastrophic war. Together, these individuals estimated that there were some 50,000 war orphans in South Korea's overcrowded orphanages. While mixed race children comprised just a small fraction of this number, they were believed to experience additional hardships. Chapter 2, "The Problem of the Mixed Blood Child," explores the narratives surrounding mixed race Koreans that emerged in the US political culture during the 1950s as American missionaries, voluntary agencies, and philanthropists advocated the removal of these children from camptowns and placement in American families for adoption. These reformers lobbied for a series of temporary bills and special acts of Congress until permanent provisions for international adoption were made in a 1961 amendment to the Immigration and Nationality Act. But in the periods between the expiration of one law and the passage of another, adoption advocates often exaggerated the conditions in camptowns in an effort to incite panic and garner more widespread support. Central to their arguments were constructions of birth mothers as unloving, hardened prostitutes; South Korea as a racist, backward society; refugee orphans as "young ambassadors" unconsciously cementing "good will between the countries of their birth and their new American families"; and the United States as a welcoming home.[68] In doing so, these Americans created a system where mixed race children could be expediently and justifiably passed on from birth mother to adoptive family—a move that caused actual harm to many Korean women and children.

Chapter 3, "Confucius' Outcasts," describes what happened in the years after 1961. By then, an estimated 2,000 mixed race children remained in South Korea. These individuals were generally older and living with their mothers in camptowns, as the younger, more desirable children had already been sent to the United States for adoption.

(14)   *The First Amerasians*

Seeking more pragmatic solutions, a small minority of international social workers rejected intercountry adoption as the ultimate solution for mixed race children and began to work with indigenous agencies to integrate these individuals into South Korean society. One notable program called Eurasian Children Living as Indigenous Residents even gained the sponsorship of the South Korean government in the mid-1960s and focused its efforts on rehabilitating birth mothers and assisting mixed race children's entry into local schools. Shortly after this initiative got under way, however, relations between local programs and American agencies began to deteriorate. Labeling South Korean efforts ineffective, many US humanitarians remained fixated on adoption and segregated institutional care, rather than integration. They used their professional and economic clout to dismantle indigenous efforts, employing a narrative of enduring South Korean racism to justify their means. Because US humanitarian intervention in the immediate postwar years had created a dependence in Korea on foreign aid to tend to the nation's pressing social welfare needs, American agencies were able to use US dollars to overpower South Korean efforts and retain control over mixed race Koreans' welfare. Ultimately, the local integrationist movement failed, and the number of children being sent to the United States for adoption would continually rise throughout the 1960s and 1970s—a reflection of US desires rather South Korea's perpetual racism.

Chapter 4, "Becoming American," follows the lives of the first generation of mixed race Koreans who were placed into US families in the 1950s and 1960s. It shows how the discursive practices that produced and justified the Amerasian rescue continued to shape the lives of these children even after adoption. As adoptive parents set out to create the American children US humanitarians promised them to be, assimilation—viewed by domestic social work and child welfare professionals as evidence of a proper adjustment—was endorsed as official policy. The figure of the happy and well-adjusted adoptee helped to further a narrative of the United States as an anti-racist nation and bolster the US military's interventions abroad. Despite this, mixed race children's entry into American families was fraught. They struggled deeply with their adjustment and with the loss of their Korean mothers; racism and segregation remained a very real and salient part of their lives; intimate knowledge about their camptown origins persisted. In fact, many female adoptees remember being told that, had they not been adopted, they would have become prostitutes like their mothers. Others reported that they were sexually abused by adoptive fathers, siblings, or male community members. While intent on exposing the anti-Asian violence of international adoption during this era, some narrators also shed light on more positive placements in what they viewed to be warm, loving, and safe adoptive homes.

Chapter 5, "The Second Rescue," investigates the reemergence of mixed race Koreans in US political culture in the aftermath of the Vietnam War. Although these individuals had more or less disappeared from the national spotlight in the mid-1960s at the height of the Vietnam War, US military defeat and ambivalence surrounding Operation Babylift—a government-sponsored initiative to rescue some 2,000 Vietnamese orphans in the midst of Saigon's fall—would bring them back to the forefront of American consciousness. While Operation Babylift had produced polarizing debates, with opponents accusing the government of "kidnapping" children as a "political ploy" to achieve a sentimental victory,[69] proponents argued that the rescue could be justified as these were half-American children, who would almost certainly have faced discrimination and intolerance in a communist Vietnam. In the aftermath of the airlifts, the question of what would become of America's mixed race progeny left behind under communist rule and a curiosity surrounding those recently adopted orphans loomed large. Searching for answers, Americans looked to an older generation of mixed race Koreans, both adoptees and those remaining in South Korean camptowns, to imagine the future of Vietnamese American children. Eventually, this curiosity and newfound public interest in mixed race Koreans would culminate in the Amerasian immigration proposals of the 1980s, in which Koreans and their champions played a crucial role as advocates for all mixed race Asians (and in particular, Vietnamese children) born from US military encounters abroad.

The epilogue of this book examines the demise of the Amerasian, which has much to do with defeat in Vietnam and the official end of the Cold War in Asia, but also the emergence of mixed race Korean subjectivity. In the twenty-first century, mixed race Koreans are speaking out about their lived historical experiences and organizing around DNA testing to undo the ideological erasure of their Korean pasts. Through these efforts, hundreds of adoptees have been reunited with their birth families. The activism and cultural work of this first generation ultimately shows how they, too, are contesting dominant narratives and finding their own origins beyond the Amerasian.

1

Managing Cold War Intimacy

When US forces first arrived in southern Korea during the fall of 1945, "Korean girls would have nothing to do with [American GIs]," recalled military doctor Crawford F. Sams.[1] In fact, as noted in his memoir, "the first girls who were seen in the company of American soldiers were stoned by the Korean people, who had protected their women from sexual contact with the Japanese for so many years."[2] While these observations are questionable, given the infamous "comfort women" system of sexual slavery in which Korean maidens constituted the vast majority of those prostituted to the Japanese Imperial Army during World War II, it reflects an initial understanding on part of US military officials that Korean women were pure, chaste, and therefore "off-limits" to American soldiers.[3] Just five years later, however, such an image of South Korean women as sexually unavailable to US servicemen had been upended completely.

In a *Chicago Defender* article titled, "GIs Spurn Korean Gals, Wait for Jap Lassies," journalist Milton A. Smith cast Korean women as loose and unhygienic carriers of venereal disease (VD).[4] "These women are streetwalkers," one serviceman claimed.[5] He clarified: "I don't mean every dame is, but the only ones I meet are."[6] Statements such as this reflected a reality in which interactions between American GIs and Korean women had been turned into that of client and prostitute in the tightly regulated confines of camptown recreational districts surrounding US military encampments. While high VD rates kept "some thinking GIs away," others risked being "eaten up by disease."[7] After all, the "new germ killing antibiotics and other safeguards" instituted by the US military allowed for them to satisfy

The First Amerasians. Yuri W. Doolan, Oxford University Press. © Oxford University Press 2024.
DOI: 10.1093/oso/9780197534380.003.0002

their carnal appetites and utilize Korean women as their temporary sexual playmates.[8] However, despite the proliferation of prostitution around US bases, the report confirmed that "no permanent relationships are built up."[9] US Army wives and girlfriends stateside need not "worry about girls in Korea," although one GI noted, "If I were in Japan it might be different."[10] The message was clear: while US servicemen might "shack up" with Korean women during the short duration of their tours, such girls were of easy virtue, unclean, and unsuitable for longer term relations.[11] Although they made decent prostitutes providing certain precautions, they were not women to marry nor women to be brought back home.

This chapter examines how the US military categorized and shaped relationships between Korean women and US soldiers during the 1940s and 1950s. A confluence of factors, including concerns about US military-civil relations, rising VD rates among troops, the local conditions of US military presence in Korea, and racial exclusions in US immigration law, contributed to a construction of Korean women, in the minds of US military officials, as prostitutes rather than decent marriageable partners for enlisted men. This, in turn, resulted in both official policies and on-the-ground practices where commanding officers deliberately oriented American GIs away from long-term relations with Korean women and instead toward regulated military prostitution in camptowns. While similar sentiments about local women were certainly present within the US military's other post–World War II occupations like Germany and Japan, the conditions in occupied and postwar Korea shaped a more rigid and severe image of Korean women than those of women elsewhere. This, ultimately, had major consequences for the mixed race children born to local women and US servicemen in Korea.

The US military presence in Korea began on September 8, 1945, when the first of some 72,000 troops from the Twenty-Fourth Corps arrived from Okinawa at the port of Incheon to transfer power from the devastated Japanese empire.[12] The following day, Lieutenant General John R. Hodge accepted Japanese surrender and the United States took control of all facilities below the 38th parallel that had been previously utilized by the Imperial Japanese Army.[13] Surrounding many of those military installations was a well-established system of regulated prostitution, developed by the Japanese during the colonial era. [14] American soldiers who found themselves at Yongsan Garrison in Seoul, for instance, inherited access to "comfort stations" that had been used previously by the Japanese military.[15] While the US military initially allowed for its personnel to visit these various prostitution facilities, it actively discouraged GIs from other public displays of fraternization with Korean women.[16] On January 25, 1947—just one year into US rule—the military leadership issued Circular No. 9 entitled, "Association with Korean Women." The pronouncement instructed "all male and civilian personnel assigned or attached to the United States Army Forces in Korea" to "refrain from association with Korean women in public," forbidding relations with local girls "other than through the lowest form of prostitution."[17] Such a contradictory stance, deeming Korean women improper romantic partners while simultaneously condoning prostitution, sums up the dominant goals (both to curtail long-term relations and to provide personnel temporary sexual gratification) undergirding US military policies toward Korean women during these early years.

Exposed within Circular No. 9 was a heightened sense of anxiety surrounding the integrity of the US-Korea relationship. In truth, the US Army Military Government in Korea (USAMGIK, 1945–1948) had, since the genesis of its rule on September 11, 1945, struggled to win the allegiances of the Korean people.[18] US military officials believed that relations between Korean women and US personnel could further challenge pacifying efforts, noting that "agitators are always present to take advantage of any such opportunities for further inciting unrest through misunderstood incidents in order to gain their own selfish ends."[19] The circular even went so far as to frame the issue as one that risked "the entire effort of the American Army of Occupation and the prestige of the American people."[20] Such intensified concerns around relations between US soldiers and local women were part of the broader issue of image maintenance for US forces in Korea. Days prior to the release of Circular No. 9, for example, the Commanding General of United States Armed Forces in Korea issued a message urging GIs not to treat Korea as a "conquered nation," reminding its soldiers to "keep [their] hands off Korean women," avoid drunkenness and other forms of mischief, and treat Koreans not as servile "gooks" but as dignified people with a "long, proud history."[21]

Korean enmity against American soldiers was colored first, by a Confucian patriarchy that tied Korean women's social status to their virtue and to male heads of household, and second, by the country's most recent colonial experience.[22] Relations between local women and US men, resembling earlier forms of colonial concubinage in places such as colonial India, signaled to Koreans their subordination to a Western nation that had, like the Japanese before it, stripped them of their sovereignty and dignity. Korean press reports drew parallels between the women newly servicing US soldiers and those "women of war" who had "fallen into the unbelievable business of selling their bodies" to the Japanese Army.[23] As a result, women sporting "exotic curls, loud popping chewing gum, and very red lipstick"[24] who were found in the company of American GIs were viewed by locals as brazen whores and could "suffer severe criticism, punishment, and deprivations at the hands of their families and neighbors."[25] Yet because camptowns were economic centers, it is also likely that many Koreans, witnessing the relative wealth of these women, were jealous of their access to American dollars. Locals created pejoratives such as *yanggongju* ("Western princess") and *yanggalbo* ("Yankee whore") that captured the ways these women were envied yet also reviled. These terms also reflected a widespread sentiment that all those seen in public with American men were of questionable moral character and, in all likelihood, were prostitutes mixing flesh and blood with foreign soldiers.[26] But beyond the ways in which such intimate encounters provoked the ire of locals, the US military had another pressing concern that would shape the image of Korean women—the issue of venereal disease among its troops.

Figure 1.1 A so-called *yanggongju* entertains US soldiers. Courtesy of Richard Bridges.

Figure 1.2 A Korean woman poses in front of an army tent. Courtesy of Richard Bridges.

Figure 1.3 Camptown women visit base. Courtesy of Richard Bridges.

Prior to the US military's entry into Korea, all major health activities of the country had been administered by the Sanitation Section of the national police force under Japanese rule.[27] This included the "periodic vaginal examinations of licensed prostitutes" as part of a VD control program in each province.[28] Police-run public health work was far more aggressive in colonial Korea than even in Japan.[29] Furthermore, because the Allied firebombing campaign never reached Korea during the Pacific War, the public health infrastructure laid by the Japanese colonial government remained more or less intact by the time the Americans arrived. As a result, VD rates among registered prostitutes were initially very low ("much lower than even in the United States") during the first few months of USAMGIK.[30] In fact, the medical officer of USAMGIK even "secured permission" to keep houses of prostitution near military encampments "on limits providing there would be weekly inspections of the working personnel."[31]

The instability of the post-colonial Korean government meant that the power of the national police force to conduct periodic examinations diminished in certain provinces amid political unrest.[32] Additionally, as US encampments became the sites of intense congregating by camp followers looking to eke out a living or find stable work, they saw the proliferation of pimp and solicitor activities. Some of the first prostitutes for the US military were women who had been impoverished and displaced during thirty-five years of oppressive colonial rule, including former "comfort women."[33] Troop replacements arriving from Japan also aggravated the VD issue in Korea.[34] There, the devastating postwar conditions combined with the relative sexual freedom of American GIs led to "skyrocketing venereal disease rates," which in turn reverberated into US occupied Korea.[35] By spring 1946, the VD problem in Korea had reached a problematic level, catching up to morbidity rates in Japan and other US occupation zones.[36]

On a very practical level, the "effective strength of the Army" had been reduced given "the hospitalization and treatment of soldiers who have contracted venereal disease," military officials announced to troops.[37] In response, the USAMGIK enacted Ordinance No. 72 on May 4, 1946.[38] Paragraph 70 of the law criminalized Korean women for "engaging in or eliciting sexual intercourse with any member of the occupying forces" while "suffering from a venereal disease in an infectious stage."[39] This distinction kept prostitution legal while outlawing both voluntary and involuntary venereal disease transmissions. Ordinance No. 72 would serve as the legal basis for the aggressive VD control regime that would structure relations between Korean women and American servicemen in the months thereafter.

In 1947, the VD morbidity rate for US Forces in Korea averaged 83 per 1,000 soldiers per annum.[40] By May of that year, VD had become such a pressing concern that the USAMGIK established a VD Control Council section under the Department of Public Health and Welfare, reinstating colonial era levels of regulation for public prostitution.[41] The USAMGIK also introduced "vaginal and serological examinations every month" for "entertainment girls" working around US encampments—a wide-ranging category including "kisaeng girls, dancers, bar girls, waitresses," and "streetwalkers."[42] This requirement reflected the US military's views that all such women were likely to participate in prostitution. Failure to comply with such examinations "result[ed] in the loss of license."[43] The USAMGIK directed twenty-six provincial hospitals and ten health centers to carry out examinations and dispensed adequate quantitates of sulfonamides, mepharsin, bismuth, and penicillin for the treatment of infected women.[44] Following the establishment of this program, a total of 14,889 women underwent examinations. Among them 59.8 percent were found to be infected with venereal disease.[45] By December 1947, the National Venereal Disease Center in Seoul opened with the primary purpose of quarantining infected "entertaining girls" until they were non-infectious.[46] All these VD control measures were directed toward women working in close proximity to US military bases rather the general population.[47] The USAMGIK exercised complete jurisdiction over Korean women's bodies and sexual health during this time. In fact, they did so to such an extent that women merely "suspected by the Military or National Police of prostitution" could be arrested and examined without trial.[48] If found to be in an infectious stage of a venereal disease "enforced treatment" was administered and woman were detained "until proven non-infectious" in local prisons or VD clinics.[49]

On February 14, 1948, Public Act No. 7, a law prohibiting public prostitution, went into effect.[50] While the abolition of legalized sex work was framed to be an emancipatory breakthrough of the USAMGIK, undoing a shameful legacy of the Japanese colonial regime that Koreans had long detested, it also served as an opportunity for US officials to rein in the VD issue.[51] Before the implementation of this public act, arrangements had been made by the Department of Public Health and Welfare to examine every licensed prostitute throughout each province.[52] It was found that 73.8 percent of the 1,985 licensed prostitutes had been infected with venereal disease.[53] The USAMGIK responded by treating all such women until they were non-infectious before allowing for their release back into "circulation."[54] By April 1948, "all known houses of prostitution [had] been closed," and the US military shifted its attention to the issue of unregulated prostitution proliferating outside its encampments.[55] But as it turns out, the 1948 abolition of public prostitution amplified the US military's troubles. Just weeks after the law was passed, VD control officers met to urgently discuss how the ban on public prostitution had created a "scattering" of once licensed and tightly regulated prostitutes, leaving "no way of holding forced inspections" and no way to ensure "that such Koreans reported for examination voluntarily."[56] The committee concluded that previously licensed sex workers (now unemployed) were turning to unregulated prostitution and "gathering outside [US military] gates" to accost and tempt US soldiers.[57]

The USAMGIK responded by stepping up its efforts to limit any possibility of GI interaction with solicitors by more clearly demarcating the spatial mappings of the camptown—where GIs spent the vast majority of their recreational time off duty. Their aims were to create a controlled and regulated environment that might limit the possibilities of VD transmission. Military officers began thoroughly tracking sources of VD by utilizing the contact tracing method. This required a GI, after having contracted an infection, to make a report about where the alleged incident occurred.[58] Military officials would then dispatch police to arrest the suspected woman and put up a sign announcing that the affiliated establishment was "off-limits" to US military personnel.[59] With every "off-limits" decree, the camptown shrank in size.

Soon after, "a study of venereal disease contact reports" noted "that soldiers are meeting women in laundries operated by Koreans, who live in the vicinity of the camp."[60] As a result, the Venereal Disease Control Council recommended "that all Korean operated laundries, houses and public places be declared off-limits to military personnel." No establishment, no matter how seemingly innocent, was exempt.[61] Matters escalated to the point that vice squads even began "mak[ing] raids on houses after positive reports" had implicated certain neighborhoods "in the vicinity" of unregulated prostitution.[62] Any Korean, woman or man, suspected of being a prostitute or procurer was arrested and then "tried by Provost Courts."[63] In the event that the prostitute was found to be infected with VD, she was turned "over to the Health and Welfare Agency of Military Government in the area for treatment."[64]

Regular patrols of restricted areas followed, with personnel "apprehended in off-limit areas" facing immediate trial "by a Summary Court Officer in Division Headquarters."[65] The standard sentence for an enlisted man caught in an "off-limits" area was two-thirds of a month's pay, while noncommissioned officers faced demotion to the rank of a recruit after the second offense.[66] Although both military officers and enlisted men contracted VD, only enlisted men were sent to the Venereal Disease Rehabilitation Center in Chinhae near Pusan on receiving a positive test result.[67] There, GIs had

Figure 1.4 Two Black GIs go on "pass" at Camp Hovey. Courtesy of Richard Bridges.

Figure 1.5 US soldiers patrol a camptown in Dongducheon. Courtesy of Richard Bridges.

their "pass privileges" revoked and were restricted to their unit areas for at least thirty and up to ninety days so as "to diminish the chances for relapse or early reinfection."[68] Infected men were subject to an intensive schedule of forty hours per week, which included four hours of daily military training, emphasis on athletic activity, and lessons focused on morality, preventative measures, and religious services.[69] Their stay in the rehabilitation center was considered a "loss of time" and not counted toward duty.[70] Yet, despite these aggressive VD control measures implemented for both Korean women and US servicemen, VD rates nearly doubled in 1948, peaking in September at 182 per 1,000 soldiers per annum.[71]

The intense VD control regime helped to homogenize an image of Korean women, in the minds of most US personnel, as potential VD carriers and thus likely prostitutes. While contact tracing reports revealed that the most frequent occurrence of VD transmission involved "solicitors" and "prostitutes," there was another problem—high incidence of "pickups," or clandestine encounters with local women. Statistics gathered from contact reports in October 1948 revealed that 39 percent of encounters resulting in venereal disease were with "solicitors," 28 percent were with "prostitutes," and 33 percent were with "pickups."[72] Warnings against "pickups" soon became part of venereal disease education. In a standard script for a VD lecture, enlisted men were alerted by their commissioned officers that "any girls whom you can pick up here in the Far East Command are almost certain to have venereal disease," adding, "there is no way you can pick out the clean ones."[73] Further, while the US military employed many educated women who could speak English for jobs on base as typists, secretaries, clerks, librarians, coffee girls, laundresses, hairstylists, and house girls, officials issued stern warnings about those women as well. "Regardless of how beautiful she may be, how well she speaks English, your chances are still the same—that you have picked up an infected girl."[74] Commanders cautioned GIs "to remember that any girl who will sell herself to you, whether you pay her in money, 'presents,' or a good time, will be doing the same for many other soldiers"—thereby vilifying even casual dating.[75] Eventually military officers were instructed to "[bring] out the fact that in most areas the rate of venereal disease is 100 [percent]" and inform their troops "of the seriousness of venereal disease contracted in Korea as compared to other countries, citing the recent discharge of five cases from medical care listed as 'uncurables.'"[76] Such thinking ultimately blurred the lines between prostitute, solicitor, camptown local, civilian employee, and steady native companion.

Beneath such official discouragement, however, was an on-the-ground culture of acceptance. After delivering such scripted warnings about

Figure 1.6 A Korean woman and her GI boyfriend. Courtesy of Korean Image Archive.

Korean women's promiscuity, officers instructed soldiers to use condoms and follow up by "taking a prophylactic within less than one hour after" exposure.[77] This reflected widespread acknowledgment by military officials that sexual contact, despite the grave risks it presented to the soldier, was all but inevitable. Further, VD control councils regularly complained that "too many unit commanders do not know or care what their men do in off duty hours—whether they engage in legitimate recreation . . . or hunt dives or molest honest Korean citizens in their 'women hunting' activities."[78] Numerous officers were even accused of failing to provide proper VD control education to their subordinates or of upholding high standards in their own conduct.[79] GIs often defended their own actions by pointing out that their superiors set a bad example for "the behavior of enlisted personnel."[80] Unit commanders were accused of "sleepwalk[ing] through the day so they can get drunk again at night" and "associat[ing] loosely with Korean women or any others they can get their hands on."[81] A note to "all officers" from Headquarters (United States Army Forces in Korea) pointed out that "a married officer whose wife is not with him, who is constantly keeping company with the same member of the opposite sex is not conforming . . . to the high standards of propriety, personal example and good taste which must prevail in this command."[82] Compounding the irony, at the same time that the US military organized vice squads and instituted aggressive anti-VD propaganda, it also directly facilitated sexual contact with local women deemed to be free of venereal disease. Correspondence between USAMGIK officials reveals that the army "haul[ed] Korean women" onto base or to enlisted men's clubs "in jeeps" and brought "Shanghai girls" into dance halls.[83] But because these women were "housed together," "taken back and forth under custody," and "examined once a month," military officials believed that they did "not contribute to our difficulties."[84]

By January of 1949, VD rates had doubled again to 319 per 1,000 soldiers per annum.[85] US military officials blamed this on the inauguration of the South Korean government on August 15, 1948, which eliminated the "authority formerly exercised by the Army Provost Court over illicit operators."[86] No longer able to legally detain Korean citizens, US officials credited the "marked increase in the activities of solicitors and prostitutes" to "the laxity of present court procedures and the insignificance of minimal sentences and fine impositions."[87] VD Control Council members noted that the new government seldom imposed jail sentences on those "picked up and turned over to the Korean police," having observed some women "back on the streets" the very next day.[88] In truth, Korean "prisons and jails were already overcrowded" in the initial days of the First Republic.[89]

Such a clash between the South Korean government and the US military reflected a stark difference in priorities. But the end of USAMGIK also

Figure 1.7 A burlesque dance show on base. Courtesy of Richard Bridges.

Figure 1.8 A Korean performer dances for US soldiers in a barracks. Courtesy of Korean Image Archive.

Figure 1.9 Korean women fraternize with US soldiers. Courtesy of Korean Image Archive.

Figure 1.10 US soldiers dance with Korean women. Courtesy of Korean Image Archive.

coincided with a gradual withdrawal of US troops from the Korean peninsula. In September 1948, the VD Rehabilitation Center had closed as part of these changes. This created "an erroneous opinion among some enlisted personnel that . . . interest in Venereal Disease control has been lessened."[90] Further, military officials attributed rising VD rates to men who had newly come forward to seek treatment (after previously hiding their infections for fear of punishment), "the mass transfer of men and officers between units," and general "uncertainties surrounding the retention of troops" in Korea.[91] During "the last few weeks of the year" this had resulted in "a temporary loss of the normal chain of command," "lowered living standards," and "lowered morale."[92] Thus, in the months leading up to June 1949, when all but about 500 high-ranking officers comprising a military advisory group for South Korean forces withdrew from the peninsula, US military officers had effectively lost control of the VD issue. This meant that the final days of the US military's initial occupation in Korea were some of its worst.

In the end, despite such an aggressive VD control regime, the US military was never able to fully resolve the crisis of sexually transmitted diseases. Comparatively, morbidity rates for VD peaked at approximately 150 per 1,000 soldiers per annum in Japan during October of 1946—an excessive figure that undoubtedly vexed occupation forces but, nonetheless, represented less than half that in Korea at its highest points.[93] Although the history of venereal disease followed a similar trajectory in Japan (including the initial unfettered use of "comfort stations" on part of military personnel, the eventual public ban on prostitution amid rising VD rates, the proliferation of private prostitution, and similar VD control tactics), the situation in Korea was exacerbated by the temporary nature of the US military's initial occupation.[94] While the USAMGIK would, more or less, leave Korea after three years, Occupied Japan was becoming a "workshop of democracy" from which the United States hoped to develop a democratic stronghold to counter Soviet ambitions in the region.[95] Although thoroughly devastated by US firebombs and atomic bombs, Japan retained its imperial advantage vis-à-vis Korea, and its political, economic, and educational systems were considered a more promising model for US capitalism in East Asia. In contrast, when Korea was divided at the 38th parallel, decades of oppressive colonial rule had left the peninsula underdeveloped, impoverished, and therefore of significantly less geopolitical importance. Relegated to the periphery of US foreign policy and Cold War concerns in the mid-to-late 1940s, Korea's importance in the minds of US policymakers had become relative to its auxiliary role in supporting Japan's postwar recovery and development.

Questions and anxieties about US commitments to Korea in the early Cold War years were reflected even in the material conditions of military housing and garrisoning which, in turn, hampered VD control efforts. For example, when General Hodge arrived on the Korean peninsula in September of 1945, he spent his first night in a former Japanese silk warehouse, where he "put down two mattresses on the floor and piled two more on top."[96] He would later move into an "old abandoned constabulary barracks."[97] Throughout the years of USAMGIK this kind of ad hoc housing continued. Troops lived in makeshift barracks as well as hotels, schools, factories, and old military facilities previously owned by the colonial government and transformed for use by US military personnel. The billeting situation, in many ways, showed that the occupation of Korea was based on "an emergency measure rather than on the basis . . . of sound planning and forethought."[98] Such conditions made for a virtual bachelor's society, comprising single, unaccompanied men on year-long stints. In areas of Occupied Japan with similar ad hoc housing such as "quonset or prefabricated huts," military officials recorded high venereal disease rates comparable to those found in Korea.[99] Commanders of the Eighth US Army in Occupied Japan (which would not arrive in Korea until 1950 at the onset of war) agreed that there seemed to be a correlation between "crowded and dingy" material conditions and "delinquencies of individuals" who in "seeking relief from these drab and uninviting surroundings" might be more likely to engage in illicit affairs with local women.[100] While a longer occupation in Japan meant that "fund[ing] for the rehabilitation of substandard troop housing and the construction of attractive local recreational facilities" would be made available, in Korea (where most of the US military would withdraw by the summer of 1949) it was impractical to combat VD with improved facilities, and such efforts remained relatively limited.[101] As a result, VD control councils in Korea regularly cited the lack of adequate housing and recreation as a major contributing factor in rising VD rates. Similarly, the "colored rate" of infection remained much higher than the "white rate" given the less than desirable living and working conditions of Black units during an era of segregation—although military officials at the time tried to understand such differences in racial rather than environmental terms.[102]

By contrast, within a few months of arriving in Japan, the US military had developed dependent housing and welcomed military wives to help support the long-term efforts of the occupiers.[103] As early as 1946, military bases in Occupied Japan began to resemble American suburbs like Levittown, complete with movie theaters, shopping centers, bowling alleys, and a host of other recreational commodities. Such infrastructure created a culture of occupation that was more conducive to childrearing and family maintenance. Differences in the material conditions of Occupied Japan and Korea shaped contrasting images of local women in the minds of US personnel, ultimately influencing military policies toward cohabitation, marriage, and paternity in each respective location. In Japan, US military officials' views of Japanese women would evolve beyond prostitute or temporary companion to include that of wife and mother. The first major indication of such a shift became evident following the passage of the War Brides Act.

When Congress enacted the War Brides Act in 1945, it initially adhered to the racial restrictions of the Immigration and Nationality Act of 1924

(32)   *The First Amerasians*

Figure 1.11 US soldiers pose outside their barracks at Camp Hovey. Courtesy of Richard Bridges.

Figure 1.12 US soldiers show off photographs of their American wives back home. Courtesy of Richard Bridges.

Figure 1.13 Permanent housing structures for US military personnel and their dependents in Occupied Japan, 1949. Courtesy of National Archives, photo no. 342-J-29-F-72533AC.

barring "aliens ineligible for citizenship" from entry into the United States.[104] Thus, while European spouses of US citizens were afforded nonquota immigration rights via the provisions of this law, Asian wives were excluded. US military officials used these terms of exclusion to categorically deny all marriage applications between US servicemen and Japanese or Korean women in their occupation zones during the early postwar years. However, in 1947, after the Japanese American Citizens League's Anti-Discrimination Committee had lobbied Congress and numerous servicemen stationed in Japan petitioned for special bills that might allow the entries of their Japanese fiancées and wives, a law was passed to extend rights of entry to Asian women.[105] On July 22, 1947, Public Law 213 amended the War Brides Act of 1945 by adding a new section that read: "The alien spouse of an American citizen by a marriage occurring before thirty days after the enactment of this Act, shall not be considered as inadmissible because of race, if otherwise admissible under this Act."[106] Under these provisions, Asian spouses of US servicemen would be eligible for entry into the United States if their marriages occurred within this brief window of time.

However, while the 1947 amendment represented an unprecedented breakthrough, it was not actually transgressive in terms of race relations.

(34) The First Amerasians

Adhering to the status quo of miscegenation, Congress deemed the intended beneficiaries to be "soldiers of the Japanese or Korean race" who had "married girls of their own race while serving in the Pacific," rather than white, Black, or other non-Asian servicemen.[107] As a result, the majority of the marriages that were approved by occupation forces in the summer of 1947 involved Japanese American soldiers, although many white and Black servicemen also successfully utilized the provisions of this law. Under Public Law 213, Asian spouses married between July and August 1947 had until the expiration of the War Brides Act on December 27, 1948, to enter the United States, although this was later extended to September of 1949.[108] According to statistics from the Immigration and Naturalization Services (INS), 757 Japanese women immigrated to the United States as the wives of American citizens between the years 1947 and 1949.[109] The very same INS statistics reveal that not a single Korean bride arrived stateside during the 1940s. This dramatic gap indicates either that news about the 1947 amendment to the War Brides Act had not reached Korea or that military officials had decided that such policies would not apply to Korean women.

The presence of Japanese wives whose marriages had been legitimated and approved by occupation commanders under Public Law 213 helped to gradually reshape military policies and soften the image of Japanese women in the minds of US military personnel. Prior to the summer of 1947, a number of marriages between Japanese women and US servicemen had taken place under local civil law without the approval of military officials. As a result, these wives were not eligible "to receive dependency housing, commissary, [Post Exchange], or other benefits except as may be specially authorized by the military authorities in such cases."[110] The 1947 law, however, changed this, creating a new category of "authorized" marriages between personnel and Japanese women for which the US military "assumed a moral obligation."[111] For example, when a sudden increase in Japanese dependents following the summer of 1947 posed a problem for the US military's goals to "provide at least a room" for its personnel and their families, the US military instituted a policy allowing its men to move into the homes of their new Japanese wives and in-laws, "provided no private rental agreement is entered" and "a sanitary inspection of the house accomplished to determine suitability" was conducted.[112] In Korea, where few, if any, such "authorized" marriages had occurred and accommodations for military dependents remained extremely limited (reserved just for high-ranking officers), a "prohibition against private arrangements to obtain housing" remained in effect.[113] Thus, for US servicemen stationed in Korea, the "definite restrictions and limitations upon the presence of dependents" helped to create conditions encouraging temporary sexual companions in lieu of long-term, marriageable partners.[114]

This is not to say that US military officials did not discriminate against interracial and international couples in Japan. In fact, as early as 1946, commanding officers were instructed to respond to personnel requests for permission to marry Japanese nationals with "reassignment to a distant station, or if eligible for return to the United States."[115] While this practice had diminished in the context of Public Law 213 in 1947, some commanding officers, because of their own personal prejudices, continued to utilize such a policy to separate GIs from their Japanese partners.[116] Consequently, US servicemen in Japan would express their frustrations about the "the lack of cooperation from the Army and all of the red tape" well into the 1950s.[117] All in all, however, these prejudices were personal and could be traced to a few individual commanders rather than to a uniform policy consistent within Occupied Japan. Although some unit officers may have discouraged their enlisted men from marrying Japanese women, the change in policy toward tolerating these relationships seemed to permeate US military culture in Japan following the summer of 1947.

Prior to the enactment of Public Law 213, standard procedure was to deny all requests for permission to marry given the lack of immigration provisions allowing for Asian women's entry into the United States "except under very unusual circumstances."[118] Such exceptions had initially been made for high-ranking officers (those deemed as essential personnel, such as linguists who needed to be retained in the Far East Command) or servicemen who had successfully convinced their congressmen to pass a private bill on their behalf. After August 1947, however, a looser interpretation of "unusual circumstances" applied, even after the expiration of the War Brides Act amendment for Asian spouses. For starters, many servicemen believed that immigration laws would eventually change to permanently allow their Japanese fiancées to enter the United States. One such soldier, Sergeant Kowashi Hirai, who petitioned to marry Yachiyo Nagata in August 1948 protested the marriage ban based on immigration laws. He argued, "This handicap can be overcome because . . . I intend to repeatedly re-enlist in the Army or stay here in Japan as a civilian until such time that the law changes permitting me to return with my prospective wife and dependents to the United States or its possessions."[119] In fact, Hirai had already "extended [his] enlistment of eighteen months to three years" hoping to wait out a new immigration bill.[120] Such arguments were seen as compelling and often proved successful in garnering the sympathies of military commanders who then "recommend[ed] approval" for the

(36) *The First Amerasians*

marriages.[121] In Korea, where tours were shorter and grittier, averaging one year, such a strategy could not be so easily employed.

While Nisei men were the primary beneficiaries of these changes in military thinking—with commanders citing reasons such as "both parties are of Japanese extraction" or "there is no language barrier"—non-Japanese servicemen also benefited from the more liberal interpretation of "unusual circumstances."[122] One such man was Sergeant William Palms, who received permission to marry Etsuko Sato in July 1948. The couple had "lived together as man and wife in a common law relationship" for three years, and bore a child whose "strong resemblance" to Palms "would convince the most dubious person of the validity of his claim."[123] Pending pertinent immigration provisions, Sergeant Palms proposed to remain in Japan or return home to "the cosmopolitan city of New York where minimum prejudice exists."[124] His commanding officer attested to Palms's "excellent character," outstanding performance of duty, and the fact "that the man has reached a reasonable mature age" after having "ample time to think" over the relationship.[125] Finally, it was suggested that "if permission to marry is not granted, I think some provision for the care and upkeep of this child should be made."[126] The marriage was ultimately approved, determined to constitute "unusual circumstances."

Other marriages were approved on the grounds that the soldiers' fiancées were pregnant.[127] One soldier who secured permission to marry in February 1948 argued his case as an issue of morality, stating "I feel very strongly against having my child born out of wedlock, and I feel that these are very unusual circumstances as outlined in paragraph 2c Circular 172 Headquarters Eighth Army."[128] After the summer of 1947, the US military kept meticulous documentation of all of the Japanese wives of US servicemen who became pregnant. The logs, which record the dates of marriage alongside expected delivery dates, confirm that a growing number of enlisted men of ordinary rank were even being granted permission to marry Japanese women at a time when no special immigration provisions for Asian spouses existed.[129] Further, they also demonstrated a commitment by the occupation forces in Japan to provide pre- and post-natal care for pregnant military dependents, including more suitable living quarters.[130] All of this attests to a more sympathetic view of Japanese women as potential wives and mothers, made possible only by a shifting military assessment that such relations between occupier and occupied could be wholesome and good.

In Korea, similar sympathies or consideration for Korean wives, fiancées, and children of US servicemen were absent, revealing a more rigid and callous adherence to military policies against interracial and

Figure 1.14 US soldiers with their Japanese partners, 1952. Courtesy of National Archives, photo no. 342-J-55-C-91322AC.

international marriages.[131] In fact, Korean Americans were not afforded the same leniency in their quest to marry their co-ethnic brides as their Nisei counterparts in Occupied Japan. In January 1949, for example, Corporal George Kim's request to marry Won Kyu Lim, "an employee of the American Mission in Korea," was argued on similar grounds as those of his Nisei predecessors. Kim's "Korean ancestry," the fact that he "speaks, reads and writes Korean language fluently," and intended "to return to Korea to live and earn his livelihood" were all highlighted in his request.[132] In a further attempt to demonstrate "unusual circumstances," it was added that "it will be difficult for George Kim to find an American, white girl for a spouse, because of existing racial barriers in America."[133] Ultimately these reasons were not considered as constituting appropriate grounds for approval, and Corporal Kim's request was ultimately denied.[134] Compounding this ironic and uneven policy, even Nisei personnel stationed in Korea (who could easily have been transferred to Japan as linguists with their prospective brides) had their petitions rejected, as was the case with Masaru Mac Morinaka in March of 1949.[135] All of this reveals that it was not the circumstances of the marriage, the character of the personnel, or even the backgrounds of the fiancées themselves that informed such a widespread

(38)   *The First Amerasians*

ban; the very fact that they were involved with Korean women was what made the US military so unwavering in its discriminatory attitudes toward these relationships.

Nevertheless, there were still numerous incidents of servicemen who had married Korean women after having been disapproved by commanding officers. Military officials responded to such insubordination by transferring personnel out of Korea on learning of an unauthorized marriage, thereby separating families. Masaru Mac Morinaka's record noted, "This marriage clearly cannot be approved under Circular 4, Headquarters USAFIK," adding "if he marries without approval, he will be returned to Hawai'i."[136] The US military also viewed such marriages as an "infraction of orders," making derogatory marks in the permanent records of servicemen like Sergeant Victor Cericole, who married Jaisook Kim after disapproval in October of 1948.[137] Such a "violation of a standing order" could be considered career shattering, serving as grounds for permanent ineligibility for promotion within military ranks.[138] The presence of children made no difference, as was demonstrated in the case of Army Corporal Nicholas Rossow who married his wife Mang Chung Hi in May of 1949.[139] One month later, after discovering such a marriage had taken place, the US military refused to assist in Rossow's aims to "legally establish and record said birth" of their child.[140] Instead, it was determined that Corporal Rossow had "married without authority" and he was ordered to "depart Korea alone" in June of 1949.[141]

On August 19, 1950, Public Law 717 revived the War Brides Act of 1945, removing racial restrictions for Japanese and Korean women. This change was part of a broader liberalization of US immigration laws in the early Cold War years and helped to construct US democracy as a harbinger of racial equality in the postwar era.[142] While initially the law was applicable only to those whose marriages occurred within "six months after enactment," it was later extended for an additional six months.[143] By 1952, the McCarran-Walter Act (also known as the Immigration and Nationality Act of 1952) granted all spouses of US citizens (regardless of race) non-quota immigration status. The law also lifted racial restrictions on naturalization and re-designated what was previously the "Asiatic Barred Zone" as an "Asia-Pacific Triangle," for which quotas, rather than exclusion, applied.[144] Such legislative changes meant that the US military, by the summer of 1950, could no longer rely on racial exclusions in immigration law to forbid soldiers from marrying Korean women. Nonetheless, exclusionary policies continued throughout the 1950s. Accordingly, despite comparable troop rates, only 2,000 Korean women are recorded in immigration statistics as immigrating to the United States as the wives of US citizens, compared to 30,000 Japanese brides during the same decade.[145]

The return of some 1.8 million US troops to the peninsula with the onset of the war only further exacerbated issues in Korea. As thousands of refugees flocked to American bases for food and shelter, private prostitution flourished. One military official bluntly stated that large population of camp followers "followed concentrations of troops wherever such concentrations occurred."[146] A formal system of regulated military prostitution, borrowed from the Japanese "comfort women" system, also reemerged.[147] These establishments served both the Korean and UN armies and were justified as a means to combat low morale in wartime settings, sexually reward soldiers for their "sacrifices," and protect ordinary Korean women from rape.[148] Elderly Korean women of this generation reiterate in their oral histories the numerous incidents of kidnapping and sexual violence perpetrated by the US military before the "comfort system" was instituted. One woman recalls:

> Virgins, married women, young girls, even grandmothers—the US soldiers would rape all the women. They wouldn't touch the kids, but if you were over 16 years old . . . My older sister even hid in a large earthenware jar at night, and my uncle's sister hid too—because they were afraid of being raped.[149]

Some "comfort stations" were erected and maintained by the Korean military and government, while others were set up by "private businesses that secured approval from the authorities."[150] "Comfort stations" preyed on destitute women, including those vulnerable to exploitation after having been separated from their families, orphaned, or impoverished by the war. Some of these "comfort women" were also captured "female communists and collaborators" forced into military prostitution.[151] Following the first year of combat, when the warfront stabilized with positional warfare at the demilitarized zone, "comfort stations" would spread across all of Korea, becoming one of the only forms of interaction between US soldiers and Koreans.[152] According to one South Korean military document, eighty-nine "comfort women" (rotating between three "comfort station" units in Seoul and one unit in Gangneung) collectively gave 204,560 "comfort services" to soldiers in 1952.[153] Such a figure represents an average of six services per day per woman.[154] Further, there was at least one division of mobile "comfort women" consisting of seventy-nine women who went "to the front lines" to service soldiers engaged in direct combat.[155] All such women were tested for venereal disease twice a week.[156]

Estimates on the total number of "comfort women" serving both the Korean and UN armies during the Korean War are largely incomplete. However, US military reports record the number of sex workers (both "registered prostitutes" and "non-registered prostitutes") within their purview who were subject to regular venereal disease testing. In November 1952, for instance, "more than 30,000 prostitutes were examined" with "approximately 30 percent show[ing] infection with one or more disease."[157] Of these, around two-thirds seem to be "non-registered prostitutes," given that US military documents from April 1953 record 10,761 "registered prostitutes" (most likely synonymous with "comfort women") and eighty-nine VD clinics to which the US military was directing assistance at that time.[158] "Comfort stations" were viewed by South Korean officials as temporary wartime measures that would eventually cease following an established peace.[159] By March 1954, the Korean government closed all of their "comfort stations," many of which were then re-appropriated as dance halls and service clubs for US military personnel, where military prostitution resumed nonetheless.[160]

The reemergence of prostitution during the Korean War helped to resolidify an idea in the minds of military commanders that Korean women were unsuitable marriage partners for American GIs, despite major shifts in US immigration policy. Such attitudes did not go unnoticed by US military officials elsewhere. In September 1951, "numerous rotatees" arriving at the Sasebo Replacement Depot, 8068th Army Unit in Japan had stated their "desire to marry" Korean women without "either an approved application or unit commander's statement that it was impracticable to process the individual's marriage application prior to departure."[161] Confused as to "why applications were not processed prior to departure" (given the "length of time the majority of these men have been in Korea" and the fact that "many were reported to be from 301 units which precludes the possibility of combat conditions interfering with submission of application"), the memorandum instructed commanding officers in Korea to comply with standard procedure.[162] This reveals that individual commanding officers were continuing to ignore soldiers' requests to marry Korean women. As a result, these soldiers were instead applying for permission after they left Korea.

Following the Korean War, such discriminatory practices by military officers would continue. The US military adapted a uniform policy to discourage marriages with Korean women rather than prohibit them—not on the basis of restrictive immigration laws since those no longer existed, but instead through "the pertinent laws of the proposed state of residence concerning interracial marriages."[163] Prospective applicants received marriage counseling in which they were advised against entering into interracial marriages. A standard script entered into a servicemen's record included a statement from his commanding officer noting: "I have pointed out to him every pitfall of the road ahead and from years of experience in dealing with these situations I have advised him strongly that the odds of a successful marriage are not in his favor."[164] Additional administrative red tape added to the arduous process, including character conduct assessments by community leaders of the prospective brides, (sexual) health examinations, letters from family supporting the impending marriage, and background checks ensuring that the fiancée had never "been a prostitute, procurer, or pimp."[165] The latter was indicative of a broader view on the part of US authorities of Korean women as prostitutes until proven innocent.

Some commanders even went one step further in their own personal convictions to prevent their enlisted personnel from marrying Korean women. Often paperwork sat on the commanding officer's desk without further processing or action. Reassignment policy also continued. In 1952, when US servicemen David Keller met Sook Kyung Ko at the GI Service Center Library in Pusan, the pair fell victim to similar tactics. After having learned that his subordinate was going steady with the local librarian employed on base, Keller's commander "transferred [him] to another base . . . also intercepting the letters [he] subsequently sent to [his Korean girlfriend]."[166] A fellow GI finally told Keller what his commanding officer had done, and the couple reconciled and married in August 1955. While the Kellers were lucky, many others were not.

In the 1950s, the camptown military sex industry would continue to grow alongside the establishment of semi-permanent military installations, transforming from large populations of camp followers servicing troops out of tents and cardboard houses in shantytowns into small cities complete with commercial entertainment districts catering to a stable troop presence.[167] By 1955, just two years after the war, there were some 60,000 Korean sex workers servicing foreign soldiers throughout the country.[168] Because the Korean War ended in an armistice agreement—a mere cessation of hostilities, rather than a formal peace agreement—the conditions of an unending war would keep South Korea designated "a restricted area" or hardship tour by the US military.[169] As a result, a military culture orienting servicemen away from long-term relations with Korean women and instead toward regulated military prostitution would persist. Despite similar troop populations, marriages between Korean women and American GIs would not reach the same numbers as those in Japan until the 1970s, indicating that the dominant image of Korean women as prostitutes established during the 1940s endured for over two decades.[170]

Figure 1.15 The Kellers just after they were married, 1955. Courtesy of Ruth Keller.

These policies, ideas, and on-the-ground realities shaping relations between GIs and local women not only influenced how Korean women were treated by US military officials but also impacted the children who would be born from such encounters. Many families were literally forced apart by military commanders who refused to approve marriages between Korean women and US servicemen, in many cases even after the babies arrived. As a result of this cold indifference, some mixed race children—abandoned by Korean mothers and GI fathers in desperate circumstances—were left on the streets, the doorsteps of police stations, US military bases, missions, and orphanages.[171] While a similar problem had emerged in Occupied Japan, it had been more or less resolved by the mid-1950s. American military government families stationed there adopted thousands of those orphans, and nongovernmental Japanese agencies also assisted in integrating mixed race children into Japanese society.

However, war-torn Korea struggled to handle the crisis on its own. By the mid-1950s, thousands of American missionaries and voluntary aid workers would arrive in Korea to assist in the humanitarian crisis following the Korean War. Together, these individuals estimated that there were some 50,000 war orphans in South Korea's overcrowded orphanages, noting that mixed race children, while comprising just a small fraction of this number, experienced additional hardships.[172] Soon Americans spearheading the postwar recovery campaign would embark on an international campaign to bring these children "home."[173] Their efforts would expand to include not only those orphaned but also those living with their single Korean mothers in camptown communities surrounding US military installations. During this process, the dominant ideas surrounding Korean women as prostitutes would be disavowed to construct a humanitarian rescue based on wholesome images of US-Korean relations but would also be employed by adoption advocates to undermine Korean women's maternal rights and create more orphans eligible for adoption in American families.

2

"The Problem of the Mixed Blood Child"

Dear Anderson,[1]

Just a few lines to let you know is I am feeling fine and everythings are getting along ok. But I don't know what I must inquire of you first for this is the first times letter ever I had been wrote you. Hope you don't have any trouble to read his unfluently letter and have understand if there is any mistaking words in this letter. Dear Mrs. Anderson how have you been feeling and all family? "fine" I hope. The baby is left from here almost 5 days now and I hope nothing to have any trouble and reach to there by time now. Because the baby is already reach or not. and I pray to the God the baby like you and all family too. And I am going to send baby clothes . . . and this clothe is made in Korea clothe because the baby was liked it. and you too. then if you receive it let me know as soon as. How is the weather there now? The weather of here today real fine and warm outside. It is very peaceful day well there is so many things to tell you. but it is to late so I am going to close for this time. Please write more often and I will try again. Then I will looking forward to having the wonderful letter from you very soon. Take care of yourself this cold weather. May lord bless you and protect you always.

With your good friends,

Lee Chun Ja
P.S. I don't know if you like this is the Korean sing (play Rocker) because she liked it very much if you like it I will send next mail.[2]

On December 28, 1959, Mr. and Mrs. Anderson of Anchorage, Alaska, received what they viewed to be a very "disturbing" letter.[3] The note, arriving just days after they had welcomed an adoptive daughter into their

The First Amerasians. Yuri W. Doolan, Oxford University Press. © Oxford University Press 2024.
DOI: 10.1093/oso/9780197534380.003.0003

home, appeared to have been sent by the child's "natural mother."[4] Like so many Americans adopting mixed race Koreans during these years, the Andersons' knowledge of so-called GI babies was limited to what they had read in the print media, seen on television, been told by social welfare professionals working on their case, or heard through the firsthand accounts of Americans participating in South Korea's postwar recovery. It was from these sources that the family learned about "the problem of the mixed blood child" and the pitiful conditions in which they lived and perished.[5] Ashamed Korean mothers "left them to die as soon as they were born" and even had the "right to kill them."[6] In institutions and on the streets, GI babies were found "stoned to death" by their full Korean playmates "as well as adults."[7] Even nurses' aides working in childcare facilities "with[held] food from these babies of mixed origin," saving what scarce resources existed for those of "full Korean" parentage instead.[8] As "children who knew only life in a Korean orphanage" and had "never known the love and affection of real mothers," champions of the "mixed blood child" called upon ordinary citizens, like the Andersons, to rescue these innocent "half-Americans" from a life of misery and imminent death.[9] This letter, however, revealing that their six-year-old daughter was not actually an abandoned war orphan but had a loving mother back in Seoul, contradicted much of what the family thought they knew about mixed race children and their desperate plight in South Korea.

In the confidential child study conducted prior to the placement of the Andersons' "Korean-Caucasian" daughter, Korean social welfare professionals noted that the young girl "lived in an environment which gave her love and security," was looked after by both her Korean mother and grandmother, and was "not badly in poverty."[10] The American agency assisting in the Andersons' placement, however, ignored all this—failing to see past what they viewed to be an "almost impossible social situation in Korea."[11] Instead, in correspondence with the Department of Public Welfare in Alaska, American caseworkers maintained that the young girl had "a very inadequate home life."[12] Her mother was vilified as a prostitute and depicted as a "simple, uneducated woman" who could not care for her daughter and might "literally 'sell' the child to about anybody."[13] Such dehumanizing portrayals of Korean mothers and exaggerations of their living conditions were commonly used to create a sense of urgency among child welfare professionals so as to expedite lengthy adoption procedures amid soon-to-expire orphan legislation.

After contacting the agency involved with this adoption about the letter they had received, the Andersons were assured by their case workers that the situation would be dealt with and the family need not respond. As for the Lee Chun Ja, the birth mother back in Seoul, she was to be reminded by a Korean social worker that releasing her child for adoption meant a complete severing of the relationship. As such, she could not continue to send letters to the adoptive family, nor should she expect to hear about her daughter again. In order for the six-year-old to "learn to belong to a new father and mother," it was emphasized that she "have no complicating ties with Korea."[14] Following this incident, the Andersons formalized the adoption of this young girl, and it seems the family never heard from Lee Chun Ja again.

This chapter examines how ordinary Americans like the Andersons came to adopt the children born to US servicemen and Korean women in camptowns, eventually bringing thousands to the United States in the 1950s and 1960s. Although American humanitarians initially failed to see the issues facing mixed race Koreans as separate from the myriad other problems experienced by the general war-torn, impoverished, and disease-ridden population, this all changed in 1954 when Oregon farmer Harry Holt and his wife Bertha made it their life's mission to rescue as many GI babies from South Korea as possible. Utilizing the special orphan provisions of the Refugee Relief Act of 1953 and a method called proxy adoption, the Holts made obtaining mixed race children quick, affordable, and accessible to US citizens who could not travel to South Korea on their own. However, in 1956, when the Refugee Relief Act expired, with no clear indication of whether another bill might be enacted to extend its orphan provisions, the lack of an expedient immigration pathway for Korea's mixed race population created a sense of hysteria among adoption advocates.

Between 1956 and 1961, intercountry adoption was facilitated through a series of three temporary laws that extended the orphan provisions of the Refugee Relief Act. But each time one of these acts expired, a period of several months followed when the future of mixed race Koreans seemed uncertain. It was during these interim moments that Americans panicked and constructed the figure of the neglected and mistreated "half-American" child to lobby Congress for the quick passage of new orphan legislation. Central to this effort were depictions of South Korea as a backward, barbaric, and racist society; Korean mothers as prostitutes and incapable mothers; and thus mixed race children as abandoned war orphans in need of loving homes. In addition to the humanitarian motivations for an American intervention, adoption advocates also emphasized to US lawmakers the foreign policy benefits of continuing to allow their citizens to adopt mixed race Koreans. Allies of the Holts argued that by extending refugee orphan provisions for these abandoned GI children, the US government would not only win friends in the Far East by proving its brand of

"THE PROBLEM OF THE MIXED BLOOD CHILD" (47)

democracy was benevolent and racially tolerant, but it would also counter communist accusations of US imperialism, irresponsibility, and immorality in the Third World.

Despite these dominant narratives constructed both to motivate the American public to adopt GI children and convince Congress to enact new orphan laws, conditions surrounding mixed race Koreans were not always as bad as adoption advocates made them seem. In South Korea, the general public's attitude toward mixed race children had begun improving by the time Americans arrived on the scene to rescue these individuals in the mid-1950s, and most Korean mothers were not actually prostitutes who could not care for their own children but were the separated wives or fiancées of US military personnel. Further, the rash behavior of American adoption advocates in South Korea actually caused harm to mixed race children, many of whom were taken from their Korean mothers and hastily placed into families in the United States. Between 1953 and 1961, over 4,000 children from South Korea would be placed with American families; the vast majority of these children were mixed race individuals, but some had full Korean parentage.[15] The movement Americans created around mixed race Korean adoptions eventually culminated in an amendment to the US Immigration and Nationality Act in 1961, which provided permanent provisions for the entry of children under the age of fourteen entering the United States for the purpose of adoption by US citizens.

———

Prior to the Refugee Relief Act's enactment in August of 1953, a small number of Americans serving in South Korea as military personnel, missionaries, and voluntary aid workers had already begun adopting Korean children through petitioning private bills in Congress. Some of these early adoptees were the so-called mascots or camp orphans seen around US bases. Units "would take on a Korean boy" to perform domestic duties for their soldiers and the last sergeant remaining ("after the others had been sent home") would bring the child with him to the United States.[16] Other children included orphans whose families had been killed or disappeared during war, as well as waifs picked off the streets, nursed back to health in barracks or hospitals, and formally adopted by US citizens living in South Korea.[17] Both mixed race individuals and those of full Korean parentage were among this first cohort of Korean adoptees. One such child was five-year-old Jimmy, "orphaned when the North Korean communists killed his mother."[18] Although Jimmy was mixed race and had been born to a white father, the Los Angeles Times article featuring his adoption found

(48)   *The First Amerasians*

this fact to be of little significance. Instead, he was described as "just another waif" until twenty-five-year-old Sergeant Paul Raynor noticed him one day and moved him into his compound.[19] The new father eventually adopted Jimmy and brought him stateside following the end of his military tour in November of 1953. Like much of the early media coverage surrounding the first Korean adoptees, the article about Jimmy's adoption failed to differentiate between the problems facing mixed race Koreans and those afflicting the general populace. This reportage was characteristic of Americans' indifference to or possibly ignorance of GI-fathered children during the immediate postwar years.

It is also possible that the lack of acknowledgment in the US media was a deliberate effort to conceal the role of military personnel in creating this crisis of illegitimate mixed race progeny left behind in South Korea. Indeed, the issues facing these children and their mothers extended beyond the poverty and destruction of civilian life wreaked by war and experienced broadly by all Koreans at the time. For the children, being born to a Korean mother did not confer automatic Korean citizenship, as this was granted by paternal *jus sanguinis* or, entry of the birth into the family register of a male head of household. Sometimes, women who had the support of extended family could get around this by convincing their fathers or brothers to register their children as their own. But in cases when they could not or when no male relatives existed and US military authorities refused to recognize such children as the legitimate sons and daughters of American servicemen, the futures of such children remained uncertain. For their mothers, even after the McCarran-Walter Act lifted racial restrictions on Asian brides' entry into the United States in 1952, military commanders continued to "discourage marriages" on the assumption that such women were prostitutes.[20] While some camptown women practicing prostitution became pregnant and a few children were the products of rape, the vast majority of mixed race children were born to the wives, fiancées, or steady partners of US servicemen. Field studies produced by child experts in camptowns regularly confirmed this fact, noting that "the true prostitute does not have babies" and that "the girl who has a baby is usually going steady with the father (the relationship being that of a mistress rather than a prostitute)."[21]

One such woman named Kim Soon Ja found work as a typist on a US military base near Seoul, where she met her GI husband sometime after the war. Although Kim at first tried "hard not to like him," owing to the custom that "Korean women should marry Korean," her husband was persistent and eventually proposed.[22] But because the military chaplain refused to marry the couple "without consent of the company commander," and the commanding officer "would not let his men marry Korean women," the situation proved to be an impossible one.[23] In 1955, when Kim became pregnant, the couple made another plea to military officials. This time, given the presence of an unborn child, the military chaplain sympathized with the pair and agreed to marry them in secret. The marriage, however, was meaningless without the commander's approval, and Kim's husband was reassigned to the United States without his wife, just two months before the birth of their daughter Carole Diane. Although Kim's husband promised that he would return and regularly sent letters and money for the care of their daughter in the initial months of separation, their correspondence tapered off in June of 1956. Kim would hear from her GI husband once more in September, when he revealed that he loved an American woman and could not continue his Korean marriage. Kim's husband would never write again, let alone return to South Korea for his family.

It is unclear whether Kim Soon Ja's husband was already married to this American woman before he began his military tour or was discouraged by family, friends, or commanding officers from bringing "an Oriental woman like that" home upon his return stateside; but numerous similar scenarios left the Korean wives and mixed race children of US servicemen abandoned in South Korea without any form of American support.[24] In Kim's case, she kept her marriage and child secret even from her parents, fearing their rejection. Desperate, she had initially relinquished Carol Diane to the Seventh Day Adventist mission, leaving her at the Seoul Sanitarium and Hospital Orphanage. Just days later, however, she changed her mind and returned, in tears, to reclaim her daughter. Although it is not certain what became of Kim Soon Ja and Carole Diane, it is possible that Kim, who would widely be considered a ruined woman with limited prospects for a decent job or marriage to a Korean man, would turn to prostitution in camptowns or enter into another conjugal relationship with an American GI in order to support her child. Such a trajectory was common for women who did not receive the support of extended family members after being abandoned by their American husbands.[25] The story of Kim Soon Ja is just one example of how a US military culture orienting servicemen away from marriage could cause distressing situations for mixed race children and their Korean mothers in the early and mid-1950s.

Single Korean mothers and their mixed race children soon became regular sights around US military bases, eventually leading to general acceptance of these families in camptown neighborhoods.[26] Proximity to US dollars and goods meant that some mothers could make a much better life there than elsewhere in postwar South Korean society. Some women, however, moved back to provincial towns or rural villages with their families after being left by their GI partners. There, mothers might have to shield their sons and daughters from prejudicial behavior by those unfamiliar with and hostile toward mixed race children. According to the testimony of mixed race Koreans growing up in South Korea during these years, some mothers kept their children within the protective confines of the home and away from the outside world. Others "made pathetic attempts to disguise the identity of their children by dyeing their hair and eyelashes black, or by keeping their hair always covered up, so that the child's forehead above the line of the cap is much lighter in color than the rest of his face."[27] Such efforts would allow Korean mothers and their children to walk the streets without being harassed or accosted by villagers who viewed such children as unwelcome reminders of military occupation and war. Nonetheless, many women made the difficult decision to give up their sons and daughters, leaving them on "the doorsteps of foreign missions, hospitals, and orphanages" to be cared for by Americans.[28] Some had been pressured to do so by their families; others relinquished their babies voluntarily, hoping to escape the stigma of having mixed race children or knowing they could not support them on their own.[29]

One of the earliest US media reports to acknowledge the unique plight of mixed race children was coverage on the adoption of twenty-two-month-old Patricia Lea by American nurse Irene Robson in December 1953. A *Los Angeles Times* article explained that Patricia Lea became a war orphan when

Figure 2.1 A Korean woman carries her mixed race child. Courtesy of Korean Image Archive.

her "frightened Korean mother ran out the doorway and vanished into the night" after giving birth at a Red Cross center in Seoul.[30] Patricia Lea was then brought to the Seoul Sanitarium and Hospital Orphanage, where Robson, the director of nurses, cared for her and ultimately adopted and brought her to the United States in July 1953. Although the article stressed that Patricia Lea was just one of the "hundreds of other war babies" among the many children "unwanted by their American fathers," it suggested that the biggest problem for GI children was South Korean prejudice.[31] Claiming there is "no place for them in Korea because the people there feel they don't belong," Robson wondered what would come of the fifty "war babies" currently in the institution's care.[32]

Media coverage surrounding Patricia Lea, Irene Robson, and the Seoul Sanitarium and Hospital Orphanage produced an overwhelming 608 inquiries from prospective adoptive parents in the United States wishing to adopt mixed race Koreans, providing an early glimpse of the powerful sentimental attachment and sense of responsibility Americans felt toward such children.[33] Just one month later, the Southwestern Union Conference of Seventh Day Adventists reported that "five of the half Korean children" from the Seoul Sanitarium and Hospital Orphanage had "gone to the states already."[34] But these early efforts to adopt mixed race Korean children would be frustrated by the lack of an intercountry adoption infrastructure in South Korea. The absence of an American agency working to facilitate the intercountry adoptions of GI babies at this time made their mass placement in the United States virtually impossible; a further complication was that the South Korean government had no policy legislating Korean children's adoption by foreigners. Up to that point, adoptions from South Korea operated through US immigration law and were facilitated by diplomatic offices on a case-by-case basis. It was not until later in 1954, when the South Korean government developed an official policy and procedure for sending its children abroad (and the Ministry of Health and Social Affairs established the Child Placement Service to facilitate those adoptions), that the mass emigration of mixed race children became a possibility.[35] But even then, the broader fundraising and philanthropic efforts of American missionaries and voluntary associations did not devote special attention to mixed race children. Instead, their outreach focused on the estimated 300,000 widows and 50,000 orphans of the Korean War, many of them "disabled or handicapped by accidents resulting from unexploded land mines and hand grenades" or suffering from exposure, tuberculosis, leprosy, parasites, and other diseases.[36]

This all changed when a wealthy Oregon farmer and his family thrust mixed race Koreans into the national spotlight and provided US citizens with a more concrete way to support the postwar recovery effort in South Korea. The effort began in December of 1954, when Harry and Bertha Holt were invited to attend a lecture and to meet Robert Pierce, then president of World Vision, to learn about the interdenominational Christian organization's efforts to assist Korean war orphans and widows.[37] During the meeting, Pierce showed the Holts two films. The first movie, *Dead Men on Furlough*, depicted the deathly persecution Korean Christian pastors faced from the communist North Korean government.[38] The other film, a documentary entitled *Other Sheep*, detailed the philanthropic work of World Vision in postwar Korea. Although the double feature exposed the Holts to pitiful images of child amputees, diseased or handicapped widows and orphans, and children dying from starvation and exposure, the images that most affected the Holts were those of the mixed race children.[39] The family immediately signed up to sponsor "3 children at $10 a month through the World Vision Orphanage plan."[40] But sponsorship did little to assuage their guilt. Holt would later write in a memoir that he was haunted in his sleep by a little girl with an American face but "almond-shaped eyes."[41] "I couldn't forget those undernourished bodies, those tiny outstretched arms. . . . Neither of us could," he recalled. "And then suddenly, without either of us mentioning it to the other, we knew we could and should do something about those little unwanted creatures."[42] With

Figure 2.2 A mixed race war orphan, perhaps similar to the one first seen by the Holts. Courtesy of Korean Image Archive.

the blessing of his wife Bertha and their six children, Harry Holt went to South Korea in May 1955 on a self-touted crusade to rescue mixed race Korean children and "double the size of their family."[43]

From May to October, Holt "traveled by jeep throughout the war-shattered country," searching South Korea's orphanages and child institutions for the abandoned children of US servicemen and Korean women.[44] Because many of these so-called GI babies were not living in orphanages but "were being hidden by ashamed Korean mothers," Holt had difficulty finding mixed race waifs like those he had seen in the World Vision presentation.[45] To create a system whereby mixed race children could be more easily gathered and passed on from Korean mothers to orphanages and American families, Holt worked with the organization to establish a reception center for these individuals.[46] Eventually, he found a total of thirteen mixed race children: eight of whom would become new additions to his family, one of whom died a month prior to her scheduled travel to the United States, and four others destined for three US families.[47] But because a maximum of two children per family were permitted to receive preferential visas as "eligible orphans" through Section 5 of the Refugee Relief Act of 1953, Holt could not immediately return to the United States with all twelve. He would require the passage of a private bill, guided through Congress by his state senators and representatives, to facilitate the entry of the six children joining the Holt family.[48] For the four children going to other families, Holt utilized a method permitted in the Refugee Relief Act whereby the prospective parents signed a power of attorney that allowed for a proxy in South Korea to complete the adoption on their behalf. These proxy adoptions, popularized by the Holts between 1955 and 1961, would become the primary process used by Americans to obtain mixed race Koreans until the practice was banned for the risks it posed to internationally adopted children. Eventually, on August 11, 1955, Private Law 475 ("the Holt bill") was enacted by the 84th Congress. Two months later, on October 14, Harry Holt arrived in Portland, Oregon with his entourage of children.[49]

Virtually overnight, Harry Holt was transformed into a national hero for his efforts to save mixed race children. His family's quest for a special orphan bill and news about his humanitarian good deeds abroad prompted *Time* and *Life* magazine photographers to follow him to South Korea and document his mission.[50] The media described Holt as "an Oregon farmer who has dedicated his life to aiding Korean foundlings," and congressmen praised him as a "Biblical Good Samaritan," humanitarian, and ideal citizen.[51] En route back to the United States, Holt was met by large groups of the press corps at layovers in Tokyo and Hawai'i hoping to catch a glimpse

Figure 2.3 Harry Holt arrives in the United States with mixed race Korean children. Courtesy of Holt International, holtinternational.org.

of him and his twelve small Korean charges.[52] When he arrived in Portland on October 14, a crowd of fifty, "including anxious new relatives of the children, reporters, radio, television and cameramen, eagerly waited to catch a glimpse of" him with "the widely publicized waifs."[53] At the family farm in Cresswell, the Holts encountered another sixteen photographers.[54] That same evening, the collective family's "first dinner in months was interrupted by a jangling telephone," with calls from prospective parents inquiring about how to adopt mixed race children.[55] In the subsequent weeks,

"THE PROBLEM OF THE MIXED BLOOD CHILD"   (55)

the highly publicized event triggered more news reports about mixed race Koreans and the efforts of their "Pied Piper."[56] Soon, "the gameroom in the Holt basement was converted into an office" and the Holts had to hire three full-time staffers to help them answer the roughly "300 pieces of mail which arrived each day" from nearly every state.[57] The flood of inquiries from families set Holt off on what he dubbed "Operation Babylift."[58] By February of 1956, Holt would return to South Korea to build an orphanage and establish the Holt Adoption Program with the singular goal to "personally bring home as many as possible of these pathetic youngsters" before the expiration of the Refugee Relief Act of 1953.[59]

Because the Refugee Relief Act was set to expire on December 31, 1956, with no clear indication of whether a new bill might be passed to extend its special orphan provisions, the work of the Holt Adoption Program in its first year of operation could be characterized as a "race against time."[60] As the agency struggled to process "all the children in the Holt and World Vision orphanages . . . in time to get them to the United States," a sense of urgency surrounded "the desperate plight of these orphans in Korea."[61] In a press report, Holt confirmed: "In planning our adoptions, we are not counting on the Refugee Act being renewed. We are going right ahead, cutting as much red tape as we can."[62] Attention-grabbing headlines such as "Oregon Farmer Brings 12 More Orphans from Korea for New Homes in America" and "Adopter of 8 Off to Get 200 More" spread across national papers, generating more interest and demand for information on mixed race Koreans with each emergency planeload of children.[63] Americans soon learned that an estimated 1,500 "American-Korean orphans" were scattered across the war-torn country, with some 600 children already in "orphan centers" and "hospitals all over South Korea . . . suffering from malnutrition and other diseases."[64]

Readers were haunted by accounts of Holt picking up babies "in orphanages over there that were mere skeletons."[65] These were accompanied by reports of "outcast" Korean mothers "turn[ing] to prostitution" and committing suicide following rejection from family and loved ones.[66] Missionaries working near the demilitarized zone where many foreign servicemen were stationed "described the woods as being full of girls with such children."[67] Sad stories also surfaced of mothers "deserting their babies in the streets and at the gates of orphan homes" and leaving them to die before they could be rescued by child authorities.[68] Even in orphanages, mixed race children were reported to be "mistreated and humiliated" by "other children" who "point their fingers at them and call them GI babies."[69] Such tragic tales "touched the hearts" of Americans, prompting thousands of inquiries from couples hoping to take in a Holt orphan.[70] But just as quickly as the campaign to save mixed race Koreans had aroused the interests of prospective adoptive parents, the small window of opportunity was closing, and a battle to extend the special orphan provisions of the Refugee Relief Act in Congress was beginning.[71]

Holt's allies, including politicians, humanitarians, Christian organizations, and adoptive and prospective parents of mixed race Koreans, aggressively lobbied Congress until the refugee law expired at the end of that year. In April of 1956, one of Holt's fiercest supporters,

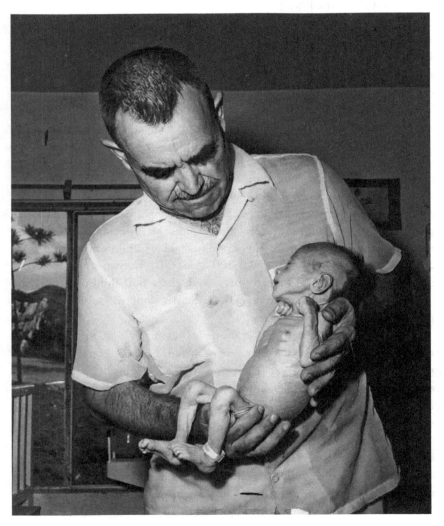

Figure 2.4 Harry Holt holds a malnourished Korean war orphan. Courtesy of Holt International, holtinternational.org.

Senator Richard Neuberger of Oregon, introduced S. 3753, an amendment to the Refugee Relief Act that would allow for a "3-year extension of the section applying to orphans."[72] The bill also proposed to permit the adoption of older children (raising the legal age limit from 10 to 14 years), while increasing the orphan quota by providing an additional 5,000 visas for children adopted by US citizens. Neuberger argued that "many of these orphans should be the direct responsibility of our people and Government, since they were fathered by American military personnel."[73] But as the end of the 84th session of Congress loomed, with no movement on the senator's bill as of July 23, the threat of leaving "several hundred children in Korea who are partially or fully adopted . . . unless the act is extended" created more desperation.[74] Another Oregon lawmaker, Wayne Morse, criticized the US Senate for its failure "to act upon any of the legislation which has been proposed to remove many of the inequities in our immigration laws and to increase the arbitrary quotas set up by the Refugee Relief Act of 1953."[75] To further underscore his pleas for a legislative solution, Morse asked that nearly fifty letters and telegrams "with regard to adoption of Korean-American orphans be printed into" the *Congressional Record*.[76]

Parents who had adopted children through the efforts of Holt argued that they would provide warm, stable, and Christian homes for "these little ones of American fathers" who were "dying of cold and lack of food and care."[77] One prospective couple asked: "Don't you think it is justifiable that we as true, honest Americans, should do our level best to give [these children] a chance in this country of ours, where they will have a good education, a wonderful time growing up in peaceful surroundings, and the heritage that will be their due—as citizens of a free nation?"[78] On July 26, 1956, dozens more letters were entered into the *Congressional Record* in support of S. 3570, another orphan bill that "follow[ed] closely the provisions of [the Neuberger] bill."[79] The testimonies, which expressed concerns "about the Korean-American babies" who "so badly need a home," stressed that it was the duty and moral responsibility of the United States government, which had "sent the fathers of these children" to South Korea, to shelter and care for these mistreated "outcasts" and transform them into "good citizens in a Christian nation."[80] Together, these pleas from congressmen and adoptive parents to extend the Refugee Relief Act were tests of the nation's dominant ideologies. As the self-purported leader of the free world—steeped in wealth, power, racial tolerance, and democratic ideals—the United States was poised to rescue these children, and Americans were keen to make sure their nation would stand up to its lofty promises. These Cold War arguments would become more explicit as continued delays in

(58)   *The First Amerasians*

legislative solutions heightened anxieties among those most concerned for the welfare of mixed race Koreans.

Although the 84th Congress ultimately left the expansion of the refugee orphan program to future lawmakers, a Judiciary Committee report entered into the *Congressional Record* during the final day of that congressional session would provide a firm foundation for later efforts to expand the program. Focusing on the Refugee Relief Act's outcomes, the report argued that the policy was "materially advancing United States foreign policy objectives in the Far East" by tending to the "tremendous population upsets," "widespread human suffering," and "displacement" wreaked by "Communist aggression."[81] Such government-produced narratives helped to absolve the US military for its role in creating refugees and orphans through its destructive air raids, bombings, and indiscriminate killings of civilians (not to mention its earlier discriminatory policies toward Korean women) by instead providing them humanitarian assistance. The report also made more specific arguments about the South Korea refugee program. Because the vast majority of the refugees entering the United States from South Korea were orphans, statements praising "the investment the United States has made toward alleviating the problem of refugees in Korea" were likely references to the popular efforts of individuals like Holt and his allies.[82] Alternatively, irresponsibility and "negligence on the part of some United States Government officials" were deemed to pose major threats to "the security of the free world and to the cause of a just and lasting peace."[83] While earlier arguments made by Holt allies and adoptive parents highlighted the humanitarian incentives for extending the Refugee Relief Act, the Judiciary Committee report focused on the law's role "in advancing United States foreign policy objectives in Asia and in creating a better understanding of United States policies by the people of Asia."[84] Later on, in the US Congress's final assessment of the Refugee Relief Act, the orphan program would be credited for bringing about "an awareness of the part citizens can play in helping their Government carry out its foreign policy."[85] Such government understanding of the political utility of refugee orphans (largely understood through the plight of mixed race Koreans specifically) would incentivize finding legislative solutions in later congressional sessions to help these individuals.

Soon after the 84th Congress came to a close on July 27, 1956, the orphan quota of the Refugee Relief Act was exhausted, halting adoptions from South Korea indefinitely "some four months prior to the program's expiration date."[86] Although only 397 children from South Korea had come to the United States during the program's three-year tenure, the vast majority (211) of them had received visas through the work of the Holt

Adoption Program over just three months.[87] While this number represents just a small fraction of the 4,000 orphans in total who arrived in the United States under the Refugee Relief Act, it was mixed race Korean children's plight and the timing of the Holt campaign—hindered by the restrictive quota in the last months of the policy's operation—that reinvigorated national discussions about refugee law and pressured Congress to eventually enact additional orphan legislation.[88] When the year-end expiration date of the Refugee Relief Act arrived with no clear indication as to whether another bill would be passed to extend the special orphan provisions of the law, hundreds of mixed race children were left in limbo in overcrowded orphanages and reception centers. The Holt orphanage, for example, reportedly bulged "with nearly 100 children" during the second half of the year, while "the World Vision reception center in Seoul also has nearly 100" despite "the capacity for each [being] 50."[89] The stress this caused Holt, his allies, and other adoption advocates was immediately reflected in the pages of national newspapers and the *Congressional Record*.

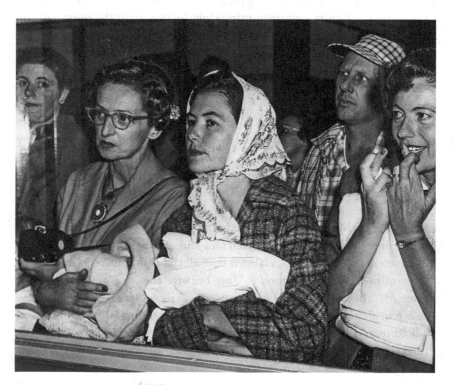

Figure 2.5 A group of adoptive parents anxiously await the arrival of their Korean children. Courtesy of Holt International, holtinternational.org.

(60) The First Amerasians

Adoption advocates depicted the delays in intercountry adoption as a grave matter of mixed race children's survival. Rumors about dying babies circulated among adoption circles in South Korea and found their way into US newspapers, causing Americans to believe that "ninety per cent of the children of mixed parentage in Korea perish," experiencing either "a slow death from disease or sudden death at the hands of their Korean countrymen who refuse to accept them."[90] In a letter addressed to Secretary of State John Foster Dulles, entered into the *Congressional Record* on January 25, 1957, Senator Neuberger wrote: "Another cold winter in Korea will spell death for many of these mixed blood orphans, who were fathered by American military personnel."[91] In the summer, as delays continued, Neuberger reminded Congress "that many children already adopted by American families [but still in Korea] will die . . . due to inadequate food and water, summer heat, and lack of medicines."[92] Adoptive families, like the Waddingtons of Portland, Oregon, wrote pained notes to their senators about the deaths of their adoptive children before they could be brought to the United States. "Please pass the orphan bill before more of us suffer such a loss," they begged, warning that "more babies will die if the bill is not passed soon."[93] Media reports quoting Holt, by this point the most authoritative voice on Korean children, confirmed the anguish of mixed race children who "die in the orphanage because they lack the desire to live without a father and mother."[94] Or, worse, they were "mobbed" and "murdered" by their "Korean playmates," their bodies left "to be found in irrigation ditches or washed up on beaches."[95]

The Holts' firsthand accounts, which were becoming increasingly extreme as legislative delays ensued, would go largely uncontested by Americans during these years. In fact, Harry Holt's statements about mistreated and murdered children would be regularly repeated by his allies and other adoption advocates in the United States, ultimately transforming them into widespread truths despite evidence of improving conditions. As early as 1955, the *Tonga Ilbo* reported on a South Korean institution caring for seventeen children of both mixed race and of "full Korean" background. The caretaker, Kim Jung Ja, claimed that all the children were "one happy family of brothers and sisters."[96] "Just because they are mixed race," she observed, "they are not any different. . . . [T]hey blend in well with the Korean orphans and eat the same way."[97] Such accounts of mixed race and "full Korean" children living harmoniously with one another under the protective custody of a South Korean caretaker directly countered claims made by the Holts that mixed race children were abused, starved, and killed in Korean orphanages.[98] South Korean narratives of progress were never shared with the American public. While the reasons for Holt's overly

"THE PROBLEM OF THE MIXED BLOOD CHILD"   *(61)*

dramatic and sensationalized accounts remain unclear, his statements were effective in guilting US lawmakers and recruiting allies. In the summer months of 1957, Holt maintained that mixed race children perished at a rate of two per week. He added: "The people in Korea cannot understand why we don't take the children to America. . . . To them, America is a land of many warmhearted people. To tell them the children are waiting here until a new law is passed is difficult, especially since it has been so long now."[99] Without government action, Holt feared, "these poor little ones will never see the land of their fathers."[100]

Amid the delays, Pulitzer– and Nobel–prize winning author Pearl S. Buck contributed to the aggressive public relations campaign with a letter to the editors published in the *New York Times* on June 9, 1957.[101] Buck, who had founded the nation's first interracial adoption agency (Welcome House) in 1949, was already a well-known champion of mixed race children in the United States before she began assisting Amerasians. Further, her ground-breaking literary works set in China and Japan positioned her as one of the nation's most credible and popular experts on US-Asia relations. Buck implored Americans to do something about orphans, whom she dubbed "the most needy children in the world today."[102] Discriminated against for "being the children of conquerors," Buck urged the nation not to allow "half-white children, most of them of half-American background, to grow up in Asia as the lowest class of citizen."[103] Such a tragedy, she argued, would not only lead to "cynicism about our brand of democracy . . . in those parts of the world where half-American children live unwanted and too often neglected," but also seriously jeopardize "the prestige of our own people, or the white man."[104] More troubling was her warning that such children, as they grew "into displaced adults," would become agitators for communist "rebellion and revolution" turning "their hatred to those who have brought them into being and then rejected them."[105] Buck's scathing critique of US governmental indifference was also a rallying cry to bring such children "home" where they would be rehabilitated and democratized into US nationals. This idea of rescuing mixed race Koreans and steeping them in American ways bears striking resemblance to earlier colonial practices— similar to the ways in which Europeans assimilated their Eurasian children in places like French Indochina and the Dutch East Indies or how Americans sought to Christianize and civilize indigenous children in native boarding schools or, later, the Philippines, so as to create docile colonial subjects to strengthen Western empire.[106]

Promoting her own brand of racial liberalism, Buck asserted that interracial and international adoptions would help to forge a more inclusive nation in an era of Jim Crow as well as serve as "a triumph of American

(62)   *The First Amerasians*

democracy."[107] Such expressions of interracial familial love would further US foreign policy objectives in Asia by repudiating communist charges that America's disreputable racial practices made it ill-equipped to lead and liberate the Third World. Although her entry in the *New York Times* framed this crisis as a problem for "the white man," Buck would make similar pleas to Black Americans in subsequent years. For instance, when it became obvious that Black families were less interested in adopting GI orphans than white Americans, leaving a disproportionate number of these children in South Korea, Buck began publicizing their plight in the Black press.[108] In the *Baltimore Afro-American*, Buck warned, "If they are left without help and guidance, they will be the natural dissidents in coming years and prey to the worst Communist propaganda."[109] Thus, even if for "selfish reasons, we must assume responsibility for these children who were fathered by American soldiers and are called 'Americans' in their native lands."[110] These concerns about communist propaganda were not completely unwarranted, as it had been reported by social workers in South Korea "that a Korean youngster was bribed by an agent from North Korea to abduct a mixed blood child from one of the orphanages so that he might be exhibited in North Korea as evidence of [America's] colonization of South Korea."[111] Even Harry Holt had his own troubles "with North Korea's Radio Communist Anti-Holt propaganda" which framed him and his efforts as that of an imperialist kidnapper.[112] Yet Americans also participated in their own Cold War storytelling, warning Korean birth mothers that if war were to break out "the communist party and Kim Il Sung would come down and kill the biracial babies first!"[113]

A combination of these various political and personal convictions by adoption advocates from Holt to Buck, adoptive parents, and senators alike fueled an aggressive campaign for legislation that would renew provisions for mixed race Koreans' entry into the United States. By July 1957, nearly 500 private orphan bills had been introduced in Congress by Holt parents and other adoption advocates, applying immense pressure on US lawmakers to finally pass widespread orphan legislation.[114] One politician even remarked, "Private legislation is time-consuming and costly, and interferes with the regular work of Congress."[115] Ultimately, the lobbying by adoption advocates was too great to ignore, and on September 11, 1957, the 85th Congress enacted Public Law 316. The act would authorize an unlimited number of visas for orphans up to the age fourteen years old either adopted abroad by US citizens or entering the United States for the purpose of adoption. However, like the Refugee Relief Act, the law was not a permanent solution, as it was slated to expire on June 30, 1959. As a result, Public Law 316 did little to alleviate the pressures under which

Korean adoption had operated in its initial years. Champions of mixed race Koreans were compelled to place as many GI babies as possible in American families before yet another temporary provision ended.

It soon became evident that the Holts and other humanitarian non-professionals, in their haste and fervor, had produced a number of problematic placements using the proxy method of adoption. Although proxy adoptions made obtaining mixed race children an affordable, accessible, and expedient process for many Americans, the practice was uniformly condemned by child welfare professionals for exposing adopted children to potentially severe risks.[116] Holt parents had bypassed the lengthy background checks, home studies, and mandatory period of adjustment whereby the emotional and physical needs of adoptive children were carefully observed in their new homes before social welfare professionals made a legal recommendation for adoption. These timely and costly procedures, considered ethical social welfare practices in this period, were viewed by the Holts as institutional red tape—nuisances, in other words—that "harassed" them and delayed their good work.[117] Child welfare professionals were horrified to learn that the Holts' procedures for vetting parents included just "a questionnaire . . . with assurance of their religious beliefs" (the Holts placed Korean children only in "born-again Christian homes") and a credit check performed by a commercial agency, in lieu of a criminal background check or proper home study.[118]

Such lax procedures accounted for the Holt program's failed adoption rate of 10 percent in their initial years of operation.[119] Studies conducted by child welfare professionals later on revealed a high rate of "immature parents" within the Holt cohort and individuals who gave up their adoptive children when behavioral or adjustment issues arose, often "in haste without any effort to resolve the problem."[120] In some cases, Korean Black children even "raised a point of not wanting to be identified as Negro in a Negro home . . . which would seem to be an indication for a need for special counseling."[121] Such post-adoption services simply did not exist or were not being provided by the agency at that time. Ironically, this awareness of US racial hierarchy on the part of mixed race children reveals the contradictions of a system that extracted them from a society which supposedly discriminated against them, only to place them in another racially hostile environment. In several cases the Holts had placed children in "psychotic families . . . after medical advice had been given demonstrating the psychotic qualities and disfavorably recommending adoption."[122] Incidents in which a family had received a second or third child following an initial failed adoption also perplexed observers who noted "a family that cannot adjust with one child would also have equally difficult time adjusting with another child."[123] Social workers even observed "unfortunately, the substantial amount of child abuse" and neglect among Holt placements.[124]

In April 1958, one incident occurring in the state of Indiana poignantly demonstrates some of the human consequences of the Holts' many questionable adoption practices.[125] Correspondence between the St. Joseph County Department of Welfare and the Indiana Department of Public Welfare revealed that "a 15 month old, female Korean war orphan who had evidently had polio and was in need of medical care" was adopted by a family with a mother who "was presenting dangerous homicidal tendencies." "A few weeks after the child was placed in the home," the mother was hospitalized and diagnosed with paranoid schizophrenia, after having "attempted to choke her husband, . . . harm the child," and "threatening suicide."[126] Although the couple was sterile and had hoped that "working with Korean orphans . . . might have a therapeutic effect on" their relationship, social workers observed that "neither parent actually had any real affection or feeling for the child and were not emotionally in a position to adequately care for the child."[127] The living conditions of their "small 15 foot trailer" were described as "completely inadequate," "filthy," and "so cold that relatives feared for the child's health."[128] The child was even discovered to have bite marks, suspected to have been made by the adoptive mother. The adoptive parents gave the child back to the Holts "on the insistence of relatives who threatened" to otherwise report the situation to a "protective service agency."[129] However, just one month later, the Holts attempted to return the child to the deranged mother, at which point the county Department of Welfare intervened.[130] Although this family could be viewed as just one extreme example of a bad Holt placement, incidents such as this were hardly isolated. In fact, some cases of abuse were so extreme that children had died at the hands of their new adoptive parents. Such was the case of Wendy Kay Ott, who was just twenty-two-months-old in June of 1957 when she was struck on the head and killed by her mother, Mrs. Howard B. Ott of Roseburg, Indiana.[131]

During these years, various organizations got more aggressively involved in counteracting the Holt program's virtual monopoly on mixed race Korean children's welfare in South Korea. One major organization that began to participate in intercountry adoption was International Social Service (ISS). Although the organization had, since 1953, been involved in some of the very first placements of mixed race children to American GIs, missionaries, and volunteer workers serving in South Korea, ISS was not directly placing Korean children with US families at the time. Rather, it served as a liaison between the South Korean government, immigration offices, and child welfare departments in the United States. Having assisted with a similar crisis

"THE PROBLEM OF THE MIXED BLOOD CHILD" (65)

in Occupied Japan, ISS took the position that while adoption was justifiable under certain special circumstances (for instance, a biological father or relative adopting their own illegitimate mixed race kin), South Koreans must come up with indigenous solutions so that the vast majority of such children could remain in their birthlands with their mothers and fellow countrymen, similar to their Japanese counterparts.[132] The organization's stance on mixed race Korean children dramatically shifted in 1956 once Holt began his placements utilizing the proxy method of adoption. ISS felt there was a strong need to provide more "sound methods" and models for Korean adoption that were informed by more conventional and ethical social welfare standards.[133] The organization's first field study on mixed race Koreans produced in late November of 1956 reflected this sentiment. In it an ISS social worker concluded "we need urgently to obtain the necessary funds to speed up our program. . . . [I]n the absence of ISS coordination the entire initiative will pass to persons like Mr. Holt as long as proxy adoption is legal."[134] In many ways ISS foresaw as early as 1956 that Holt's methods would produce disastrous results and moved quickly to document and counteract them.

Figure 2.6 A chaotic scene of mixed race children brought to the United States by the Holts. AP Photo/Ernest K. Bennett.

(66)   *The First Amerasians*

For the next few years, ISS continued to maintain "several very thick files on Mr. Holt and his activities in Korea," revealing that beneath the veneer of his humanitarian rescue were practices that harmed mixed race children and Korean mothers.[135] In an attempt to make adoption more accessible, the Holts cut costs and corners at every stage of the adoption process.[136] To bring down transportation costs, for instance, Holt chartered his own transpacific flights from South Korea to the West Coast. These charismatic airlifts not only made for a sensational news story, adding to the Holts' celebrity status, but also saved adoptive parents hundreds of dollars in air-fare and individual child escort costs.[137] The downside, however, was that these famed babylifts could be quite dangerous for children. ISS reported that Holt flights were severely understaffed and chaotic with "teenagers," rather than child welfare professionals, looking after unmanageable groups of children who "should have had better medical care immediately prior to plans for their departure" in the first place.[138] Babies were transported in "white, heavy cardboard boxes, approximately three feet long and perhaps two feet wide" containing "small round holes in the ends of each box."[139] The holes were "to enable the boxes to be stacked one above the other" so as to save space and load the planes with as many children as possible.[140] Because of all this, it was not uncommon for infants to perish before ever reaching their adoptive homes in the United States. Rather than blame the conditions of the babylifts, the Holts and their allies (including adoptive parents who lost children) often scapegoated congressional delays in orphan legislation, believing that had the laws been passed sooner, their children might have survived the transpacific voyage.

In June of 1958, a Korean pediatrician who once worked for the Holt Adoption Program on one of their transpacific flights expressed to ISS serious reservations about some of Holt's questionable methods for procuring children in camptowns. An ISS report from that meeting noted: "Dr. Rho was particularly concerned now about the efforts in Korea to force mothers of mixed blood children to give up these children. She stated that she had witnessed on three different occasions the mothers actually being physically forced to give up their children."[141] A 1958 case file, involving a Korean mother seeking assistance from ISS and an army chaplain in dealing with the Holt Adoption Program corroborates Dr. Rho's claims and provides further insights into some of the on-the-ground practices of the organization:

> Although Miss Kang knew that Kyung-ok had already been adopted by proxy and was scheduled to leave Korea the following day, she went on that same Tuesday to the Holt Agency to ask that Kyung-ok be given back to her. . . . However, yesterday she came again to the office in my absence, her face swollen and bruised

"THE PROBLEM OF THE MIXED BLOOD CHILD" (67)

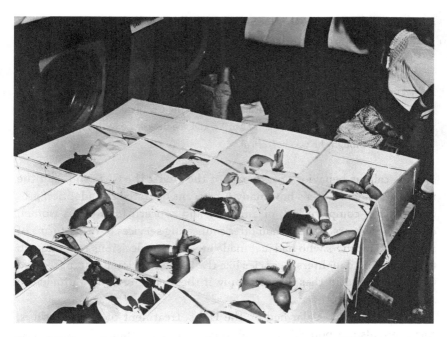

Figure 2.7 Korean infants crated in boxes for travel overseas. Courtesy of Holt International, holtinternational.org.

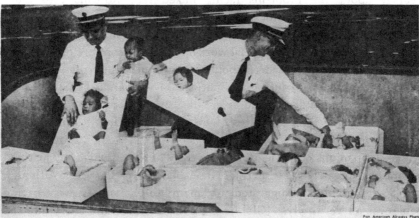

Harold Schultz, left, and Dick Robinson, right, take roll call of some of the members of flying nursery, during Honolulu stopover yesterday of 91 orphans.

Figure 2.8 Pan American pilots arranging baby boxes. Courtesy of Holt International, holtinternational.org.

and alleged to Mrs. Rhee that she had been struck by Miss Holt [the daughter of Harry and Bertha Holt] and by a GI who is Miss Holt's boyfriend. She stated that they had also tried to drug her. In considerable perturbation and anger I called the chaplain when I later learnt this. He told me that Miss Holt and her friend had admitted to striking Miss Kang as a measure to stop the hysteria she displayed at not having her child returned to her. The Chaplain seemed to accept this explanation though I made it clear I could see no excuse for slapping Miss Kang even though she was hysterical.[142]

Such callous behavior on the part of the Holts, the GI friend, and the military chaplain reveals how many Americans operated the adoption program with a complete lack of empathy and concern for Korean women during these years. Rather than offer counseling services or other forms of support to mothers who had just made life-altering decisions to relinquish their sons and daughters, agencies like the Holt Adoption Program seemed to be interested in these women only if they had children to provide to American families.

Although ISS was alarmed by the Holts' treatment of birth mothers, they were also responsible through their own field studies for depictions of Korean women as hardened prostitutes who did not even love their own children. In fact, the optics of their professional methods transformed hearsay about the problems facing mixed race Koreans into more legitimated pseudo-scientific and scholarly truths, which in turn informed how many adoption professionals treated Korean women and their children. A report made by ISS social worker Anne Davison in 1961 is representative of some of the ideas about Korean mothers circulating among adoption professionals during this period. Davison argued that "most of the mixed racial children in Korea are illegitimate because their mothers are casual or regular prostitutes of foreign servicemen."[143] Such claims aligned with US military understandings of Korean women as temporary sexual companions rather legitimate mothers or wives, which had justified separating Korean wives from their GI husbands in earlier years. Although the ISS representative suggested that many Korean women were having babies "as a lever to press [GIs] into marriage" and secure entry into the United States, she also stated that some women actually had "no intention of leaving [their] way of life."[144] Ignorant about the actual challenges faced by interracial couples in legitimizing their marriages, Davison argued that Korean wives blamed "legal offices, friends, and welfare workers as excuses for her own indecision."[145] In her view, mixed race children were "not loved by the mother," but were "held for blackmail purposes" to collect "money for debts, living expenses, and school fees" from responsible GI partners stateside.[146] In this narrative, the US military and American soldiers bore little of the blame for the problems facing mixed race children.[147] Instead, the questionable morals and conniving behavior of Korean prostitutes were primary causes for their troubles. Such logic justified adoption by suggesting that mixed race children would be best off separated from their mothers and placed in adoptive American families instead.

In truth, Korean mothers were no longer "wishing to give up their children for adoption" because "attitudes towards these children are changing."[148] One ISS-Korea representative even stated to a stateside colleague that "it is difficult to perceive in most cases any discrimination against these children on part of family or friends or other children."[149] This was particularly the case in the "villages where the mixed blood child is no longer a rarity and when the villages are in relatively close contact with the nearby army installation."[150] Despite such evidence appearing in the organization's field studies as early as 1958, legislative insecurities compelled ISS representatives to focus their efforts on adoption reform, and such internal information did not seem to change the organization's major goals for the US-Korea program. But the reluctance of mothers to relinquish their mixed race children deeply frustrated adoption professionals who were trying to make a case in Congress that there were thousands of abandoned and mistreated orphans available for adoption and in need of loving homes in America. These desires of Korean mothers to keep their children were believed by adoption advocates to be lacking in foresight. In their eyes, many of these women were just lowly, uneducated prostitutes who did not know what was in the best interest of their own children. ISS workers predicted that many women, in time, would change their minds when their children reached school age. Then, they could be refused entry by the headmaster "or, if admitted, teased or maltreated by school mates."[151] But by that point, the child would be "5, 6, or 7" years of age, making "further problems in terms of adjustment to an adoptive family" likely and their entry into the United States all the more difficult.[152]

To counteract this, adoption agencies like the Holts' began employing more coercive tactics to procure children while they were still young and desirable for adoptive families stateside. This was further exacerbated by an increased demand for mixed race children (particularly Korean white infants) amid such an aggressive public relations campaign back home.[153] Adoption advocates entered camptowns where they went "to the front lines" on "baby hunts," surveying all mixed race children in the area and confronting their mothers to relinquish them for adoption.[154] One mixed race woman whose adoption seems to have been the result of one of these "baby hunts" remembers:

(70) The First Amerasians

> Molly Holt came to my village and met somebody—a man, who had a clip-board. . . . She asked if my mother was around. And then we went into the court-yard into one of these great big rooms where everybody sat on the floor. And they talked, and they asked me questions. And my mother asked me: "Do you want to go?" And . . . she said to me: "You will go to school, you will have pretty clothes to wear, and you will have lots to eat." And, and I said "Yes!" Of course, I wanted to go, it sounded fun and exciting. I remember the women in that room, just kind of gasping and shaking their heads. What does a six or seven year old, know about any of this? But the promise of going to school, having pretty clothes, and lots to eat was very appealing. And I remember the women, them all crying. And my mother crying, and I . . . I don't remember crying. I just remember being con-fused as to why everybody was crying. And then I remember getting into a Jeep. And I don't know if it was that very same day . . . I just remember getting into a Jeep without my mother.[155]

In some instances, these missions to scour the camptowns for mixed race Koreans could also result in actual kidnappings. One birth mother who lost her child this way recalls the following scene:

> Some Jeep car came and there were people who said "hello" and so forth, and I wasn't good at English and so I just said in Korean: "Yes, isn't my baby good? Isn't she pretty?" She really was quite pretty. And they said: "Yes, yes, give the baby to us!" They asked me to give them my baby. So, I thought they just wanted to hold her and I gave her to them. But thinking back on it now, they were asking me if they could take the baby. But I didn't know what they were saying, I was young and stupid and so I ended up just giving them my baby unknowingly. My baby! Then they quickly got in their car and left.[156]

Soon rumors began circulating that some organizations were even so "desirous of securing the mixed blood" that they had begun paying for their relinquishment.[157] One woman who grew up near Yongsan Garrison in Itaewon during these years recalled her own mother's insistence that she not step outside the home alone.[158] Although one might first assume that this was based on a fear that the child might encounter prejudicial behavior in public, there was actually a fear of "Holt"—or abduction by an adoption agency.[159] Word spread among mothers that mixed race children were being stolen in delivery rooms at hospitals.[160] Some believed that doctors were deceiving them, claiming that they had delivered a stillborn child and later releasing a healthy infant to an adoption agency.[161] While it is difficult to evaluate the validity of all such rumors, what they convey is that many mothers had developed an extreme distrust of American adoption advocates by the latter half of the 1950s. Consequently, adoption agencies began hiring and sending Korean staff into the camptowns instead. Women, particularly those who were mothers themselves, proved to be the most successful in gaining a birth mother's trust.[162] The memoir of one Korean woman who participated in this makes clear that although the optics of using Koreans to conduct American business were far better, the tactics were just as coercive. She regretfully expressed:

> I really believed, in my youth and naïveté, that I was doing the best I could for these children. I was giving them a better chance. I misunderstood my job and thought I was supposed to make the birth mothers relinquish their children; I pushed those mothers to sign the papers.[163]

Whether these women were pressured by Americans, Koreans, or both, birth mothers were faced with impossible decisions. How could they, in good conscience, keep their children, when they were being told by all those around them that loving them meant relinquishing them for a better life in America (and to not do so was selfish)?

> They kept trying to convince me to send the kid for adoption abroad. Thinking back on it now, I can't believe the nerve and gall they had coming to tell me those things. They said because my child was mixed race, there would be no opportunity for him to develop here. They kept saying to send him to the United States for the good of his future and his life. I never thought about why they kept trying to convince me to give up my baby and since they said it was for my baby's future and life, I agreed to give him up. They said they would come pick him up one day. I said okay . . . and they came . . . but being the fool I am I didn't even think to give them any information or anything.[164]

Although ISS did not participate in baby hunting themselves, the organization had contributed to an early understanding of adoption as "the only solution for the children of mixed parentage," concluding that "in the absence of such placements" these individuals "will not live or will have nothing to live for."[165] Claims like this relied on dehumanizing caricatures of Korean mothers and Orientalist constructions of South Korea as a decadent society "five thousand years old . . . isolated . . . and priding itself upon the purity of its racial lineage." Juxtaposed with descriptions of the United States as a "multicultural" and "heterogenous" nation, these characterizations furthered American claims of its own racial pluralism and blurred the US military's patriarchal and discriminatory practices that had contributed to mixed race children's troubles (like condoning military

Figure 2.9 Harry Holt approaching the mother of a mixed race child in a camptown. Courtesy of Holt International, holtinternational.org.

prostitution and separating interracial families).[166] Claims of South Korea being a backward, traditional country helped to explain prostitution and illegitimate children as the product of South Korea's societal structure (which made it difficult for women to get jobs but "very easy for them to become prostitutes"), rather than as a problem of US empire.[167] Although ISS would eventually change their perspective, developing more nuanced understandings of Korean mothers and South Korean society in the 1960s, such arguments were utilized to justify the organization's early entry into the intercountry adoption program and resembled many of the same ideas proffered by Holt and his allies. As a result, ISS actively participated in creating consensus that adoption was the best solution for mixed race children no matter what the costs and despite organizational disagreements about what constituted the best practices in procuring and placing these orphans into US homes.

When the expiration date for Public Law 316 loomed in 1959, champions of mixed race Koreans rallied once more to secure the future of intercountry adoption. This was further complicated because the work of ISS had brought to the forefront of government discussion the question of whether adoptions via proxy should be continued under the existing conditions. Because proxy adoptions were more or less synonymous with the Holts, and mixed race Koreans constituted the single largest group of internationally adopted children entering the country annually, they became the focal point in national discussions surrounding orphan legislation again.[168] Consequently, in the lead-up to the expiration of Public Law 316, familiar actors emerged once more to reprise similar arguments made in the Refugee Relief Act hearings, so as to remind Americans and lawmakers of the urgency and desperation of mixed race children's plight and the continued need for lax and accessible provisions in adoption law. These individuals actively obscured the anti-Asian violence wrought by these early American efforts to extract mixed race Koreans from camptowns, building on earlier constructions of South Korean society as racist and barbaric in their treatment of these individuals, mixed race children as abandoned motherless orphans on the brink of death, and the United States as a welcome home.

In congressional hearings on orphan legislation, Senator Neuberger was one proponent of immigration reform who repeated statements made some three years earlier. Such testimony was already of questionable validity at the time of its initial presentation, as the senator based his talking points on secondhand knowledge acquired from individuals like Harry Holt and World Vision's Bob Pierce rather than firsthand accounts recorded during his own visits to South Korea. Nonetheless, Neuberger reiterated that "despite the abuses that have been shown to exist . . . 90 percent of the children admitted under the program are leading happy, fruitful lives in our country."[169] Because children "sired by our GIs" are "deliberately left to die of starvation or neglect or even abuse" by those who regard them "with contempt and fear and hate," the alternative to proxy adoptions was "a life of abuse and perhaps even no life at all."[170]

Pearl S. Buck also reemerged to express similar sentiments in a hearing before the Joint Legislative Committee on Matrimonial and Family Laws. The novelist argued that "half-American children abandoned by their GI fathers and Korean mothers" were "detested by Koreans" and "dying like flies in orphanages."[171] She also claimed that South Korean president Syngman Rhee wanted these children removed "even if we have to drop them in the Pacific Ocean."[172] Such extreme comments, utilized to elicit outrage and gain wider public support for proxy adoptions, angered the South Korean government. You Chan Yang, the Korean ambassador in 1959, wrote to the

New York Times stating emphatically that the author's contention that GI babies were dying was completely "unfounded" and demanded "a retraction of this slanderous statement."[173] The ambassador maintained that Syngman Rhee's "prime purpose in the area of social justice" was "to serve these innocent children" and that "the very cornerstone of the Korean Ministry of Health and Social Affairs program is to help the Korean orphans."[174] This exchange is one example of how Americans advocating proxy adoptions continually ignored evidence in South Korea of "improv[ing] living conditions in orphanages," adjustment "to the reality of GI babies," and near full acceptance of these individuals "in the large cities."[175] Instead, Holt allies like Pearl S. Buck and Senator Neuberger relied on static depictions of mixed race children's plight to convince US lawmakers and ordinary citizens alike of the ongoing need for proxy adoptions.

During a Senate hearing before the Subcommittee on Immigration and Naturalization held just one month prior to the expiration of Public Law 316, one missionary and adoptive father suggested that extending the orphan program was a matter of gaining ground in the Cold War. He argued: "If we are concerned about making friends abroad, we certainly cannot do it by having our own servicemen father children and then leaving the responsibility up to the country in which they live."[176] Renewed orphan legislation would "prevent the very fact of our neglect from going into the hands of the Communists over there who are eager to pick up any opportunity to besmirch the name or the way of the American people."[177] In another hearing, the chief of the US Children's Bureau (an organization that was aligned with ISS in its concerns about proxy adoption) utilized similar Cold War rhetoric, concluding that because these children were "young ambassadors" unconsciously cementing "good will between the countries of their birth and their new American families," the adoption program should continue with some additional safeguards.[178] Ultimately, Congress agreed with that assessment and proposed a revision to Public Law 316 that would extend its orphan provisions. Taking into consideration the abuses that had occurred in the former program, the new law would require Immigration and Naturalization Service and a social welfare agency to conduct a home investigation of the prospective family before an orphan visa (proxy or otherwise) was issued to a child. On September 9, 1959, more than two months after the expiration of the previous orphan policy, Public Law 253 was passed by the 86th Congress. The act was later extended another year by Public Law 648 on July 14, 1960, leaving the orphan program intact until June 30, 1961.

Each cycle of expiration, delay, and reenactment involving this series of temporary laws created new platforms to revisit the problem of refugee orphans, where advocates reiterated the same arguments about mixed race Koreans and their rescue. But in their fervor to prioritize adoptive families, champions of mixed race Koreans had failed to make mention of institutional barriers that made it nearly impossible for even American fathers to exercise their paternal rights. In fact, because the Refugee Relief Act and its subsequent amendments allowed only married couples to adopt, and military commanders regularly denied soldiers' requests for permission to marry Korean women, many single unmarried GIs came to the heartbreaking realization at the end of their tours in South Korea that they could not even adopt their own biological children. While some GIs lobbied for private bills in Congress to get around this, many did not know this was an option. Furthermore, the process was long and arduous and gave American fathers no fool-proof guarantee that an adoption would be successful. Other GIs tried to convince relatives, including their parents or married siblings, to adopt their mixed race children on their behalf. In the end, however, biological grandparents or aunts and uncles of mixed race Koreans often refused to cooperate, making perhaps more logical arguments that the children would be better off in South Korea with their mothers and in their birth nation. Even for those soldiers married to American women and therefore legally eligible to adopt through the refugee orphan program, it was difficult to convince their wives to adopt mixed race children who served as uncomfortable reminders of the husband's extramarital affairs during deployment (although there were, of course, some exceptions). In the end, the lack of acknowledgment from adoption advocates of even GI fathers shows that rescuing mixed race Koreans was not simply about placing children into the best possible homes but instead was about constructing Amerasians and promoting American ideologies. The active obscuring of mixed race Koreans' camptown pasts, including the ideological erasure of both Korean mothers and GI fathers, ultimately privileged adoptive parents and created a system that normalized severing these children from their biological families.

On September 26, 1961, Public Law 301, enacted by the 87th Congress, incorporated orphan provisions permanently into US immigration law. The act also finally outlawed proxy adoption, finding the practice no longer justifiable given the improving conditions in South Korea and the diversification of the orphan category to include children from other countries. By then, although Koreans still constituted the largest category of orphans entering the United States compared to children from any other country of origin (and it was indeed their champions who had seen to the extension of permanent orphan legislation in US law), the number of mixed race Koreans entering the United States had declined dramatically.[179] In the initial years of the adoption program's operation, as many as 92 percent of the children adopted from South Korea were mixed race. As Korean mothers held onto their children in hopes that Americans might help them to find indigenous solutions, that percentage declined to 39 percent by 1959.[180] Despite this, the demand for mixed race children remained high, as the intense public relations campaign by the Holts and other adoption advocates had made the GI baby a powerful symbol in US society. To meet this demand for mixed race children, adoption agencies began sending children of full Korean parentage to the United States in lieu of their GI baby counterparts. Ultimately, between the years of 1956 and 1961, as many as 2,600 mixed race Koreans had been adopted by American families. More than half of that number had been placed by Holt, while ISS had placed only around 5 percent.[181]

In the 1950s and early 1960s, Americans constructed and used the figure of the abandoned and mistreated mixed race child to lobby for laws that would facilitate and promote their adoption by American couples. Although the motivations and methods of these reformers varied greatly, there was consensus that adoption served as the only ethical solution. As thousands of mixed race Koreans entered the country as the children of US citizens, their placements into American homes promoted an image of the United States as a paternal, racially tolerant, and benevolent nation ready and eager to accept its global responsibility to lead and look after the new free world. These narratives, advocating adoptions on both humanitarian and Cold War terms, were so compelling that even prospective parents—like the Andersons—were shocked to find that their adoptive children were not the abandoned and mistreated orphans they had hoped them to be. Through the creation of the imagined orphan and the ideal American home, advocates of adoption obscured the realities and often-times profound anti-Asian violence at the heart of these transnational encounters. By positioning themselves as heroes of hopeless and pitiful children, Americans caused actual harm to Koreans. Not only were mixed race children hastily placed into incompetent homes resulting in their abuse, negligence, and sometimes death, but Korean mothers were also forced, even physically, into relinquishing their children for adoption. Eventually, this American insistence on intercountry adoption would also harm indigenous efforts to absorb and incorporate these individuals into South Korean society.

3

"Confucius' Outcasts"

In May of 1961, the United Presbyterian Mission prepared a report anticipating the congressional hearings slated to decide the fate of the refugee orphan program. The organization expressed grave concerns about the future of mixed race children should proxy adoptions be outlawed, leaving these individuals to "pile up" in South Korea's already overcrowded and filthy orphanages.[1] The report argued that the "difficulties facing the mixed blood orphan are so violent and so deep-seated . . . that no approach shows any signs of success in overcoming them in any reasonably immediate foreseeable future."[2] Should these individuals be allowed to grow up in a society "organized on Confucian lines," they would have "no way to obtain a spouse; no way to obtain a job; no source of support when unemployed; no place to go when sick; and no one to bury [them]" upon death.[3] As both a "moral responsibility" and "a challenge and opportunity" for Americans everywhere, the report concluded, "no program which allows mixed blood orphans to accumulate in Korea can be considered a rational, moral, or Christian approach."[4] The only solution, then, was "to place the adoptable mixed blood children into the best possible families in the United States," no matter what the costs.[5]

This stance, taken at a critical legislative juncture, is representative of how key American interest groups used what they viewed as "a radically impossible situation in Korea" to mislead the US public and advocate their own humanitarian, religious, professional, and political agendas.[6] Although the United Presbyterian Mission argued that mixed race children "cannot be absorbed into Korean society," there had long been evidence

The First Amerasians. Yuri W. Doolan, Oxford University Press. © Oxford University Press 2024.
DOI: 10.1093/oso/9780197534380.003.0004

of improving conditions in camptowns.[7] As early as 1958, social workers noted that mixed race children were receiving near full acceptance in the villages around military bases and, as a result, their mothers were becoming less likely to relinquish them for adoption.[8] Ignoring such positive developments, the United Presbyterian Mission and others continued to publicize the image of the mistreated and abandoned orphan in order to promote intercountry placements.

Following the 1961 congressional hearings on the refugee orphan program, Public Law 301 would be enacted by the 87th Congress, making international adoption permanently possible in US society and culture. The law's passage marked the end of an era in which legislative insecurity had so universally distorted narratives surrounding mixed race children's welfare and enabled new thinking and policies. As social workers began producing more realistic and normalized assessments of the conditions in camptowns, these alternative ideas gained traction, and some foreign agencies considered innovative solutions to the problems facing mixed race Koreans. International Social Service (ISS) was one organization at the forefront of this policy reform.

Beginning in 1962, ISS would argue that the previous focus on intercountry adoption was no longer an adequate approach for meeting the needs of mixed race Koreans. In their field studies, social workers noted that most of the children who remained in South Korea were approaching school age and were not actually orphans "but living with their mothers."[9] Believing that these youths should be integrated into South Korean society and that such an effort must come from South Koreans themselves, ISS transitioned from a foreign organization into an indigenous agency with a fully Korean staff and a mission of developing in-country alternatives to adoption. As they implored other foreign agencies to follow their lead, there were several major breakthroughs. Most notable was a collaborative effort between foreign and Korean social workers to assist mixed race children's entry into the South Korean school system called Eurasian Children Living as Indigenous Residents (ECLAIR). However, this program, which gained the sponsorship of the South Korean government by the mid-1960s, proved short-lived. Soon after ECLAIR was turned over to Korean leadership, the positive relations between international agencies and Korean social workers began to deteriorate as American organizations disagreed with indigenous integrationist policies and used their economic and professional clout to overpower these efforts.

Throughout the remainder of the 1960s and well into the 1970s, individuals like Pearl S. Buck and the Holts remained fixated on adoption and segregated institutional care—solutions that Koreans argued only further isolated mixed race children. Other US voluntary organizations such as the Foster Parent Plan (FPP) assisted mixed race Koreans through sponsorship programs whereby children were virtually adopted and financially supported by American families stateside but lived with their mothers in South Korea. Through the exchange of pictures, correspondence, and gifts, US donors created sentimental bonds with mixed race Koreans that incentivized their monetary contributions but also sometimes yielded actual adoptions. Korean social workers criticized these programs, which they viewed as pipelines to intercountry placement that ultimately undermined the local integrationist movement. Americans responded by defaulting to earlier constructions of mixed race Koreans as abandoned and mistreated orphans to justify their methods and label South Korean efforts ineffective. As South Korean agencies and social workers struggled to enact their own policies and perspectives, Americans retained control over mixed race children's welfare. In some cases, they even established organizations that directly competed with the work of indigenous programs, using US dollars to bribe Korean mothers and steal clients. As a result of these efforts, the local integrationist effort ultimately failed, and adoption remained the best available solution for many mixed race families. Consequently, an enduring image of South Korea as static and unwavering in its discrimination toward mixed race persons endures.

Dominant narratives about the immutability of South Korean racism not only exist in Korean and American social memory but also inform even the most critical of scholarship on the origins of international adoption. Citing ideologies like *tanil minjok* (a unitary ethnic nation), which emerged in the 1930s as a reaction to Japanese colonialism, and President Syngman Rhee's policy of *ilguk, ilminju* (one nation, one race), which served as justification for the reunification of the Korean peninsula in the postwar era, ethnic nationalism is often overemphasized in explaining the first intercountry placements of mixed race Koreans.[10] This chapter, however, complicates this narrative, arguing instead that it was Americans who further isolated mixed race individuals from South Korean society during these years and perpetuated a myth of innate racism to advocate their own humanitarian, professional, and political interests.[11] This is not to suggest that ethnic nationalist ideologies bore no relation to the country's initial participation in intercountry adoption but rather to critique the notion that South Koreans were unable to move past ideas about their racial purity to absorb the few thousand mixed race children who remained in-country during the 1960s and 1970s.

To be clear, this analysis of South Korean racism is not intended to undermine the lived historical experiences of mixed race Koreans. Many of these individuals continued to face harsh, dehumanizing rejection or economic hardship, even as the camptowns became more accepting of them. Furthermore, although Americans caused much harm to indigenous efforts, their assistance—including intercountry adoption, institutional care, and sponsorship—provided relief to some children in extreme circumstances. Nonetheless, the experiences of mixed race Koreans of this generation are more varied than previously understood. And as Americans retained control of mixed race children's welfare, they snatched from South Koreans the opportunity to assimilate their own mixed race population and, by extension, chances for Korean mothers to raise their own children. Ultimately, the number of these children leaving for the United States each year steadily increased throughout the 1960s and 1970s. As the image of mixed race Koreans as "Confucius' Outcasts"[12] became cemented in the minds of Americans, few alternatives beyond adoption were pursued in earnest, profoundly shaping the paths available to mixed race Koreans and their mothers.

———

When the 87th Congress enacted Public Law 301 in September 1961, proxy adoptions were outlawed, and refugee orphan provisions became a permanent part of US immigration law. During the hearings, ISS had been vilified by Holt constituents and proxy adoption allies for lobbying against their unethical practices. Even so, ISS emerged as one of the most highly respected organizations operating in South Korea in the eyes of professional social workers and the US child welfare establishment. Emboldened by the outcome and committed to upholding the highest standards of ethics and professionalism in their international casework, ISS sent its field workers back into the camptowns in June of 1962 to reassess the living conditions there. The insights gained would change the trajectory of child welfare in South Korea and completely transform the goals, leadership structure, and programs of ISS as they pertained to mixed race children. In the coming years, the organization would pioneer new solutions, and their representatives would work tirelessly to deconstruct some of the dominant narratives about Korean mothers and South Korean society that underpinned longstanding American perspectives.

In June 1962, ISS representatives from the United States estimated that there were approximately "2,000 to 3,000 mixed bloods" living in the "so called 'prostitute communities' surrounding US military installations" in South Korea.[13] The majority of these children were not abandoned and mistreated orphans, as they had been portrayed, but were well-cared for

"CONFUCIUS' OUTCASTS" *(81)*

by their Korean mothers. The notes of one field worker, recounting what was described as "rather typical of prostitute pavilions," provided revelatory information:

> The prostitute rooms surround a closed court, in the center of which is a well and washing facilities, a common stove for cooking. The relationship is like a large family and the children are mothered by all. Problems and plans of one are shared and discussed with the group. All the children seem to get plenty of love from their own mothers as well as from the others. They appear to be relaxed and contented, emotionally secure. They appear to be insulated from prejudice which is directed against them from the larger community only feeling the impact of this as they get older.[14]

One man, who grew up in a setting not dissimilar to this place, explains: "It was a community . . . basically, it felt like I had 20 aunts. My primary family was just me and my mother, but I also had all these aunts who would take care of me in various ways."[15] Insights like these, corroborated by the oral histories of mixed race individuals, reveal how earlier anxieties about the US-Korea orphan program distorted assessments of the camptowns, even by trained social welfare professionals. The 1961 report written by ISS representative Anne Davison is a useful barometer of this dramatic shift in rhetoric. Casting Korean women as hardened prostitutes who did not even love their own children, Davison's account raises major questions about the credibility of ISS reporting just one year prior.[16] While it is not clear whether the women described here were actually practicing sex workers (or were just stereotyped this way by social workers), it seems that ISS was at least recognizing what mixed race children would later express in hindsight: "So maybe my mother was a prostitute, but that doesn't mean that she wasn't also a fantastic mother."[17]

ISS social workers were in fact so impressed with these Korean mothers that they described the material conditions in camptowns to be "better than in the average Korean family."[18] Many mixed race children of this generation also recall being "well-to-do compared to other Koreans."[19] They remember their mothers as generous and compassionate members of their communities who helped others in need. One poignant example of this is recounted in an incident when a beggar with "matted hair and lice" came to the doorstep of a mixed race woman's childhood home:

> My mother went directly into the kitchen and found whatever we had to eat and warmed it up. She rolled out a mat, set the food down on the *papsang*, laid out the same silverware we used—the *chŏtkarak* and *sutkarak*—sat the man down,

and sat next to him. When he tried to eat with his hands, she stopped him and placed a spoon in his hand, and then he just ate and ate. My mother always said you should treat people how you want to be treated. And she treated him just as she treated us. I never saw her turn anyone away.[20]

Mimicking her mother's generosity, the daughter emerged as a leader of the village children,[21] often sharing with her friends the American snacks and school supplies she received from a nearby base.[22] At school, she even swapped a new pair of shoes with another girl for ones with holes in them, knowing full well that her mother could replace them and that that girl's family was needier. When she returned home wearing the tattered shoes, her mother was not upset but proud of her daughter's behavior.

It was not uncommon during the 1960s for the mothers of mixed race children and the children themselves to be viewed as a privileged class of Koreans, much like the in-between social status occupied by native wives, concubines, and Eurasian children in other imperial contexts.[23] Proximity to the camptown generally meant proximity to US dollars, and this was especially the case when an American father was present or when it appeared that a mixed race family was receiving the financial support of an American GI. One mixed race woman, born in 1962, recalls her mother even being asked by her schoolteachers to procure luxury American goods, including a "made in the USA wig" and a "US-made refrigerator" (to which she responded: "What were they thinking? We didn't even own a refrigerator! Nor a telephone or any other electronic household gadgets").[24] While the family was "not poor," she recalls that "they were not rich either," for the American father was a fleeting and inconsistent presence in their lives.[25] Eventually, his obligations to his wife and four children in the United States made it impossible for him to continue to provide for his second family in South Korea.[26] Although the girl's Korean mother struggled in subsequent years, the wealth she had accumulated during the decade-long "love affair" meant that she was still able to provide well enough for herself and her children.[27]

Advantageous material conditions could also shield mixed race families against prejudicial behavior. In the camptowns, some mixed race individuals recall seeing poorer children of full-Korean parentage bullied more than they were or claim that they themselves had not been subjected to such intimidation.[28] If and when mistreatment did occur, they remember that their mothers, as respected members of their communities, were able to demand accountability. One oral history narrator recounts how her mother responded to an incident involving a neighborhood child:

My mother went into the house, and she told the parents: "This little boy—your son—called my daughter, a word that is not even her name, *kŏmdungi* [darky], and he needs to be disciplined."[29] They immediately apologized, to which my mother responded: "No, no . . . just telling me sorry is not enough. I want you to discipline him. I'm not leaving until you discipline him because otherwise, he's going to do it again." And so, they spanked him right in front of her.[30]

Another mixed race Korean remembers the stark contrast between his life in a small village, where he was teased and excluded by the other children, and his life after he and his mother moved to the Bupyeong camptown. There, he went "from being a nobody to a somebody" as he gained access to American goods like "Coca Cola, Oreos, and Ritz crackers," which he described to be like "gold on the streets of New York."[31] As his mother gained status and stature by accumulating wealth from her relations with US military personnel, her position within the community helped him to make friends and overcome the "pain" and "isolation" he had previously felt.[32]

Of course, some women continued to experience hardships in their camptown lives, leaving many to struggle with whether to give their children up for adoption and the chance for better lives. During the same 1962 field visit, ISS officials met with Korean mothers to study their perspectives. Social workers found that the vast majority of women considering adoption did so only due to lack of alternative options. The mothers were noted to have strong "affectional relationships" with their children, so much so that few "would never give up their children, but for the pressure of prejudice and the damage it may do to the child."[33] Mixed race Koreans also remember their birth mothers this way—describing them as "gentle," "loving," "kind and delicate"—and reiterating in their recollections how "she absolutely made sure that I knew that she loved me."[34] Many women verbally expressed to ISS representatives their hopes "that something [else] be worked out to give [mixed race children] a future here."[35] Some remained skeptical about adoption and whether their sons and daughters would have the "same status and treatment as those born into family" or even "equal rights of inheritance under American law."[36] Having learned about racism through their close interactions with the US military, Korean mothers were not convinced that life in America would actually be better than what they could provide in South Korea. They requested that ISS representatives provide photographic evidence of adoptive families in the United States to prove that mixed race children were indeed "healthy, happy and being well cared for" as social workers adamantly insisted.[37]

(84) The First Amerasians

Even in instances when adoption seemed to be the obvious solution, such as those involving mothers who were completely impoverished and indebted to their "brothel keepers," ISS observed women in deep anguish at the thought of relinquishing their children.[38] By the 1960s, many women had witnessed years of bad case work involving their co-workers, neighbors, and friends. They had also seen, firsthand, how these mothers suffered after giving up their sons and daughters. Traces of these women in retrospective sources provide some insight into what it might have been like for those who lost their children. One mixed race adoptee recalls the following scenes near Yongsan Garrison in Seoul, where she grew up during the 1960s:

> I saw a lot of women like that in my neighborhood because it was so close to the base. Even as a young child, I could tell that many of these women were in love with these soldiers—some of them were actually married to these guys as well. And when these men would leave Korea, the girls would just be sitting outside crying. If they never came back, they'd have to give up their children too. And they would cry. I saw that often. Sometimes those women would come up to me. They'd grab me and ask, "are you my daughter?" Even when I told them "No, no, I'm not," some of them would pull me closer; they wouldn't let me go. They'd say "well, why don't you be my daughter now? Come with me." Then they'd try to drag me off with them.[39]

This harrowing account from Jeong Ja Kim's camptown memoir is also instructive:

> Even a day or two later, I still didn't feel as if I had sent my child away to another country. I just felt as if they were taking care of my child for a little while. That's what I thought. And then I just started to go crazy. Every time I heard a baby crying I couldn't stand it. So, I would run out to the store and start drinking *makkŏlli*. I would come back drunk and ask my friend "Where's my baby?" . . . So, I thought "Oh my God, I'm going crazy. My poor little baby." . . . After that my friend started to get rid of all the remaining diapers, baskets, and everything else that I had for the child. She just got rid of all that stuff. And then I went even crazier. I would go out to this little stream. I would just go out into the water and drink. . . . I was crazy like that. I was just out of my mind. . . . I told my friends to just go away and leave me alone. But they kept coming to me every day and they kept trying to knock me to my senses. They told me to eat. They would put spoons full of food into my mouth and tell me to swallow. . . . I decided I should just die. So, one day, I took some pills, drank the *makkŏlli*, slit my wrists and I just laid there.[40]

"CONFUCIUS' OUTCASTS" (85)

Unfortunately, scenes of women in deep emotional distress or experiencing psychosis over having just relinquished their children seem not so uncommon during these years. It is not difficult to imagine how camptown women might have felt as they saw countless mixed race children like their own taken away from their communities or why so many of them resisted adoption for as long as they could.

Camptown women were not alone in developing adverse views of adoption; Korean child welfare professionals were skeptical as well.[41] An interview with a nineteen-year-old mother who had been seen by social workers three times, but could "not make up her mind" about sending her seven-year-old son for adoption, proved informative for ISS representatives:

> She is a prostitute but is not working as much now, as income has dropped off, debts have mounted. Outlook is so hopeless, she lives only from day to day. She has given much thought to giving up her boy for adoption in an American home. She knows it would be best for him, but he is all she has. She wept several times during the interview. . . . I discussed what might be done to help the mother, but resources are limited. Miss Lee [the Korean social worker] was much interested in working on this angle, but ISS has not gone very far in helping mothers with their problems. Emphasis has been upon getting the release as soon as possible, and Miss L has had supervisory criticism for taking too much time in getting a mother's release. . . . Mother asked Miss L to come back again as she still couldn't make up her mind.[42]

This encounter illustrates how difficult it was for mothers to make a decision to relinquish their children to foreign agencies, as well as an American ISS field worker's critique of the state of child welfare in South Korea. In addition to feeling pressured to achieve closure on adoption and a quick release, Korean social workers like Miss Lee were often at the mercy of foreign agencies, with little ability to impact, at a policy level, the case work in which they were participating.

The 1962 field visit would prompt ISS to completely restructure its major goals and programs in South Korea. In the coming years, the organization would move away from its almost exclusive focus on adoption and toward integrating mixed race children into South Korean society and offering assistance to mothers who were impoverished or practicing prostitution. Believing that these efforts would be most successful if they came from the Korean employees, ISS immediately began transitioning its South Korea branch into an indigenous agency. These policy recommendations were nothing short of revolutionary at the time. ISS was perhaps one of the first organizations to realize that "the need for intercountry placement" was not the result of South Koreans wanting to send their children abroad but rather "the lack of basic welfare services within" the country.[43] While there had been a "rapid increase of foreign welfare agencies, mostly American" since the Korean War, few of these organizations had contributed "to the development of basic community welfare services by and for the Korean people."[44] In the 1950s, for example, foreign relief aid totaled more than 80 percent of the South Korean government's own social welfare expenditure, peaking at 105 percent in 1957.[45] This would continue into the 1960s and 1970s when that figure ranged from 43.9 to 216 percent.[46] In other words, intercountry adoption was not an objective solution to the problem of South Korea's many child welfare issues, including the most pressing question of mixed race children. Rather, it was the South Korean government's dependence on material and financial support from foreign organizations, in addition to US humanitarian and government interests in maintaining a refugee orphan program, that underpinned this major international effort and stunted the development of alternative possibilities.[47]

To address this unevenness, ISS urged other foreign agencies to follow their lead in the "training and development of Korean leadership" so that local solutions could be effected. Examples of these proposals included the rehabilitation of birth mothers and the integration of mixed race children into the national school system.[48] However, ISS was well aware of how difficult it would be to implement such a radical change in the way that child welfare was administered in South Korea. For example, by 1962, the Korean Association of Voluntary Agencies (KAVA) included sixty-four organizations that were responsible for much of South Korea's social welfare, but not a single one was an indigenous agency. In addition, ISS representative noted how KAVA "seems not to have any concept of training Koreans to take over."[49] This was a source of great frustration for Korean social workers. With this in mind, ISS increased its Korean staff from just seven in 1962, to seventeen out of its team of nineteen workers by 1964. But few other American organization made comparable moves during that time. Over these three years, the total number of foreign welfare agencies increased from sixty-four to eighty-four, and "except for one or two," there seemed to be "no perceptible move on the part of these programs to train and develop Korean leadership in their programs."[50] Of these twenty new organizations, one "had been added to the six already engaged in the intercountry adoption of children from Korea to the United States."[51] As a result, one ISS representative reported that "the feeling of hostility by Koreans toward Americans on this issue, that I noted in 1962, has intensified considerably."[52]

Despite these disappointments, just two years after the organization's 1962 field visit, ISS had turned itself into a quasi-indigenous agency and reported having made several major "breakthroughs on the problem of integrating racially mixed children into Korean society."[53] While the organization continued to carry out intercountry adoption, placing an average of 100 children per year, it also developed a Foster Care Family program offering "pre-placement care for children in [the] process of adoption."[54] ISS argued that such a development was "a significant departure from the previous practice of leaving children with their birth mothers until time to fly them to the United States, or the other alternative of placing them in an institution in Seoul."[55] As these former policies were the result of earlier claims that mixed race children were murdered by their "unscrupulous" countrymen, starved by Korean caretakers, and thus in need of separate accommodations, foster care signified the progress and professionalization of child welfare practices in South Korea.[56] Further, because "these are racially mixed children in Korean families," the organization believed that "the program has had the added very significant effect of gaining acceptance of these children in many families and neighborhoods in Seoul."[57] In 1964, approximately sixty to seventy mixed race children were being looked after by Korean foster parents, with eight months being the average length of time for their care before their international move.[58]

In addition to the Foster Care Family program, ISS was instrumental in promoting a more integrationist stance among the broader social welfare community in South Korea. In January 1964, for example, the KAVA Resolution on Children with Racially Mixed Parentage was adopted.[59] The statement and plan of action, carried out by the association's Social Welfare Committee, acknowledged the presence of a growing number of mixed race children now older in age, no longer in orphanages but living with their mothers and "therefore not as visible as they were several years ago."[60] The resolution recognized the "encouraging trend within the greater Korean community toward acceptance of these children" and expressed "hope that with help these children may someday be accepted in the land of their birth."[61] As such, KAVA urged its agencies to expand their efforts beyond intercountry adoption services. They recommended "educational funds for qualified older children" so that mixed race Koreans might "complete their education in the land of their birth," advocated the development of "programs to encourage the acceptance and assimilation of children of diverse national parentage," opposed the premise "of schools that only accept racially mixed children," and urged their members to assist the Korean government in their "commendable effort to develop prostitution rehabilitation centers and expand social welfare services to needy girls" who, in many cases, were or became the mothers of these individuals following separation from their American husbands.⁶² While not all organizations took up these recommendations and many remained fixated on intercountry adoption and segregated institutional care, the resolution was a significant departure from earlier understandings of the problems plaguing mixed race children and an official recognition that adoption was just one of many solutions worthy of being pursued.

Perhaps the biggest "historic milestone" in social welfare pertaining to mixed race individuals occurred when the ISS-Korea director became involved in an initiative called Eurasian Children Living as Indigenous Residents in 1963.⁶³ With the assistance of George Whitener, a field treasurer for the United Presbyterian Mission, ECLAIR was founded with the objective of integrating an aging mixed race population into the South Korean school system. Although Korean mothers worked hard to protect their children from experiencing societal prejudices during their younger years, new problems could emerge when they reached school age. One mixed race woman recalls how difficult it was to walk to school in the mornings: "You were just constantly teased. The boys would stop to look at you, they wanted to have fights. They would say *"T'wigi! T'wigi* [halfbreed]!"⁶⁴ For other mixed race Koreans, school problems were not limited

Figure 3.1 The Harry Holt Memorial Orphanage in Ilsan. *The Mixed Names (Holt's Orphanage)*, 1965, gelatin silver print, © Joo Myung Duck. Courtesy of the artist and Miyako Yoshinaga Gallery, New York.

Figure 3.2 A mixed race boy takes his school lessons at the Holt orphanage. *The Mixed Names (Holt's Orphanage)*, 1965, gelatin silver print, © Joo Myung Duck. Courtesy of the artist and Miyako Yoshinaga Gallery, New York.

to bullying but could also be legal matters. Educational authorities sometimes blocked mixed race children's enrollment into their schools because they were "not registered under a Korean father" or did not have South Korean citizenship.[65] While some mothers got around the lack of official paperwork by bribing officials, providing fraudulent documents, or convincing male relatives, friends, or neighbors to register their mixed race children, these options were not always available.[66] For many women, their inability to provide legal status to their mixed race children and to ensure their enrollment at local schools was yet another factor pushing them to place their sons and daughters in institutional care, where they would be entered on the orphanage director's family register and thus gain citizenship under their surname instead.[67]

Individuals working on ECLAIR were well aware that deep concern about mixed race Koreans' future educational prospects was one of the main reasons that Korean mothers relinquished their children for adoption. Yet some women only did so believing that their sons and daughters would eventually return to them in South Korea after finishing their schooling in the United States. It is unclear whether these mothers were intentionally deceived by adoption professionals to view their children's intercountry placement simply as a study abroad opportunity rather than as a complete severing of parental rights and relations. But one birth mother reveals how

(90)   *The First Amerasians*

the intercountry placements of her two sons were not what she understood them to be:

> I said . . . No matter how much you study in Korea, you can't make money here. If you could go right now, how great would that be? *Ŏmma* is not throwing you away, she's sending you to study in America, so go. But in exchange, you must behave and listen to your American adoptive parents. After you graduate high school and become an adult, *ŏmma* will be waiting for you. If you tell your adoptive parents you want to see your *ŏmma*, they'll bring you when you're 20 years old. Don't try to steal or lie or cheat to make money to come see me, tell your adoptive parents and come. Hold your adoptive mother's hand. Be nice to her. If she says "No" then don't do that. Go to school when you're told and eat what you're given and once you're as big as *hyŏnga*, you'll be able to come see me. See . . . Look at that neighborhood *hyŏnga*, he can't find a job, he just delivers cigarettes, is that a good life? If you stay here, all you'll be is a delivery boy. So you have to go. *Ŏmma* is not throwing you away. You're going to America to study. You'll be comfortable with your adoptive mom and dad. Listen to *ŏmma*, let's promise. Once you're 20 years old and you're done studying you can come back, and in the meantime, we can write letters and send photographs.[68]

Shortly after her children were sent abroad, the letters they promised to exchange stopped. In old age, the birth mother remains anxious wondering if she made the right choice and whether her two boys are "dead or alive."[69] Stories such as these show how concerns about mixed race Koreans' educational prospects were opportunities to prey on their mothers' insecurities and take children away from loving home environments.

The integrationist movement was driven not just by these abuses but also by more positive developments in the camptowns, which provided social workers a glimpse into what might be possible for mixed race children in South Korean society more broadly. Some mixed race Koreans had good school experiences. One woman who finished her primary and secondary education entirely in South Korea recalls that she "never seriously thought about" the fact that she was racially different from her peers.[70] Another recounts similarly how she "really was not teased at all" and found favor among her teachers:

> I remember my first-grade teacher who was also my second-grade teacher. And in those days, the military base would sometimes bring cornbread to school for the children to eat. And when there were leftovers, my teacher would take my books out of my bookbag and stuff it with all the leftover food, so that I could take it home for myself. . . . He spoiled me that way and I felt he treated me like

I was his daughter. And so, in school, I don't really recall experiencing any kind of prejudice from the teachers or from the other children. It was a small village, and everyone knew each other, and we all played together. Never once did I feel like I was an outsider even though I was darker skinned. I was one of them.[71]

Perhaps it was insights like this that helped social workers to see beyond Orientalist constructions and instead recognize a humanity among the Korean populace who, in some places, were already embracing these children with open arms.

Keen to prevent more intercountry placements as the result of mixed race children's limited educational prospects at home, ECLAIR began by "securing their admission into public schools."[72] The program also offered financial aid, covering entrance fees, tuition, books, uniforms and clothing, medical fees, transportation, and incidentals for families in need. To fund this work, ECLAIR secured "financial contributions . . . from interested persons in the United States, personally solicited by Mr. Whitner" of the United Presbyterian Mission.[73] By spring 1965, the program was sponsoring thirty-seven students in Seoul middle schools. ISS representatives praised these developments and celebrated the success of the program. In just one year nearly "all middle and high schools which had previously excluded racially mixed children opened their doors to these children."[74] In July 1965, two years after its founding, the program was handed over to Child Placement Service (CPS). CPS, established by the Ministry of Health and Social Affairs in 1954, was the only indigenous agency participating in intercountry adoption at the time. It carried out the Korean side of casework: interviewing birth mothers and children, making arrangements for relinquished children's care, preparing the necessary Korean and US government documents, checking on children at orphanages, and escorting children to hospitals for medical examinations.[75] With a subsidy from the South Korean government, CPS immediately hired two Korean caseworkers to work exclusively on ECLAIR projects and made plans to hire an additional eight trained child professionals by 1967, "when it is anticipated that there will be at least 500 racially mixed children in Korea reaching middle school age, and needing assistance to continue their education."[76] CPS also pursued a "two-year extension of service" that would expand the ECLAIR initiative beyond Seoul, open an office in the city of Pusan later that year, and establish more offices in other cities by 1966.[77]

In many ways, the efforts of ECLAIR in these early years were exactly what ISS envisioned in 1962 when it urged Americans to assist Koreans in developing their own solutions for the nation's many social and child welfare problems. As an initiative that had gained its footing through the

(92)   *The First Amerasians*

sponsorship of American humanitarians and philanthropists, was built up by both Korean and American social workers, and was then passed on to an indigenous agency with support from the South Korean government, ECLAIR provided ISS with a model for the role of foreign agencies. But the progress of Eurasian Children Living as Indigenous Residents and what it represented for the future of child welfare in South Korea would soon be undermined by a powerful American philanthropist who established a program in direct competition with the indigenous integrationist movement.

In January 1964, the Pearl S. Buck Foundation was founded by the seventy-three-year-old author and philanthropist who had previously come to the rescue of mixed race Koreans.[78] In the late 1950s, Pearl S. Buck was perhaps second to only Holt in her impassioned defense of proxy adoptions. She advocated mixed race children's expedient removal from South Korea and began placing them through her own agency, Welcome House, in 1958. Her goals for the foundation were purportedly different. In its promotional materials, the Pearl S. Buck Foundation expressed every indication that it would continue its "past policy in regard to adoption," but also establish a new program to assist the "children that must remain" in South Korea (so that they might "grow-up to be educated and useful . . . honest citizens, doing their share for the good of their country").[79] Opening its first office in Philadelphia, the organization hoped to raise enough funds by the end of the year to establish a South Korean branch. By the spring 1964, a "campaign for $10 million dollars in five years through a series of balls sponsored by the Arthur Murray Dance Studios in 50 states" was well under way.[80] In the following months, reports of Buck "traversing America to bring the orphans' plight to sympathetic listeners and potential contributors" were publicized in almost every major national newspaper.[81] The lavish galas, 200 in total, thrown in major cities including Philadelphia, New York, Chicago, Washington, and Los Angeles, attracted crowds of around 2,000 each.[82] At each event the author discussed her devotion "to the finding and rescue of the children and their mothers" and explained how "the children can be adopted," before gracefully ending her evening "with a waltz."[83]

With every new extravaganza came another opportunity to raise awareness about the plight of mixed race children left behind in South Korea. But the narratives furthered by the Pearl S. Buck Foundation were out of touch with the more recent child welfare initiatives in camptowns, even though the agency had been provided with reports detailing progress made by KAVA and CPS in the hope that it might cooperate with the existing integrationist movement.[84] Instead of discussing the organization's efforts as part of these more positive developments in South Korea, spokespeople for the foundation deployed outdated stereotypes of mixed race Koreans.

They claimed "these illegitimate children are outcasts. . . . [T]hey die at an alarming rate. They aren't allowed to go to school, and they can't get jobs. The oriental children call them 'those American kids.'"[85] They "roam the streets, live in caves, and eat out of garbage cans."[86]

In the press, Americans also read about "little girls, eight and 10 years old" who "become prostitutes . . . or they die."[87] The story of a half-caste teenager turned sex worker provided millions of Americans with a glimpse into the lives of children South Koreans "would rather forget about."[88] Published with the assistance of the Pearl S. Buck organization, an article in *Time* magazine titled "Confucius' Outcasts" began with this haunting anecdote:

> At six, she followed her Korean mother to a ramshackle bar and discovered that her mother was for sale to US servicemen. On the way home, alone, the little girl had an even more traumatic experience: a man lured her into an alley and assaulted her. At eight, she learned why classmates jeered "half-caste!" at her: her father had been a white GI. At 16, she was a full-fledged prostitute working among American soldiers who liked her slim Occidental legs and ample breasts. Now, at 19, after six abortions and uncounted liaisons with every variety of GI, Annie Park is the most-talked-about girl in South Korea.[89]

Accounts of young children dying or practicing prostitution were not quite sensationalist enough to get donors to open their purse strings. The Pearl S. Buck Foundation also constructed mixed race Koreans as white despite the fact that the majority of those left behind were Black, and invoked national pride so that Americans would feel racial familiarity and a political obligation to aid these pitiful children. Stories of "blond hair, blue-eyed" beggars filled the Pearl S. Buck Foundation's promotional materials, where the author herself gave the following account:[90]

> I visited Korea recently and took time to investigate the status and condition of the American-Korean children. It makes me feel strange, I can tell you, to have a beggar child put out his hand for a penny and to look down, not into a Korean face, but into a face unmistakably American. Aside from the humanitarian aspect of the situation can this be good for American prestige?[91]

To embellish its claims, the organization declared that it had "uncovered some astounding figures" on the number of "illegitimate children left behind" by US servicemen.[92] Throughout 1965, the Pearl S. Buck Foundation would continuously assert that there were 50,000 mixed race children in South Korea, the number "increasing at a rate of 1,000 a year."[93] The foundation reported this grossly inflated figure despite "reliable Korean sources [telling them] that the total number most likely did not exceed 5,000."[94] In fact, "in 1961 the Korean government was able to locate only 869 racially mixed children," and in 1964 child welfare agencies made a conservative estimate of 2,000.[95] Such "irresponsible reporting," fed to the press by Pearl S. Buck Foundation representatives, utilized the most extreme and exaggerated accounts of mixed race children's suffering so as to move Americans to care about what they were being told was an inhumane and desperate situation in South Korea.[96]

All of this severely troubled social welfare professionals in South Korea who accused the foundation of "misleading publicity for fundraising purposes" and "misrepresent[ing] the plight of these children."[97] ISS representatives assured their colleagues elsewhere in the world that "the Annie Parks are relatively few" and that "in the past three years . . . there have been virtually no racially-mixed children begging on the street."[98] They claimed that "the old Confucian values are giving way as South Korea joins the modern world" and that "the country is assimilating the relatively few racially mixed children in her midst" at an "astonishing[ly] rapid pace."[99] In fact, mixed race Koreans were now "accepted in the public school" and "their community acceptance depends less on their appearance than it does on the stability of the family with whom they are living—like children anywhere."[100] In addition, important efforts to extend "a helping hand . . . to mothers still entertaining" soldiers were also being made by responsible social welfare agencies.[101] ISS representatives charged the foundation, with their gross exaggerations, of undermining "the quiet revolution of acceptance" that had been achieved through the collaborative work of Korean and American child professionals in recent years through initiatives like ECLAIR.[102]

Indeed, hyperbolic claims made by Buck were not genuine concerns about American prestige but more likely attempts to solicit funds from middlebrow constituents and to "live up to the boast that the Pearl Buck Foundation is the only agency exercising concern for the integration of [the] racially-mixed child," in the words of her contemporaries.[103] It was a combination of these professional interests and feelings of national and racial superiority—cloaked in the language of humanitarianism—that pushed the organization to publish stories that highlighted the most disturbing accounts of mixed race children in South Korea.[104]

Organizations like KAVA, ISS, or CPS were not devoting their energy to campaigning or funding a major public relations campaign in the United States, leaving the Pearl S. Buck Foundation's account of mixed race Koreans largely uncontested among the American public. The media promoted Buck as a credible expert who had spent much of her life in mainland China "where her parents were Southern Presbyterian missionaries."[105] In addition to being a Nobel Prize–winning author of beloved novels and celebrated works of non-fiction by 1949, Buck was also a renowned philanthropist who had founded the nation's first interracial adoption agency, using her personal money to fund the work. By 1958, Welcome House had begun its intercountry placement services with South Korean children. Buck promoted this work by giving heartfelt accounts of mistreated orphans and ardent defense of proxy adoption to the press and in legislative hearings.[106] As Pearl S. Buck and her team toured the nation, her status helped to earn the foundation enough social, cultural, and economic capital to catapult it into success.

The information she circulated about mixed race Koreans quickly became conventional truths within and beyond the United States. Even mixed race Koreans who grew up in South Korea during this period remember learning "about Pearl S. Buck and how she was working to save mixed race Korean children from terrible things."[107] After reading an article in the military newspaper *Pacific Stars and Stripes*, one mixed race Korean woman recalls, "I started to panic and cry because I thought she was talking about me. I thought my parents were going to abandon me and give me to an orphanage. Even after my dad reassured me, the fear stayed with me because every now and then I would see mixed race children on the streets who were dressed poorly, wearing rubber shoes, and often collecting bits of something in big tin cans."[108] By June 1965, Pearl S. Buck representatives had arrived in South Korea where they were "making a survey of where the children are and what can be done for them." In November, the organization began covering "educational costs for racially mixed children going into integrated schools" and supporting younger children "in need of aid such as food or medical care."[109]

When the Pearl S. Buck Foundation registered with the Ministry of Health and Social Affairs in November 1965, ISS began monitoring the organization's activities as it had done with Holt earlier. After an investigation of the agency's initial months of operation, ISS concluded that "the Pearl Buck Foundation has demonstrated a total lack of concern for the welfare of programs already in Korea and would seem to have made every effort to disrupt local [efforts]."[110] The foundation had "given top priority to working in prostitute communities surrounding units of the US Seventh Division" located north of Seoul near the towns of Uijeongbu, Dongducheon, and Uncheon.[111] In doing so, they had set their program up in direct competition with "three established social agencies" already concentrated "on helping mothers of racially mixed children," whose services

(96) *The First Amerasians*

included "intercountry adoption, rehabilitation counseling, help with separation problems stemming from GIs rotating to the US, and the integration into Korean society of racially mixed children."[112] Social workers had even helped mothers find alternatives to intercountry adoption when they were practicing prostitutes, encouraging the child's "transfer to a relative's home away from the debilitating atmosphere of these villages."[113] The established organizations referenced—the ISS, CPS, and Korean Social Service (KSS), an adoption agency founded in 1964—were all considered indigenous or quasi-indigenous agencies at the time.

Rather than cooperating with these societies' efforts, the Pearl S. Buck Foundation "systematically contacted mothers" previously known to these agencies and bribed them with $25 per month "in return for a promise to keep the grant a secret yet at the same time refuse any further contact with" the other organizations.[114] The foundation offered no other services aside from the money, which ISS called "deplorable as it does nothing to rehabilitate the mother" nor help "children whose material needs" were already better met "than the average Korean child."[115] Further, ISS charged the Pearl S. Buck Foundation's policy of direct cash grants with "placing a premium on producing illegitimate children."[116] Indeed, many women withdrew from integrationist programs and instead signed up for the foundation's stipend. Because only one child per family could qualify for the grant, mothers even began lending "extra children to motherless friends."[117] In at least one instance, "a family receiving help from ECLAIR" was persuaded "to accept a large grant from [the foundation] in return for discontinuing further contact with ECLAIR."[118] The Pearl S. Buck Foundation even made trips to schools scouting for ECLAIR-sponsored children. In one case it outed a child "who was racially mixed but passing for full-Korean," seriously upsetting the family and making "her subsequent school adjustment more difficult."[119] In other instances, the heart-wrenching process of putting a child up for adoption was further complicated by monetary considerations. Social workers feared that adoption agencies might soon try to outbid the foundation's cash grant to obtain the release of mixed race children. The outraged ISS argued that the Pearl S. Buck Foundation was using "Western funds" to destroy "Korean agencies which are struggling to develop indigenous child welfare programs."[120] Ultimately, the foundation's activities upended the progressively successful integration and rehabilitation work of local organizations; it nearly eliminated the entire intercountry adoption program of CPS and severely damaged the integration program of ECLAIR by stealing their clients.

Perhaps most tragic was the South Korean government's decision to reduce its financial support for the ECLAIR effort as a result of the foundation's work. In August 1965, the South Korean Economic Planning Board disapproved a subsidy request to CPS made on behalf of the Ministry of Health and Social Welfare on the basis that the ECLAIR program was no longer necessary because the Pearl S. Buck Foundation operated a similar program.[121] In response, ISS remarked, "This has been a most unfortunate development as it has been felt by responsible social workers that the initiative for the integration of half-American children must come from the Korean people, as represented by their government rather than from a foreign agency imposing its humanitarian views."[122] While "the official recognition by the government of its responsibility for racially-mixed children in Korea was seen as a dramatic departure from a previous attitude that these children could never be absorbed in the culture of their birth," the damage to the viability of ECLAIR was actually caused by Americans.[123] In the coming years, CPS would be forced to solicit funds from foreign agencies such as the Wilson Foundation, the United Presbyterian Mission, United World Mission, and FPP to keep the ECLAIR program operational.[124] That money would come with obligations to the granting institutions. As a result, ECLAIR would no longer be a completely indigenous effort emphasizing local solutions but rather a program working to assist mixed race children within the parameters established by its many American donors. Throughout the 1960s and 1970s, this dependence on American aid deeply frustrated CPS social workers who continually noted in their reports disagreements "between chief of the voluntary agencies and us."[125]

Correspondence between the CPS director Youn Taek Tahk and FPP director James L. Pullman illustrates this friction between Korean social workers and American voluntary agencies in South Korea during the late 1960s. By February of 1968, ECLAIR officials were highly disturbed by the recent trend in intercountry adoption placements among their clients. The organization had just lost "two ECLAIR children . . . going to America by arrangement of Pearl S. Buck," two others were adopted "in secret" through Holt and the Seventh Day Adventist Mission, and another two supported through FPP sponsorships were "adopted . . . suddenly" as well.[126] Although FPP had no direct role in the arrangement, Youn Taek Tahk became involved in an embittered battle with James Pullman about two FPP policies he believed to have contributed to the loss of his ECLAIR children to adoptive homes in the United States. These included "the child and his mother" being "immediately asked" (and encouraged in CPS's views) "if they would consider adoption in an American home" and FPP's requirement that sponsored children "write a letter to the foster parent or sponsor once each month."[127] In spite of Tahk's concerns, Pullman maintained that FPP would uphold its requirements and that ECLAIR children receiving

(98)   *The First Amerasians*

the organization's support should continue to "acknowledge every gift received."[128] Tahk's scathing response to the FPP director began: "You will never know, I dare say, the mental suffering I and the ECLAIR workers have to overcome because of such conflict between the foreign agencies."[129] Although Pullman did not view correspondence between ECLAIR children and American sponsors "as a means to promote [the] adoption of mixed blood children into American families," Tahk argued that "close contact with overseas sponsors . . . inspires the intentions of going overseas. The children [lose the] intention of staying here and adjusting into Korean society."[130]

In a shocking move that captures the depth of ECLAIR's frustration and resentment toward American voluntary agencies, CPS director Youn Taek Tahk rejected the FPP director's offer of fifty sponsorships that year, averaging $10 a month per family. Among his FPP colleagues, Pullman would mock Tahk's unintelligible English and criticize ECLAIR's inability to accomplish "any significant Korean support." Claiming that "there is little good in the program in respect to integration of the children into Korean society," he dismissed the entire CPS-ECLAIR effort as ineffective.[131] His derisive commentary would spread throughout the child welfare community in South Korea, tarnishing ECLAIR's reputation and undermining the credibility of the indigenous integrationist movement. Although the CPS director had stood up to an American sponsor, defiantly rejecting money that his organization so desperately needed, little would change in the coming years. ECLAIR would continue to be funded almost entirely with American dollars, and the organization would continue its operations under the auspices of foreign sponsors. This would be a perennial thorn in the organization's side as richer and more powerful American institutions fixated on their own professional and humanitarian ambitions would continue to undermine efforts to integrate mixed race Koreans into South Korean society.

By July of 1968, estimates of the population of mixed race children in South Korea ranged from a conservative government figure of 2,500 to the Pearl S. Buck Foundation's new projection of 10,000 (a dramatically lower figure that the organization's earlier claim of 50,000).[132] Although ECLAIR retained a government subsidy to be used for integrating mixed race children and rehabilitating single mothers, the amount was minimal compared to American contributions.[133] In addition, organizations with more social, cultural, and economic clout overshadowed their work. For example, in 1968, ECLAIR was supporting just 106 children in South Korean schools, and only thirty-four mothers were involved in their rehabilitation program, receiving such services as vocational training, loans for small businesses, housing assistance, and medical care.[134] By contrast, the Pearl S. Buck Foundation was providing 1,200 mothers with cash grants.[135]

Although, in the eyes of most observers, the Pearl S. Buck Foundation appeared to be invested in the integration of mixed race children into South Korean society, Korean social workers saw much of their effort as working in opposition to this goal. ECLAIR had embraced a "policy of anti-institutional care," arguing that using segregated facilities "bars integration to Korean society or at least slows it down."[136] Increasingly, Korean social workers saw the intercountry placements of mixed race children into adoptive families in the United States as detrimental to the integrationist effort, contending that such a practice only further "secludes" these individuals "from Korean society."[137] By 1968, the Pearl S. Buck Foundation was housing approximately eighty individuals, ranging in age from five through adolescence, at their Opportunity Center in Sosa.[138] Similarly, Holt had established a center in Ilsan to accommodate some 100 "mixed blood" children; the vast majority were Korean Black ranging in age from ten to thirteen.[139] Although these institutions provided schooling and promoted vocational training (including knitting, sewing, nursing, and driving) for older children, they often served as pipelines to adoptive families in the United States rather than efforts to prepare mixed race individuals for entry into South Korean society.[140] When these American humanitarians fell short on their promises and suddenly withdrew monetary support and closed orphanages and institutions housing mixed race Koreans, as the Pearl S. Buck Foundation did in Paju on July 5, 1971, the children were left abandoned before being "driven out of the orphanage unattended."[141] As delinquent mixed race children roamed the streets and got into trouble, constructions of these individuals as troublemakers, gangsters, and violent criminals further isolated them.

By the 1970s, CPS representatives observed that despite the successful implementation of services to rehabilitate Korean birth mothers and facilitate mixed race children's entry into local school systems, these individuals were still not assimilating into South Korean society. In a 1971 report produced by the agency, Korean social workers noted that many of their clients did not identify as Korean and had developed a longing to immigrate to the United States. They believed that such a "tendency of mixed blood children [was] not solely caused by exclusion [from] Korean society" but was also the result of systems orienting these individuals toward the United States.[142] "American fever" spread throughout the broader Korean population during these years, though mixed race children experienced it even more intensely.[143] One mixed race man remembers how he was "hell bent" on getting to the United States, having experienced the kindness and

Figure 3.3 A mixed race girl at the Holt orphanage. *The Mixed Names (Holt's Orphanage)*, 1965, gelatin silver print, © Joo Myung Duck. Courtesy of the artist and Miyako Yoshinaga Gallery, New York.

wealth of Black soldiers, who "would almost go out of their way" to gift him money or American goods.[144] He explains:

> We had the taste of America through the soldiers. He was validation of how superior America was.... [I]n Korea we have these little ass Koreans, but in America, they have these superheroes! In our minds that was proof positive ... and then to experience American products... it all fuels the imagination of what America could be.... [T]he technology is superior.... [T]here's flying cars, there's gold everywhere, everyone is rich, people are fat all the time because there's so much food. That's what we thought.[145]

Mixed race Koreans had long been the beneficiaries of the US military's wealth and power and had grown up being constantly engaged by American humanitarians. Many had witnessed others like them being adopted abroad, their mothers pressured by social workers to follow suit, and their friends being sent to study "in the United States after being invited by American citizens."[146] In other words, there was a pervasive culture and well-established infrastructure that made sending mixed race children to the United States the normalized and oftentimes expected path for these individuals. One woman who was adopted into an American family during her early teenage years in the 1970s recalls always knowing that intercountry placement was a possibility for her. She remarks:

I heard it over and over again. People saying things like: "You should go to America for adoption. There was someone like you, but she got adopted to America. You should go as well. Your life will be better." People in the neighborhood said it, people at school. I didn't know anything about adoption or America, but I asked my mom if I could go too.[147]

CPS also observed that their clients expressed a deep sense of gratitude and indebtedness toward the United States for the support they received, including "school tuitions, living expenses, vocational training and housing."[148] Even when these services were delivered by indigenous programs like ECLAIR or were administered by Korean social workers, they were accompanied by "letters filled with love and warm-hearted" messages from Americans and requirements that the children regularly correspond with their sponsors in the United States.[149] Such a "counter-presentation" imposed on indigenous agencies by their foreign donors deeply frustrated social workers, who argued that the dichotomy between "Korean society's indifference" and "America's deep concern" only further "estranged" mixed race individuals from South Koreans and oriented them toward the United States.[150] These perspectives were consistent with earlier views and predictions on the part of organizations like ISS and CPS that a US monopoly on mixed race children's welfare would prevent their integration

Figure 3.4 Children pose on a brick wall at the Holt orphanage. *The Mixed Names (Holt's Orphanage)*, 1965, gelatin silver print, © Joo Myung Duck. Courtesy of the artist and Miyako Yoshinaga Gallery, New York.

Figure 3.5 A mixed race girl being visited by an American GI, who later became her adoptive father. Courtesy of Estelle Cooke-Sampson.

into South Korean society. Throughout the 1960s and 1970s, a continued fixation on intercountry adoption, segregated institutional care, and study abroad and sponsorship programs in the United States would overpower the efforts of CPS and ECLAIR. As the years went by, more foreign services were established, rivaling indigenous efforts. Ultimately, Korean social workers lacked the power, clout, and money to retain their hold over mixed race children's welfare.[151]

By the mid-1970s, the promising economic and social advances observed by American social workers in camptowns during the previous decade had been reversed, closely connected to changes at US bases. While in the 1960s the number of American soldiers stationed in South Korea averaged 60,000 annually, by the early 1970s, that figure had dropped to about 40,000, as the US military withdrew the 7th Infantry Division and its 20,000 troops from South Korea, with plans to soon remove an additional 10,000. This massive reduction was in part due to the Nixon Doctrine, a policy that mandated steady disengagement from South Korea alongside troop withdrawals in Vietnam.[152] Neighborhoods that were dependent on GI patronage deteriorated, from once bustling entertainment districts to shantytowns where thousands of Koreans were left displaced and without livelihoods. As many flocked to other bases, camptowns were quickly overwhelmed by new residents looking to cater to the dramatically shrinking troop population. In just one year (1970–1971), real estate prices in camptown regions plunged, 6,000 (out of a total of 32,000) Koreans employed at US bases lost their jobs, 100 clubs had been put out of business, and the salaries of camptown women catering to GIs at bars and clubs decreased from an average of ₩100,000 per month to a mere ₩5,000.[153] Having enjoyed financial security relative to the general South Korean population, camptown women fell into impoverished circumstances. As Korean mothers became poorer, they became less able to protect their children. The economic devastation wreaked by US troop withdrawals underscored the unequal nature of the US-Korea military alliance. As both the symbolic and physical embodiments of this relationship, mixed race children and their mothers became the targets of anti-American hostilities and bore the brunt of local resentment.

The situation was particularly desperate for Korean Black children who were disproportionately left behind in South Korea and less likely to racially pass than their white counterparts. Their mothers occupied a lower position in the camptown social strata, as Black GIs were seen as poorer and inferior to white GIs. This racialization of Black GIs in South Korea affected their local romantic partners as well the children born from such

Figure 3.6 Mixed race Koreans cherished the toys given to them by their American sponsors. *The Mixed Names (Holt's Orphanage)*, 1965, gelatin silver print, © Joo Myung Duck. Courtesy of the artist and Miyako Yoshinaga Gallery, New York.

Figure 3.7 Mixed race children, mostly Korean Black, at the Holt orphanage. Courtesy of Holt International, holtinternational.org.

relations. One oral history narrator witnessed a Korean Black girl who was teased so mercilessly about her dark skin that she self-harmed:

> There was another girl in my neighborhood. I was maybe 7 or 8 and she was about three years younger than me and part Black. They used to tease her because her skin was dark. They'd tell her to go shower because she was dirty. And then they'd spit on her. And one day I saw her on the sidewalk somewhere and she was rubbing a piece of stone on her skin just up and down, up and down. And I said, "What are you doing?" And she was crying but she just kept rubbing her arm. It was bleeding but she wouldn't stop. And she said, "I need to [scrub] my skin." And I will never forget that. And you know, to this day, I can hear her voice and I can hear her crying. I see her tears and I see the blood just dripping. Just a little girl, maybe 4 or 5 years old, crying and trying to peel her skin off.[154]

By the mid-1970s, camptowns went from being neighborhoods where mixed race Koreans were "insulated from prejudice," to places where their presence was detested.[155] They were stoned, spat on, taunted, and told "Go home, Yankee!"[156] One mixed race women, recalls an incident in which she was attacked by a local elder somewhere near Yongsan Garrison in Seoul in the mid-1970s:

There was this one time when I was 8 or 9 years old. It was *Ch'usŏk* and I had my *hanbok* on, my mother had braided my hair, and I remember feeling really good about myself. I think I was just standing in one corner, opening up a candy or something when all of a sudden all of these people came over with rags and they were hitting my head. Well, it turns out there was an old man lighting a cigarette and he decided to light my hair on fire because my hair wasn't black. I had red hair. Good thing my hair was long. I don't have any burn marks or anything, but to receive that kind of hatred . . . it really does something to you. He was just a grandpa, some older man. I didn't even know who he was. And then he just disappeared. Maybe he was just a passerby. But people just hated you because you looked different.[157]

As hostilities increased, Korean mothers began keeping their children indoors to shield them from outside prejudice. Others placed their children in orphanages and institutions that served as pipelines for immigration to the United States. Soon, villages near US bases once "crawling" with mixed race children became places where the sight of these individuals were rare.[158] In schools, mixed race Koreans were targeted—their hair yanked, noses bloodied, bodies beaten. In some instances, the bullying was so extreme that Korean mothers pulled their children out and homeschooled them. Other times, children dropped out of school to find work or help their mothers at home. With limited economic and educational prospects, older children worried about their futures. They begged their mothers to send them to the United States, as two different narrators remembered:

I made her. I made my mom send me to America. She was not going to give me up. I pressured her. I said you have to let me go for a better life. I didn't know anything about America except that everyone said America is better. America is a rich country. I didn't even know if Amerasian kids actually had better lives there. I knew nothing. I didn't know anything about that. In Korea at that time, that's just how people talked about America. They'd say, "People sleep on beds in America! It's a wealthy country!" That was in my mind, a child's mind not knowing anything. But I knew my family was struggling. My mom was struggling. My brothers are struggling. We had no relatives. We had nobody but each other. I told my mom, "You have to let me go." I couldn't even go to school because my youngest brother was not even a year old. I was carrying him around my back and looking after my other three brothers too. I told her, I'll study hard, get a good job, send money back home and help the family that way. So, she finally let me go.[159]

It got to the point where eventually I just stopped going outside because I was tired so of being taunted and being called names. Even when I was older people

(106) *The First Amerasians*

would throw stones at me. They wouldn't come to me and punch me or yank my hair anymore because I was older and bigger and taller. But they would come and spit, they would throw stones at me, and tell me to go away, that I'm no good. So, I just stopped going outside. The only time I would go outside was if it was dark, like 8 or 9 o'clock at night time. . . . I remember one time I was looking at a dog and I thought, you know your life is better than me. You're a mutt and nobody throws stones at you and no one bothers you. So, I took a bunch of pills. I tried to commit suicide. . . . And so by that time I told my mom I can't live like this anymore. There's no future here. I have no school education. What am I going to do? And I actually asked her to put me up for adoption so I could come here and go to school and have a chance at life. And that's how I came. I asked.[160]

Although statistics for mixed race Koreans adopted annually were not kept by the South Korean Ministry of Health and Welfare after 1970, there are indications that the figures increased as the social and economic conditions in camptowns worsened. Already, the trends were clear: in 1962, there were 158 adoptees and in 1970 that number was 361. As mixed race Koreans and their mothers struggled through this chaotic period, they looked for relief and found nothing but American solutions available. Among institutional care, segregated schools, sponsorship programs, and intercountry placement, all paths led to the United States. While indigenous agencies had tried to provide local solutions so that mixed race Koreans might remain in the lands of their birth, they had been completely overpowered by American humanitarian intervention. Eurasian Children Living as Indigenous Residents was nothing more than a promising but naïve idea. The local integrationist movement had ultimately failed.

The narrative of South Korean racism persisted, as adoptees would grow up being told by their American parents that they were lucky "to leave Korea because they hated mixed children there."[161] While the conditions in which mixed race persons lived were not always good and Korean mothers pursued adoption for a variety of economic and social reasons, the integrationist movement did not collapse solely because of South Korean racism. As indigenous initiatives were overshadowed by foreign agencies with more money and more professional and political clout, intercountry placements would increase instead. This inability to absorb mixed race individuals into postwar South Korean society was less a matter of South Korea's desire to excise its national impurities via adoption and more a reflection of the strength of American humanitarian, political, and material power. Nonetheless, Orientalist constructions of mixed race Koreans as "Confucius' Outcasts" have endured and continue to shape the ways in which this history has been remembered transnationally.

Figure 3.8 Korean mothers often took photographs with their mixed race children prior to giving them up for adoption. Courtesy of Nena Adams Benhoff.

Figure 3.9 A Korean mother with her mixed race son before he was sent to America. Courtesy of Joel L. A. Peterson.

Figure 3.10 A Korean mother and her child part at the Holt orphanage. *The Mixed Names (Holt's Orphanage)*, 1965, gelatin silver print, © Joo Myung Duck. Courtesy of the artist and Miyako Yoshinaga Gallery, New York.

4

Becoming American

Mrs. Smith is in agreement with her husband with regard to adopting a part Oriental child, providing its coloring and features are more Anglo than Oriental.[1] They have a strong preference for a blue-eyed girl with blonde hair. When I pointed out that few of the children have that coloring, she said she understood there are some who do, and does not believe her husband will accept one who is very dark or one who has strikingly Oriental features. She mentioned their plan to have an operation to produce a fold in the upper eyelids should they adopt a child with the characteristically Oriental eyes. She said that a slight slant is not objectionable to them, and she thinks that characteristic adds to a child's attractiveness. . . . My impression is that she is a stable person with a wholesome attitude toward life. I believe she will be quite accepting of a carefully chosen Korean child.[2]

By the time of this report in 1956, International Social Service (ISS) was fully participating in the intercountry placements of mixed race Koreans and had begun doing so to counteract the activities of humanitarian non-professional agencies like the Holt Adoption Program. The organization prided itself on maintaining the highest standards in its international case work while criticizing rivals for using the proxy method of adoption to bypass bureaucratic red tape. In fact, ISS worked with local and state child welfare authorities to match mixed race Korean children with American families through a lengthy procedure that included a series of home studies and interviews with prospective adoptive parents, criminal background checks, and financial evaluations of adoptive homes. Yet despite the protective measures in place to vet families and conduct quality placements according to what was viewed to be ethical and up-to-date child welfare protocols, social workers and adoptive parents developed harmful

The First Amerasians. Yuri W. Doolan, Oxford University Press. © Oxford University Press 2024.
DOI: 10.1093/oso/9780197534380.003.0005

(110)   *The First Amerasians*

processes to shape the identities of mixed race Koreans. This was informed not only by the prevailing American racial attitudes of the day but also the dominant Cold War ideologies that had justified these adoptions in the first place.

Indeed, adoptions like that of the Smiths depended on children's perceived ability to successfully become American—even if this meant augmenting their physiognomic features through surgical procedures. Plastic reconstructive surgery was pursued by the US military following the ceasefire in the Korean War as "visible evidence of American goodwill in Asia."[3] Military surgeons first reconstructed bodies injured from US napalm attacks and bombings, and when this proved effective in "[winning] the heart[s]" of the Korean people, they also began correcting other "deformities" or "anomalies," such as "flat noses" and "Oriental eyes."[4] Following these cosmetic procedures doctors proudly noted how their patients could now be "mistaken for Mexican or Italian" and were ready to become Christians or "travel to the United States."[5] Korean nurses, interpreters, entertainers, and war brides—given their proximity to the US military—were among the first to trade their "slant eyes" for "round eyes."[6] But as plastic reconstructive surgery became yet another way for Americans to disavow the violence of US imperialism in the name of democracy, liberation, freedom, and humanitarianism, it seemed a natural progression that adoptive parents could suggest this for mixed race children too.

Shortly after their interview with state social work professionals, the Smith family was approved for an adoption. Five months later, a mixed race child arrived in the United States and was placed in their custody. It appears that the family received no counseling to redirect their thinking. Instead, because the case worker believed the mother was speaking about "what it would mean to a child to be different from other children in the community," the gift of plastic surgery was most likely viewed as an appropriate and generous expression of American identities and ideologies.[7] Furthermore, because this was an ISS placement, many adoption professionals would consider this endorsement to be the product of responsible vetting and social welfare practices.

Using ISS case files, memoir, and oral history, this chapter explores the transformation of mixed race Koreans from the war-torn and war-damaged Asians that many US citizens imagined them to be into the all-American children whose adoptions and assimilation into US society were continuations of the anti-Asian violence they first experienced in South Korea. As adoptive families were recruited to take in mixed race children and encouraged by social workers to erase their Korean pasts, the intimate confines of the American home became a microcosm of the Cold War—a symbolic battleground in which the dominant ideologies undergirding the US military commitments of this era could be justified and reproduced. Consequently, the lives of mixed race children were profoundly shaped not only by the narratives surrounding their so-called rescues but also by the more localized US prejudices present in South Korea, including understandings of Korean mothers as camptown prostitutes. While the Cold War construction of the Amerasian was a powerful force that structured the lives of mixed race children in their new US homes, there were many adoptees who resisted this change. Thus, this chapter also showcases the perspectives of individuals who, as young children, fought against the ideological erasure of their Korean pasts.

In focusing on the discourse surrounding the Amerasian as a concept and how it shaped the lives of actual people, the narrative offered here does not represent the entirety of the mixed race Korean or adoptee experience in America. Adoptive families are not a monolith, and there were, indeed, parents whose views differed from the policies of social workers as well as those who pushed back against the dominant ideas. They respected their children's racial difference and acknowledged their Korean pasts. These experiences are already well-expressed in popular representations of adoption as well as in the memoirs of adoptees who pay homage to their loving adoptive families.[8] Because most accounts of adoption often do focus on the happy and well-adjusted child rescued from a life of poverty, this chapter instead highlights what this narrative can obscure. Further, while the epigraph to this chapter is about plastic surgery for adoptive Asian children, it is unclear how widespread these practices actually were.[9] Nonetheless, they illustrate the very real anxieties many Americans felt surrounding mixed race Koreans' racial differences as well as the extent some adoptive parents might have gone to get rid of those differences. What follows is an investigation into the various ways mixed race Koreans became American and how adoptive parents—bolstered by the institutional power of professional social work and the ideological power of US empire—furthered the problematic work of humanitarians, the military, government officials, and other adoption advocates in the making of the Amerasian.

———

Almost complete racial and ethnic isolation marked the experiences of mixed race Koreans in the early years of the intercountry adoption program. When these children first arrived in the United States during the mid-1950s, their status as dependents of US citizens made them rare exceptions to the severely restricted immigration from Asia. Although their numbers far surpassed those of most other Asian immigrant groups between 1952 and 1968, they followed American sponsors rather than ethnic kin into the country.[10] Social workers did very little or could do very little to cluster multiple children within the same communities. Consequently, mixed race Koreans were often kept apart from existing populations of Asian Americans as well as from one another. As these children were thinly dispersed throughout the country, they joined families in rural regions where few, if any, Koreans, let alone Asians, had ever lived before. At a time when the nation still upheld Jim Crow racial segregation and laws against miscegenation, observers considered these interracial and international adoptions to be truly revolutionary.[11]

ISS celebrated their early Korean placements, in particular their adoptive parents, who they praised as individuals with "the capacity to accept and to love a child toward whom others might have alien feelings."[12] Case consultants were amazed to find that many prospective families had not, in fact, previously been interested in adoption but "were asking specifically for a Korean child because of their humanitarian and religious concern."[13] Many had "strong religious affiliations" and "had learned of the miserable plight of the children through the missionary groups in Korea."[14] Others had "read articles and seen pictures in the press or had been aroused by the reports of American servicemen who had given firsthand accounts of the devastation of the Korean War and the appalling conditions under which these orphans live and die."[15] Indeed, political, humanitarian, and religious convictions prompted ordinary citizens to bring children of a markedly different racial "stock" into their families. ISS noted that this was a truly "remarkable fact" despite the "multicultural background and heterogenous population of the United States.[16]

However, the racial liberalism heralded by ISS social workers was, in fact, limited and perhaps less disruptive to color lines than most observers initially believed. During the early years of the Korea program, ISS refused to place fully Korean children in American homes because of their racial differences, as did other humanitarian non-professionals like the Holts, who prioritized the adoptions of mixed race Koreans.[17] White prospective parents also made clear their unwillingness to cross Black-white racial divides. In interviews with adoption professionals, they requested any Korean child so as long as it was not "partly-Negro."[18] In actuality, such expressions were unnecessary as ISS already followed an organizational policy of placing "Korean-Caucasian children" exclusively with "Caucasian Americans, and the Korean-Negro children with Negro Americans."[19] These practices and attitudes reveal how mixed race Koreans were desirable to Americans not for their Koreanness or racial difference but for their proximity to dominant US racial categories and their ability to fit into the status quo of America's existing racial landscape.

Furthermore, while ISS claimed to the international social welfare community that their adoptive parents had prioritized political, humanitarian, or religious reasons in their grounds for accepting mixed race Koreans, their early casework reveals that many Americans actually came to consider these children only after pursuing domestic adoption without success. In 1961, nearly 800,000 more American families wished to adopt each year than there were adoptable children in the United States.[20] The majority of these families were white Americans seeking white American children. Given the daunting odds, the process for getting a child through international adoption, particularly mixed race Koreans, was easier in the 1950s and 1960s, so long as prospective parents were willing to accept one who was racially different. This was certainly true for humanitarian nonprofessional organizations whose use of proxy adoption allowed families to bypass a strict evaluation process and avoid demonstrating the psychological, emotional, or financial ability to successfully care for a child. But even for those parents who would eventually get through ISS's stringent vetting, many were first denied placements of white children by other organizations, which led them to consider mixed race Koreans as a second choice. This desire for replacement white children was evident in some of the organization's early case work. Meanwhile, African American couples, who had access to a domestic surplus of adoptable Black children in state institutions, were more likely to express an explicit desire to raise mixed race Koreans exclusively.[21]

Additionally, constructions of mixed race Koreans as "American-faced" or blonde-haired and blue-eyed furthered by individuals like Harry Holt and Pearl S. Buck helped to emphasize the Amerasian rescue as a mission to bring these children back "to the land of their fathers."[22] These dominant images created a sense of racial familiarity that enabled Americans to imagine mixed race Koreans as racially passable members of their families. Respect for US paternity on part of Americans translated into a desire for "half-American," rather "half-Korean," children. Requests for children with "Caucasian" features were hardly isolated in ISS's early casework. In fact, ISS or state child authorities only mildly scrutinized prospective adoptive parents who expressed racist desires for children of a specific "coloring."[23] In most cases, social workers representing state departments of public or social welfare were happy to oblige these requests. They believed that matching adoptive children to adoptive parents' desires would ensure a

Figure 4.1 A portrait of a Korean girl who might have racially passed as white. *The Mixed Names (Holt's Orphanage)*, 1965, gelatin silver print, © Joo Myung Duck. Courtesy of the artist and Miyako Yoshinaga Gallery, New York.

successful placement in the long term and thus considered this practice to be ethical social work.

As mixed race Koreans were incorporated into white middle-class domesticity, their adoptions were based not so much on the formation of a new multicultural family but more on the basis of complete and total assimilation.[24] Immediately upon arrival in the United States, mixed race children with names such as Il-Sung, Mi-Ja, or Jung-Sook were legally given all-American names like Bobby, Susie, and Sarah. This was done not only for infants who would grow up with no memory of the change but also for children who were school-age or teenagers and had identified with their Korean names for their entire lives. Social workers also advised that, for more successful English language acquisition, children should be encouraged to forget the Korean language; this was held up as evidence of proper adjustment to their new country.[25] One adoptee recalls that the emphasis on English language learning was so intense in her household that "I wasn't allowed to sit in the chair until I said chair; I couldn't go to bed until I said bed."[26]

Figure 4.2 A photograph of adopted children with old Korean and new American names marked. Courtesy of Holt International, holtinternational.org.

Another aspect of assimilation that was particularly difficult for mixed race Koreans related to food. One woman, adopted at eleven years of age, recalls this when describing the details of her arrival in Minnesota in the 1960s:

> I was so hungry because we were not fed throughout the entire plane ride. Maybe they thought we would get sick if they fed us, I don't know. But by the time we arrived to my adoptive family's home, it was really late—way past supper time. So, my parents, as Americans, they thought, "Oh, what do all children like to eat late at night? They like milk and cookies!" But that's not what Korean children

(116)   *The First Amerasians*

like—we don't eat sweets. But I was so hungry and so I ate the cookies and milk, but I wound up sick. And then the next morning for breakfast, what do you think they fed me? Cereal and milk! And I'm thinking "Oh my God, I need some rice and soup. This is a crazy country. They eat cookies and milk at night and then you wake up and you have cereal and milk for breakfast!" And I wasn't used to drinking milk, so I was constantly getting sick. And I remember thinking, "How on earth am I going to survive here?"[27]

Indeed, many children have memories of "vomiting constantly" during their first weeks in America as they were placed on diets heavy with lactose and sugar.[28] It seems that adoptive parents were not instructed by the agencies about common foods in South Korea and, consequently, the children were not slowly introduced to American cooking but had their diets completely altered.

As mixed race Koreans became extremely homesick without their usual meals, they scoured gardens for cabbage in hopes of making kimchi;[29] they went outside to hunt for grasshoppers and asked their adoptive parents to roast them instead;[30] they requested rice, which adoptive mothers almost always topped with milk and sugar until "finally I was able to convince her to at least let me have it with butter, and salt and pepper."[31] Almost universally, mixed race Koreans of this generation report hating oatmeal, which they first tasted in the orphanages, but later would also be served in their adoptive homes.[32] One mixed race woman remembers finding the taste of oatmeal so "disgusting" that she once "spat it out on the floor," shocking her adoptive mother.[33] It was the only time this preciously polite and tidy child had ever been "that rude about food."[34] While it is possible that milk sensitivity was the primary reason for this large-scale taste aversion common among so many children of this generation, there was also probably some deeper psychological meaning for its rejection by mixed race adoptees. Oatmeal was often the first meal children were given following their separation from their Korean mothers. It remained a constant in the American orphanages in South Korea (along with "the scent of urine") and a constant on the breakfast tables of their new homes.[35] To mixed race Korean children, oatmeal tasted like their relinquishment. It was a reminder of all that they had lost and all that they would continue to lose.

Mixed race children were often misunderstood for behaviors they brought with them from South Korea. They confused their adoptive families when they slept on the floor instead of on their beds.[36] Some hoarded food under their pillows, in closets, or in blankets, a habit picked up while living in the orphanages among many other children.[37] Many cried for their birth

BECOMING AMERICAN (117)

mothers every night or asked their adoptive parents to return them to South Korea.[38] The adoptive parents, of course, knew no Korean language and could not understand them. As adults, mixed race adoptees of this generation recount:

> It was when I laid down to go to sleep—when my soul would kind of settle—that I would start to think about my mother. Because that's when it got kind of quiet and that's when you think about your blood. I cried myself to sleep for probably a good year . . . almost every night . . . I had dreams all the time about climbing over a fence and wading through the rice paddies to eventually find my way back home to my mother. That was a recurring dream throughout my childhood.[39]

> My adoptive mother bought me all these clothes and I had never seen so many nice clothes before. So that kept me occupied for a while. But then, after the clothes got old, I was ready to go back to Korea. And, now, I can just remember the feelings. I remember being in despair . . . just a little girl crying. . . . Because I just missed my birth mother. Wow, I really missed her. . . . I missed what I knew. You know, everything here. . . . I didn't know anything. People didn't talk like me. And what I would do is, I would grab some of the clothes that I liked and I would put them in a pillowcase. And you know, I was always stealing food. . . . And every time I would hear an airplane, I would grab my little bag and I would run out into the yard and try to flag the plane down . . . to take me back to Korea. When I tell that story now, it brings tears to my eyes for the little girl that was so, so homesick. But the plane, it never . . . the plane never would come and get me. So, I guess at some point I accepted that I was here.[40]

> I am five. I'm pulled away from all that I know. I would play those memories of my mother over and over in my head. Every night I would cry. I don't know what I was thinking exactly, other than the feeling of longing for her. So, I just cried myself to sleep. I don't know how long I did that.[41]

Such retrospective insight provides a small glimpse into the minds of young children who were experiencing the ideological erasure of their Korean mothers and Korean pasts.

Many adoptees also carried with them memories of their tearful departures from South Korea. This is because their mothers often only agreed to relinquish them provided they would remain in their protective custody rather than in institutional care.[42] As such, some children lived in their homes up until the day they left for America or, if they were in orphanages, they had been visited regularly by their mothers who then also accompanied them to the airport.[43] One mixed race Korean woman,

Figure 4.3 Mixed race children sleep on the floor at Holt orphanage. *The Mixed Names (Holt's Orphanage)*, 1965, gelatin silver print, © Joo Myung Duck. Courtesy of the artist and Miyako Yoshinaga Gallery, New York.

adopted at age seven in 1959, details the final moment in which she was prised from her mother:

> My mother and I rode a bus to the airport. She had bought some gifts for me but was not allowed to give them to me. She was told by the Holt staff that it was important to make a clean break. . . .When it was time to board the plane, my mother tried to get on with me, but the staff stopped her. She begged them to let her on because she wanted to see what the inside of the plane looked like. When that didn't work, she wanted to know where I was sitting so she could wave to me. She became hysterical and they had to hold her back. Someone took my hand and almost dragged me up the long steps to the plane. I got on the plane and cried so hard that I threw up before the flight even took off.[44]

Another women adopted at an older age recalls:

> My mother wouldn't let go of my hand on the way to the airport. She was crying. As soon as I got on the plane I just cried and cried. I cried the entire flight over here. I didn't know where I was going. You can't imagine how scared I was. I wasn't old enough to understand, but also not young enough to forget.[45]

Figure 4.4 Cheerful flight attendants pose with bewildered soon-to-be adopted children. Courtesy of Holt International, holtinternational.org.

It was these emotional scenes of separation that left many adoptees with lasting impressions of their birth mothers' love. One woman explains: "I don't know what I would have remembered if she had been cold to me on that day. Maybe I wouldn't have held on to my memories. But, because of her tears, I know that she loves me."[46]

Adoption case workers, such as those working on ISS placements, interpreted children's persistent crying and unhappiness rooted in the trauma of losing one's mother as problematic behaviors. They praised children who adjusted more quickly and appeared happy in their new American

(120)   *The First Amerasians*

homes. In particular, social workers agreed that "for the younger children, it is naturally easier," which in turn made infants appear more desirable than older children.[47] This, of course, produced even greater demand for younger children and accelerated on-the-ground coercive "child finding" practices in South Korea.[48] ISS case files also note that some parents who "felt the language barrier to be a real difficulty" brought interpreters into their homes.[49] These Korean language–speaking individuals "sometimes 'lectured' the child—telling him to forget the past, that he must be good."[50] In extreme cases, it was not unheard of for parents to give up their newly adopted children on the basis of being "unable to bond" with them.[51] Some mixed race Koreans were even re-homed for reasons as superficial as lactose intolerance.[52] This occurred not just among humanitarian non-professional agencies but also in organizations like ISS.

One mixed race woman, who came to the United States at the age of two, recalls her own adoptive mother's failed attempts to physically bond with her, and her own inability to accept her adoptive mother as her own. Although not re-homed herself, she describes what it felt like as a young child to have an adoptive family physically forced upon her:

> I remember even as a small child my adoptive mother would try to bond with me, and it was almost like daggers going through me when she would try to hug me and kiss me. . . . I think in my heart I still belonged to my Korean mother. I cried for my mother very often. I remember at school they had *National Geographic*. So any *National Geographic* issue on any Asian country—not just Korea, but any Asian country—I would read and look at the pictures . . . and I remember looking at pictures of older Korean women and I still do that to this day, but I did it even more as a child. . . . I would look at pictures of older Korean women and wonder if that was what my mother looks like . . . if that was my mom. And you're just a child so, you fantasize. There was this one special *National Geographic* issue specifically on Korea and I would just use those pictures to fantasize about my mother. At home I would get yelled at for looking at something like that, so I could only do it at school.[53]

Many mixed race children of this generation report not being able to talk about their lives prior to adoption or to ask about their birth families without hearing angry retorts such as: "I don't want to hear you talk about your Korean mother again, I'm your mother now."[54] In some extreme cases, the word "adopted" was even banned in families.[55] Instead, mixed race Koreans resorted to learning and remembering in secret.[56]

Social workers not only embraced assimilationist tactics in indirect ways but also explicitly instructed adoptive parents to do so. While an adoption via proxy would have meant no follow-up after a child's immigration to the United States, an adoption through a professional organization like ISS could mean adoptive parents would encounter a state social worker who might say: "Don't expose them to their Korean heritage, just raise them as American kids."[57] Even if those instructions were not delivered, it is difficult to imagine how adoptive parents could have paid meaningful homage to mixed race children's backgrounds given their general lack of knowledge or access to resources about Korean culture. In ISS case files, adoptive parents often admitted to knowing very little about South Korea or never having met a Korean person prior to their adoptive child. While later generations of adoptees had heritage camps or language schools that helped to keep their birth cultures somewhat intact, many mixed race individuals reflected on never having met or seen another Korean person during their childhood. Some never tasted Korean food again or discovered what kimchi was until late into their adult years.[58] Yet, despite the tragic loss of their birth culture, assimilation afforded these children little escape from the racial hostilities of 1950s and 1960s America.

Mixed race Koreans were often placed in the Jim Crow South and states upholding anti-miscegenation laws, and social workers provided parents with little direction on how to raise Asian children within this racial landscape. For example, one adoption professional simply accepted a white parent's assessment that these children "should not marry a white person" and would have few, if any, future marriageable prospects if brought into the country.[59] Social workers relied instead on the parent's own positive racial attitudes (loosely interpreted) to determine whether a placement would or would not be successful. In the end, adoptive parents were left to navigate segregated America on their own with their new family members. In Jim Crow states, some confusion emerged about where mixed race children might attend school. Korean Black children recall being barred entry into white schools or being on the receiving end of racial pejoratives and other hostilities upon entering newly integrated institutions. To get around this, some adoptive parents sent their children to predominantly white, private religious schools with affiliations to missions in South Korea that admitted mixed race children and were familiar with their plight. While this allowed mixed race adoptees to enter communities that were more willing to accept their racial differences, they might be reminded of their status as Amerasians. One mixed race woman who was adopted through the Seventh Day Adventist mission in 1956 was teased mercilessly by her peers as a "welfare child" and recalls how uncomfortable she felt when her mother would "get praise from her church members" for having "rescued" her from South Korea.[60] This experience was certainly not isolated to

(122)   *The First Amerasians*

individuals whose parents maintained strong ties to religious missions but was one that was perhaps most pronounced in communities where adopting Amerasians was equated with "God's work."[61]

Other mixed race Koreans who attempted to racially pass into the dominant racial categories of their families were confronted with hostile reactions from locals who objected to the presence of Asians within their communities. One woman who grew up in Texas during the 1960s recalls that even though she was viewed by whites as a Black person and she identified as Black herself, her Black neighbors were suspicious of her and often questioned her presence in Black spaces:

> We didn't have a car and so we would take the city bus to downtown Dallas with my mother and I remember having to sit in the back of the bus and I still recall the Black and white water fountains because when I, as a little girl, almost went to drink out of the white water fountain, my mother snatched me by the arm so quickly and so hard. And I remember the Black and white bathrooms all the way until the 1970s. . . . But we were just these odd looking kids. So, my mother had to be very protective of us, because, you know the little Black girls from my neighborhood would try to start to fight with us or pull out our hair. . . . My parents also caught a lot of flak for adopting. Many of their friends were like, "There are so many Black kids in need of adoption here, why would you adopt those little Orientals?" That was literally the word they used. Not all had that attitude, some were very supportive.[62]

Indeed, the Black families who adopted mixed race children received less social, cultural, and religious capital from their communities than their white counterparts. The Cold War imperatives that encouraged many Americans to see the adopting of mixed race children as a "cultural celebration" increasingly "benefited white adoptive families more than African American families."[63] A surplus of Black children in need of adoption also influenced these feelings. Consequently, Black families were less likely to get a "pat on the back" for welcoming mixed race Koreans into their homes, and Black communities had less incentive to perform racial colorblindness.[64] Another woman with similar experiences explains: "I was teased more by the Black kids. . . . And in retrospect, it's because the Black kids saw the nuance in my face that suggests my Korean ancestry. And so to them, I was a chink. But to the white kids, they just saw my brown skin and saw me as Black."[65] At the same time, mixed race children's inability to racially pass as fully Black did not prevent them from more violent forms of prejudice and institutional racism by white supremacists. Many remember

Figure 4.5 A Korean Black girl's American kindergarten school photo. Courtesy of Shirley Chung.

being called "niggers" and denied the right to use public accommodations reserved for whites in the Jim Crow South.[66]

Local hostilities and instances of racial violence, similar to those that had occurred in South Korea, highlighted the irony of removing children from one racially hostile environment only to place them in another. One woman remembers being stoned by American children in her neighborhood, just as locals did to mixed race children in South Korea:

> They'd say things like, "Go home Chink, go back to China, you slant-eyed Jap," and it was just horrible. I didn't even know how to react to that, but I thought, you're not supposed to throw rocks at people. That I knew. They picked up little rocks and threw them.[67]

Another mixed race Korean woman recalls a similar scene from her childhood:

(124)   *The First Amerasians*

The kids on my bus loved to sing to me. They gleefully sang, "Chinese Chink!" over and over for the forty-five-minute bus ride. Some of them had never seen a real-life Asian up close, albeit half Asian. I desperately tried to tell them I was also white, just like them. But I don't think they heard.[68]

Mixed race Koreans whose educational prospects were limited in South Korea also faced disruptions in American schools, where anti-Asian racism had detrimental effects on their scholastic success.

In 1950s and 1960s America, US school teachers and administrators were generally ill-equipped to handle or identify racialized bullying or to tend to the very specific educational needs of internationally adopted children. Mixed race Koreans were often thought of as troublemakers for displaying behaviors at school that were actually rooted in self-defense. They were disciplined by teachers and parents or suspended by school administrators when they fought back against verbal or physical assaults from their peers, which they identified in hindsight as racially motivated. Additionally, those children who had come to the United States after their critical period of language acquisition struggled to learn English. Without infrastructure in schools to help non-native speakers attain native levels of proficiency, many of these individuals were never able to fully adjust to life in America. As they lost Korean language as well, they remain, to this day, without fluency in any language. This in turn meant that some would have limited prospects for economic and social mobility despite American promises that the Amerasian rescue would enable mixed race children to become fully fledged members of US society.

At home, mixed race Koreans could also find themselves being raised by emotionally and physically abusive parents, some of whom had substance abuse or mental health issues that were not discovered during lax vetting processes. One woman, who revealed that her father's alcoholism had culminated in his suicide attempt, recalls how difficult this was for her to deal with as a young child:

I started acting out during my teen years. I would run away from home, I got into drugs. That's not uncommon, you know. From the literature that I've read, you've got the orphan heroes or high achievers and those who go into the dark. I kind of went into the dark, but I don't think I was intrinsically that way. I think I was acting out on a lot of hurt and a lot of confusion.[69]

Another mixed race man, who faced relentless emotional abuse inflicted on him by his adoptive mother, reflected on how much this had affected his own development and sense of self:

BECOMING AMERICAN   (125)

I spent most of my youth having no friends. . . . I've spent pretty much my entire
life being bullied by my mother and my brother, and to a lesser extent even my
dad. . . . I just have exceptionally low self-esteem, low self-image. Looking at it
in hindsight, I think that because of that treatment, I suffered from depression
most of my life. I spent an awful lot of time alone as a child and, in fact, the vast
majority of time I spend now is alone.[70]

By far, the worst cases of abuse reported by mixed race Koreans seem to
come from those individuals who were adopted via the proxy method. One
mixed race woman graphically details the physical abuse she experienced at
the hands of her mentally unwell adoptive mother:

I literally have physical scars on my body from her. She put my hand on a red
glowing stovetop burner. She slammed the garage door down on my toes. When
I was in kindergarten—that was about a year after they adopted me—I acciden-
tally caught my tights on a splinter on the bench in the kitchen. She beat me
black and blue. She'd tickle me until I wet my pants and then she would beat me
for wetting my pants. She once picked up a three-legged stool and hit me on the
head with it. I have an inch and a half mark on the back of my head from that.
When I ran to the bathroom and locked the doors, she got an axe and started
axing down the door. . . . I was 8 years old when she got multiple sclerosis.
I cleaned the entire house, I did laundry for everyone, and I made every meal.
There was a time I didn't vacuum the floor well enough. This was a six bedroom,
four bathroom house . . . two stories with a formal living room, a soundproof library, a family room, a dining room, and a kitchen. She had me on my hands and
knees licking the floor clean. . . . The abuse was just so violent and constant.[71]

As an adult, she reflects: "I have a lot of bitterness because there was
never any follow up. Nobody ever came to the house to see if I was okay.
No social worker came to see if it worked out."[72] Instead, she ran away from
home, "slept under bushes," and "ate out of garbage cans" just as Americans
alleged mixed race children did in South Korea.[73] After that she spent "the
next four years in the juvenile court system" until she married at the age of
sixteen for the explicit purpose of gaining legal emancipation.[74]

As a result of all the mistreatment they experienced at home and elsewhere, many mixed race Koreans became severely depressed or mentally
unwell, even as young children. One woman explains:

When I was ten I was adopted to this woman who would just constantly beat me
for no reason, several times a day. There were times I couldn't even go to school
because I would have bruises, or my eyes would be swollen from the beatings.

After two years with her, I said to myself "God, I can't take this anymore" and then I just stopped eating. I refused to eat, I stopped moving. I just sat on my bed in silence and that scared her so much that she gave me up. And when I came to be with my mom after that, she said I was not okay. She said I would just sit in a chair and stare into nothing for hours straight. I guess I learned to just tune things out because in the other home, I was beat up for anything—if I got up too fast, if I looked at her a certain way, if I didn't smile, if I did smile. Whatever I did she'd find a reason to beat me up. So, I just stared into nothing. That was my safety mode. And I continued to do it for years after.[75]

Unfortunately, some mixed race Koreans even turned to self-harm and suicide attempts: "I was just so tired of being treated badly by everyone. I had enough. I started believing death would take it away because it didn't look like things were getting any better."[76]

Other children were able to channel their energies more positively, by turning inward and focusing on the aspects of their lives that they could control, like school and planning for their futures. They studied hard with the hope that they could get good jobs that would enable them to become independent from their abusive adoptive parents or so that they could afford to return to South Korea to find their Korean families once more. Indeed, in spite of all the difficulties they faced in America, many adoptees report that it was the memory of their birth mother's love that they believed saved them. They explain:

Even as a small child, I can remember being five or six years old—beaten up and just sitting in the corner crying for my ŏmma. . . . Over the years, I've thought about how I turned out okay. And I think I probably turned out the way I did eventually, because of the love and care that I had, up until I came to America.[77]

I was so loved. And I think that my compassion toward other people comes from what I learned from my mother, my grandmother, and my aunt. You know, I tell people that I have bowed legs now because none of them let me walk when I was a child. Either my grandmother or my aunt or my mother would carry me. . . . I believe that if I didn't have that wonderful childhood, I probably would have been lost.[78]

In retrospect, some adoptees wonder why their abusive parents even pursued adoption in the first place. If "not for us to have a family" then perhaps it was to collect government subsidies, exploit older girls' domestic labor, or receive praise from their neighbors for having rescued Third World children. [79]

Throughout the 1960s, it became more and more common for older mixed race children to be placed in adoptive homes in the United States. Although the kinds of families and the treatment they received varied greatly, these adoptees often found that their new lives in America, while perhaps exciting at first, were not quite what they were expecting nor what they were told they would find. America was not an idyllic land of "flying cars, moving sidewalks, and mountains made of ice cream," nor a place immune from "racial discrimination" and "hunger."[80] After the excitement of "living in a big house," "sleeping in a bed," and having lots of new belongings wore off, many could not shake the feeling of wanting to return home: "I just started missing Korea and I started missing my family, my mom. . . . There was nothing familiar around me. I wanted to go back."[81] Others could find that their material conditions in the United States were hardly better, as financial criteria had been overlooked by some agencies to prioritize adoptive parents with certain religious affiliations.[82] Indeed, for these older mixed race Koreans who had immigrated in their late childhood or early teenage years and retained memories of their former lives many felt they had been misguided by social workers and others in South Korea who pressured them to leave for the United States. Assumptions of national superiority played a large role in orchestrating the Amerasian rescue, in particular constructions of the United States as a welcoming home for mixed race Koreans. This helped to justify adoption as the only ethical solution for children experiencing hardship or poverty in South Korea, even though their lives in America might not actually be better.

Furthermore, adoptive parents' knowledge of South Korea often hinged on what they had learned about the country via the Amerasian rescue, a fact that they often used to shape the identities of their children. Many adoptees "grew up hearing how I was lucky I got to leave Korea because they hated mixed race children there and would have treated me badly."[83] ISS reports stated that parents "sometimes with the best intention . . . may have teased the child about going back."[84] This had a detrimental effect on mixed race children's development. As adoptees felt that their positions within their families were precarious and conditional on their behavior within the home, social workers noted that some had even begun to "scream in terror" at the sight of Korean adults.[85] Americans familiar with the plight of mixed race Koreans probably assumed this behavior to be rooted in the children's experiences of mistreatment in South Korea. However, it is also possible that stories told to adoptees by adoptive families colored their perspectives. Indeed, many parents simply drew on the figure of the Amerasian with all of its myths about Korean society and people to teach

The First Amerasians

mixed race children about their heritage and origins. Understandings of Koreans as hateful toward mixed race children would continue to follow some adoptees well into their adulthoods. They recall how they felt "dirty" when first encountering Koreans or Korean Americans many years later, or how they have spent most of their lives ignoring other Asians or avoiding them altogether.[86]

Most unfortunately, for mixed race Korean women, a "camptown shadow" also lingered.[87] Even as young children, many adoptees remember being told by their adoptive parents that their birth mothers were most likely prostitutes for the US military. One mixed race woman, adopted at age four, recalls the following scene:

> When I was seven or eight years old I asked for a red dress to wear to a Christmas party. I wanted this red dress in the worst way and I literally threw myself on the floor and had a crying tantrum because I wanted this dress. I was told "no, because it'll make you look like a whore, like your real mother. You should be grateful because if we hadn't adopted you, you would have lived the life of poverty and probably been a prostitute like your mother."[88]

Another oral history narrator remembers being told something similar:

> There are some things children should never be told. When I was twelve years old my mother told me that my birth mother was a prostitute and that my father was someone in the Army who came back to America and probably didn't even know that I existed. She told me that if she hadn't adopted me, I would have just been another Korean prostitute like my mother. Those were her exact words. And it was told to me out of anger.[89]

Such comments could escalate to assumptions on the part of adoptive parents that their daughters were of questionable morals and deviant sexuality. These ideas might become most pronounced as a young girl approached adolescence. Mixed race women suspect that their adoptive parents' assumptions that their mothers had been prostitutes were reflected in their strict efforts to keep them "chaste."[90] One hypothesizes:

> My mother would chastise me for the way I did my hair, the way I dressed. She'd tell me that I looked like a whore and make me go change. I think underlying that was this feeling that my birth mother had been a whore and that's how I had been created. I guess, in her mind, she was trying to break me from being that kind of person. So, she beat me, or she made me look plain jane ugly. And this was my mother's way of preventing me from being that kind of woman.[91]

BECOMING AMERICAN   *(129)*

While it is unclear why adoptive mothers might have shared this information with such young children or behaved so cruelly, one mixed race Korean theorizes that her adoptive mother resented the way that others in the community saw their family. She felt that it was clear that she did not belong to her white adoptive mother but was the product of war.[92] Such insight might point to the ways that the "camptown shadow" was even cast on the entire adoptive family unit. Considering it was not uncommon for US servicemen to have second or third families from their military tours abroad, such an assumption by observers would have been reasonable.

Some women also speculate that their adoptive mothers were "jealous" of their relationships with their adoptive fathers.[93] To their minds, when adoptive fathers would show affection for their mixed race daughters, the American mothers of these young girls would perceive them as sexualized threats. While certainly most adoptive fathers did not have inappropriate relationships with their daughters, jealousy of adoptive mothers could indicate a suspicion that maybe some girls were adopted precisely so they "could be used by dad in 'that way.'"[94] Sadly, constructions of Korean mothers as prostitutes (and the subsequent "hypersexualization" of their children as a result)[95] were not only used to inflict emotional and physical abuse on mixed race women, but Korean adoptees also report being sexually abused by adoptive family members:

> My adoptive father was a truck driver and when he'd be out driving, I'd be sent on the road with him. The excuse that I remember being told was because I could stay up as many hours as he needed to stay awake for driving. One of the things I do remember my adoptive sister telling me was that those truck rides were part of why she left our family . . . because she didn't like what would go on during those trips. Well, because I was so much younger at that time, my memory of those drives is really spotty. But I do remember that I hated storms, lighting, thunder—it all scared me so bad. And my father would volunteer to come sleep with me in my bed so that I wouldn't be scared. But then I remember I wouldn't like what would happen when he would come to sleep with me. Because of the touching. I must have been four or five when that started. It was not an easy childhood . . . and it continued until I was fourteen when one night I was told I had to sleep in my father's bed. I woke up the next morning and I knew I was no longer a virgin. That's when I got put up in a hospital because I finally told my parents that I would kill myself.[96]

> My life turned for the worst when I was 12. . . . My mother was an evangelist. She would run revivals. One of the times she was away . . . we had what we called a den . . . the family room where you watch TV. I was awakened by a little pain, and

(130)   *The First Amerasians*

it was my father molesting me. I didn't know what to do. I just acted like I was still sleeping. Turned my body, squared my body so he stopped. I told my best friend. She told her mother. Her mother told my mother. My mother took us for a ride, and confronted my father. Of course, he denied it. . . . But from that point forward, my life was hell living at home. Because my mother took everything out on me. Like she resented me. . . . I confronted my mother about that. . . about five years ago. . . I told her, "You weren't there for me. Your husband molested me." And she starts saying, "You're lying, you're lying, you're lying, you're lying." And I just hung up. Then she repeatedly called me, left all these messages. One of these messages. . . she was very sarcastic. She said, "You were the perfect daughter. You rescued us. We didn't rescue you. You rescued us." But it was in . . . a sarcastic manner. . . . I never confronted my father. I thought I would on his deathbed. But I didn't. I forgave him years prior. Because I would read up on. . . incest. From the stories I read, I felt I was fortunate. Because it was a single incident, and it was not . . . actual sex. He just . . . was touching me down there. So I forgave him. Because it was a single incident. [97]

Sexual exploitation occurred not only within the intimate confines of the home but also the broader communities adoptees became a part of. It seems to be more prevalent among those placed via proxy adoption, in strictly religious homes, or in small rural towns where child abuse was more easily hidden. This is further demonstrated in the following narratives made by four different oral history narrators:

I was told that little girls in Korea sit on grown men's lap and fetch candy out of their pockets, and that that was the norm and that it was okay. The men in my church expected me to do the same. [98]

When my brother raped me and I told my adoptive mother about it she said, "well, at least he's not your real brother" and walked away from me. . . . I was eleven and that's when I started running away from home. . . . I used to come back and I would rope the end of my bed to the door knob, so that my brother couldn't get into my room. [99]

During the holidays the Seventh Day Adventist church has something called "in gathering" where everybody in the church has a set goal that you're supposed to collect, or if they work they can just pay it as a check to the church during the holidays for spreading the gospel. At that time, it was about $200 a year. Well, not working and being in the ninth grade, I had two options. I could either go out in front of stores, stand there, and ask people for money or I could go out in a car load of people to different neighborhoods where we could go door to door.

BECOMING AMERICAN   (*131*)

This is winter, it's night, pitch dark out and here we are wandering the street going door to door. Well one night, it was super cold and when I went back to the van, there was my friend's father. I sat down in the back seat but he told me to get up in the front so he could get me warm faster. I was fourteen at the time. The next thing I know, I had a tongue down my throat, a hand under my top, another hand going down in my pants. So, of course when I got back to the church and was counting up my money, I was pretty much in shock. And when I got home I wasn't going to tell them what happened. So, I just more or less kept it to myself. But I talked to this other girl who was also an adoptee and she mentioned the same thing had basically happened to her after he took her home from a school function.[100]

I left home when I was fifteen years old because some bad things happened to me. My best friend from ninth grade—her brother served in Vietnam. And when he got back from Vietnam, because it was a small town, he thought he could get away doing some of the things he did to the girls over there to me. So, he did some bad things to me that my parents didn't know about. And I wasn't happy at home, so I decided to marry him and leave.[101]

While childhood sexual abuse within families and close-knit communities has been experienced by too many American women, the centrality of race should not be discounted in these cases involving Korean adoptees. Korean and other Asian women were first coded as sexually available to American men via the US military. As Asian Americans and the real or imagined children of sex workers, mixed race adoptees would experience the consequences of this racialization, even as young girls and even by their family members. Across all of these examples, it seems that Americans who interacted closely with these children maintained some awareness of the camptown as a hypersexualized space of US Cold War intimacy. They connected these ideas—first introduced to Americans by the US military—with adopted girls which, in turn, mediated how they would understand and relate to them.

The question of where adoptive families might have gotten the idea that Korean birth mothers were prostitutes is perhaps best explained by one mixed race woman, who recounts: "That's what it said on my paperwork. It listed her profession as 'prostitute.'"[102] Later, when reunited with her biological family through a DNA match, this adoptee learned from her aunt that her mother had not been a prostitute but was in a steady, long-term relationship with her biological father. For the first three years of her life she lived with both of her parents in a house her father built for them near Camp Casey. He was lucky in the sense that he received three

(132) The First Amerasians

back-to-back tours to South Korea, which enabled him to stay with his Korean family for an extended period. When he left for the final time, he planned to divorce his American wife. However, when the divorce process was protracted, the Korean mother panicked and was pressured by those around her to give her daughter up for adoption. At the time, she worked in a textile factory. Nonetheless, on the child study, the mother's profession was listed as prostitute. Whether this was done in error, was the result of sloppy recordkeeping, or was the outcome of a more deliberate, widespread stereotyping remains unclear. However, what is evident is that this documentation, which was reviewed by case workers and made available to the adoptive family, would color this narrator's perspective on her own biological mother for years to come and inform others' views of her as a daughter and child of the camptowns. Countless other mixed race Korean adoptees also have paperwork that lists their mother's profession as prostitute. And for many, this is all they will ever know about their biological origins.

The "camptown shadow" is so pervasive that it continues to belie the memories of many mixed race Koreans, who wonder about their mothers' pasts, despite having no recollection of "being around that kind of environment" as children.[103] One mixed race woman who spent the first seven years of her life with her birth mother remembers her as a textile worker, not a prostitute. She recalls:

> I would ride the train with my mom sometimes. And I remember her taking me to the place where she worked, which now I understand was a textile place. Because inside there were machines with all these bright, huge spools of colored threads. And then outside the building, were these great big plastic tubs with brightly colored water. And when the women were done with the water they would pick up these big plastic bowls and just throw it all on the side of the hill. And so I'm assuming that must have been dye that they would dye the fabric in and then when they were done, they just threw it because the side of the hill where they would throw all this water was quite colorful.[104]

Yet despite these memories, when she was a teenager, her adoptive parents told her that her Korean mother was "probably a prostitute."[105] Following this, she spent much of her life feeling deep shame about her origins. She remembers: "It took me many, many years to come to terms with the fact that if she was a prostitute that it was okay. That those were desperate times and people did desperate things to survive. And I wasn't going to judge her or hold that against her. Her or any of the other women in similar circumstances."[106]

In addition to forced assimilation; racism; unstable homes; physical, emotional, and even sexual abuse, another trauma related to mixed race children's immigration to the United States was that their placement in American families did not automatically confer upon them US citizenship. While adoptive parents were supposed to naturalize Korean adoptees one year following their placements, many parents simply forgot to do so or were not instructed to do so by the agencies that aided in their children's adoptions. This was more common among individuals placed through humanitarian non-professional organizations, but it also occurred in a few ISS cases as well. Some adoptees became aware of this fact after being threatened by their adoptive parents when they misbehaved and have lived their lives in fear of immigration authorities and run-ins with the law since childhood.[107] Others discovered their legal status late in life when they went to collect the government assistance available to seniors but were denied.[108] Although a few adoptees have achieved naturalization through various ad hoc measures of their own, including marriage to a US citizen or the sponsorship of a US senator, there are many mixed race Koreans who remain undocumented to this day. Their anxieties about immigration authorities have been reinforced as several high-profile cases involving the deportation of Korean adoptees have surfaced in recent years, the most infamous of which culminated in the tragic suicide of Phillip Clay in South Korea.

In 2000, the US Congress passed the Child Citizenship Act, which allowed adopted individuals born no earlier than February 27, 1983, to receive automatic citizenship. However, the law left out internationally adopted individuals who arrived before that time and were living in the United States as adults and even seniors. Since then, numerous proposals such as the Adoptee Citizenship Act of 2021 have been proposed to include internationally adopted individuals of any age, but no law has yet been passed. While adoption into American families was supposed to grant legitimacy, status, citizenship, and refuge from a racist South Korean society that denied these rights to children without Korean fathers, the Amerasian rescue actually produced many stateless individuals—children who were taken off legal registers of male heads of households or orphanage directors in South Korea and were then sent off to the United States with no more than a US passport. Such precarious legal status prevents undocumented mixed race Koreans from doing many things, but perhaps most tragic, from returning to South Korea to find their birth mothers:

> I would like to be naturalized so I can get a passport and go back to Korea again before it's too late. I want to find my Korean mother. I want to conduct my birth search. My Korean mom would probably be in her eighties by now. . . . I hope she's still alive.[109]

Figure 4.6 Mixed race Korean children in their adoptive American home. Courtesy of Susie Whitford Hankinson.

Of course, not all placements of mixed race Koreans were so negative. Many adoptees attest to having warm and loving homes and what they viewed to be good adoptive parents. These individuals are certain that they had better lives in the United States than they would have had they remained in South Korea. They are well educated, many of them working as doctors, academics, engineers, or other highly skilled professionals, and lead fulfilling lives with loving families of their own. Yet still, many adoptees express an intense feeling that there is something missing in their lives, that "they have no beginning."[110] They hope to be reunited with their birth families to find those origins—to discover where their lives began. The following testimonies of two mixed race Koreans poignantly captures the complex ambivalence about adoption and about the Amerasian rescue that so many of these individuals continue to feel in their late adult years:

> My adoptive parents sent me to the best schools. I went to private schools my entire life; I've never been in the public school system. I also took piano lessons. They saw a talent in me when I was three or four years old and they cultivated it. So, I am a classically trained pianist. My mother exposed me to the finer things in life. I had beautiful clothes. Even though she went into debt for it, my clothes always came from Nieman Marcus or Lord and Taylor. She, herself, was a very well-dressed woman from the shoes to the designer clothes and perfume, her gloves, her everything. It was all beautiful and it all had to match, and she dressed us the same way. And so, I lived quite a privileged life. We weren't rich, but my mother was a spender—she had credit cards. I knew how to set a table; I knew how to use which fork for what. And as I became more and more accomplished in piano, I began traveling and meeting important people. And I knew how to carry myself in front of them. So, my adoptive parents gave me a good life and I am very grateful for that, but I just . . . I miss my mom. I will always wonder what my life could have been like had she had the resources to keep me.[111]

> I am over sixty years old and so I have given up on ever finding my Korean mother. But all I ever wanted was to thank her and tell her that I was grateful to her for giving me life . . . that I'm okay that she gave me up for adoption and that things turned out all right in my adoptive family. I'll always miss her.[112]

By the late 1960s, Americans had used the concept of the Amerasian to remove nearly 5,000 mixed race children from South Korea and place them in adoptive homes in the United States.[113] This chapter can capture only a fraction of their complex and varied lived historical experiences in America.

5

The Second Rescue

I was born in Paju, Korea. . . . From pictures I could tell my father was an older man, dressed in a US Army uniform. . . . The earliest memories I have are of living with an old lady in a small house. My mother paid this lady to keep me. I think I was about four. One day, while I was out playing, the lady disappeared. . . . The next thing I knew I was living in an orphanage where I remember people sometimes coming to pick out children, but never me. That is where I first remember being called Yankee and [t'wigi]. I had to fight a lot, and so I ran away from there. . . . While I was out on the streets, an older boy came up and offered me food at his home. I went and lived there in the basement with several other older boys. . . . Upstairs lived the captains of this gang and the girls who had men coming in to sleep with them. One girl was an American like me. She was about 14. . . . My job was to run in the market and bump into someone, causing them to fall. Then the older boys would take their purse and money. . . . If I made a mistake or did something wrong, the boys would kick the front of my legs. I still have scars. . . . I did not like it there, so one day in the market I hit a lady and went on running far away. . . . I came to a place with lots of Americans on the streets and lots of nightclubs [Itaewon]. . . . A girl taught me how to beg for money. I lived inside a wooden box in the market. . . . Sometimes Americans would buy me clothes or give me money. . . . One day I saw a half American, half Korean, young man who followed me and kept calling: "Do you go to school?" I said, "No." . . . My new friend took me to Amerasian Club and a man took me to Father Keane's orphanage. I had my first real home and was so surprised to see how many half and halfs there were just like me. Father Keane sent me to school, taught me English; and for the first time in my life, I was happy. I came to the United States [two and a half] years ago, and live with my parents, and two sisters, and four brothers in Georgia. My life is really happy now, but I am here today to tell my own story because I don't want my brothers and sisters who I had to leave behind to be forgotten and to live with people always pointing their fingers and calling them names. Please, please, help us.[1]

The First Amerasians. Yuri W. Doolan, Oxford University Press. © Oxford University Press 2024.
DOI: 10.1093/oso/9780197534380.003.0006

On November 17, 1981, John Keller was brought before the Subcommittee on Immigration, Refugees, and International Law to provide the first testimony in support of HR 808, a new bill that would amend the Immigration and Nationality Act to extend preferential immigration rights to individuals in Asia illegitimately fathered by US citizens. The bill would eventually be considered by the Committee on the Judiciary alongside its senate counterpart (S. 3198) on June 21, 1982, culminating in the enactment of the Amerasian Immigration Act, signed into law by President Ronald Reagan that October. In the numerous hearings on Amerasian immigration proposals, American politicians would consider testimony, both oral and written, from dozens of mixed race Koreans like John Keller. But while these individuals took center stage, it was the 8,000 mixed race children who had been left behind under oppressive communist rule in Southeast Asia just six years earlier ("adorned with cowlicks and spattered with freckles" and "ineligible to attend public schools, hold a job, or receive a government ration card") that remained the top concern of state senators and representatives as they looked at the faces of mixed race Koreans.[2] Lacking access to an older generation of mixed race Vietnamese who could speak, firsthand, about the discrimination they faced back in communist Southeast Asia, it was the story of the Koreans—the first Amerasians—that provided Congress the

Figure 5.1 President Ronald Reagan signs the Amerasian Immigration Act of 1982. Courtesy of Ronald Reagan Presidential Library and Museum/NARA.

(138)   *The First Amerasians*

human evidence necessary to construct a post-Vietnam story of rescue and redemption.

When the last US helicopter took off from the roof of the Saigon embassy in spring 1975, so ended some twenty years of brutal American military, political, and economic action in Vietnam—and for naught—for the war was all but lost. Nearly 60,000 US soldiers were dead or missing as a result of the conflict and over 1,000,000 other civilian and foreign military personnel had become tragic casualties of war. For decades, Vietnam tore the United States apart, but at its end, with little or nothing to show for the carnage, it brought about an "American reckoning."[3] The war raised central questions about American identity and ideologies. It upended the master narrative of the postwar era that the United States was a force for good in the world—equipped to deliver democracy, strong enough to achieve its ends, and worthy to lead. Sociologist Yen Le Espiritu has argued that in the absence of a military victory or a liberated people, Americans produced a substitute to recuperate American identities and shore up US militarism: "the freed and reformed Vietnamese refugee."[4] In the aftermath of Korea, a war that ended in disappointment some twenty years earlier, a similar figure had also emerged. Displaced from communist aggression, but saved by US democracy, mixed race Koreans captivated national audiences in the 1950s and 1960s. Their placements into American homes via adoption provided the nation with a sentimental victory in the aftermath of a war not quite won by the US military. Like the refugee orphans who followed the Korean War, mixed race children fathered and then abandoned by US servicemen in Asia would allow Americans to have another chance for redemption—this time as Amerasians following defeat in Vietnam.

During the fall of Saigon, the US government sponsored a series of orphan airlifts to bring thousands of Vietnamese children stateside, reminiscent of efforts made by Harry and Bertha Holt in the 1950s. For weeks, Americans were bombarded with media coverage of the government-sponsored initiative called Operation Babylift. While many were touched by heartfelt stories of pilots and nurses risking their lives, humanitarians and philanthropists displaying their generosity, and adoptive parents opening their hearts and homes to rescue innocent Vietnamese children from the ironclad grip of communist tyranny, not all were so moved. The highly publicized babylifts were immediately criticized by an American public that had grown increasingly skeptical of the nation's altruistic intentions throughout all the years of war. As Americans debated whether Operation Babylift was a rescue or a kidnapping, proponents silenced even the staunchest of critics by highlighting the mixed race children fathered by US servicemen. While some argued that mixed race Vietnamese would be slaughtered by the communists if they were to remain in Vietnam, others rejected such unsubstantiated claims, pointing instead to North Vietnam's good record of child welfare. But most all could agree that the United States had an obligation to assist these "half-Americans" and that, for those children, at least, the orphan rescue was justified. Although the specificities of Operation Babylift soon faded from national headlines, the fierce public debates had brought "the problem of the mixed blood child" back to the forefront of the American consciousness. Throughout the remainder of the 1970s, curiosity about what would become of the thousands of mixed race children abandoned and left behind in a now communist Southeast Asia prompted journalists to reenter the camptowns to see what had happened to their Korean predecessors.

As renewed attention was paid to these individuals, Father Alfred V. Keane, Maryknoll priest and director of St. Vincent's Home for Amerasians in South Korea, began campaigning for immigration reform that would allow those too old to be adopted by US citizens to find an alternative pathway to the United States. Organizations that got their start in South Korea, such as the Pearl S. Buck Foundation and Holt Adoption Program (renamed Holt International Children's Service), reemerged once more to champion the Amerasian in Congress. As these individuals and groups lobbied on behalf of all "half-American" children left behind in Asia, it was the Vietnamese children from America's most recent war who remained the most pressing concern to the American public and US lawmakers. But because the United States lacked diplomatic relations with the communist nations of Southeast Asia, mixed race Koreans stood in to provide firsthand accounts of the discrimination and desperate conditions that these children were subjected to in Asia. In Congress, the Amerasian immigration hearings not only allowed US legislators to revisit debates about the controversial orphan airlifts, but also offered an opportunity to achieve the symbolic, sentimental, and long-awaited victory that had fallen short at the war's conclusion. Highlighting communist inefficiency, barbarism, and economic failures, members of Congress argued that Americans were the rightful and moral protectors of mixed race Vietnamese children. It was from this complex interplay between mixed race Korean's human suffering and Vietnamese children's symbolic power in light of a recently lost war through which the category of Amerasian was legally constructed.

(140)   *The First Amerasians*

Six years before the first Amerasian immigration hearings, Operation Babylift, a government initiative "to fly 2,000 South Vietnamese orphans to the United States" amid an imminent communist takeover of Saigon, had raised public consciousness about America's mixed race progeny born during the Vietnam War.[5] Justified on the grounds that anyone associated with the Americans would be the targets of communist bloodshed, the government's plan to direct $2 million toward the effort was announced by President Gerald Ford on April 3, 1975.[6] The initiative triggered an outpouring of donations from various voluntary aid organizations, adoption agencies, private citizens, and even celebrities like Hugh Hefner and his Playboy bunnies. Taking advantage of the temporary emergency measures that cut through the bureaucratic red tape that had long curtailed adoptions from Vietnam, these rescuers chartered private flights to deliver planeloads of orphans to American families stateside. Coverage surrounding the dramatic arrivals of emergency airlifted children was dominated with images of "bewildered orphans strapped inside flying boxcars," "tearful parents straining to catch a first glimpse of their adopted infants," and "travel-weary but happy tots settling in at their new homes."[7] The Pentagon and State Department were flooded "with calls from people all over the country wanting to adopt orphans."[8] In their efforts to make sense of this sudden fervor, observers explained that Vietnamese children provided ordinary citizens, who had for years believed that US participation in Vietnam was "immoral, illegal, and not worthwhile," with a chance to "atone, even in the most tentative way, for the collective sins of governments."[9]

To the public, President Ford cast the effort as a "mission of mercy" for "the victims of Southeast Asia," positioning Americans as their saviors and benevolent protectors.[10] The powerful symbolism of Operation Babylift—in which the US government, unable to rescue Vietnam from communism, could instead rescue its children—was intended to provide Americans with a sentimental victory following nearly twenty years of catastrophic warfare and, ultimately, a humiliating defeat in Southeast Asia. It was supposed to deliver closure ("it is true that we have suffered setbacks at home and abroad"), clarity ("but it is essential that Americans retain their self-confidence and perspective"), rehabilitation ("this is the time to mobilize our assets and to call upon our greatest capacities"), reconciliation ("let no ally or friend fear that our commitments will not be honored"), and remasculinization ("now or in the future let no potential enemy of the United States be so unwise to wrongly assess the American mood and conclude that the time has come when it is safe to challenge us").[11] But instead, the policy proved highly divisive. While it received high-profile acclaim, Operation Babylift was also met with ambivalence and accusations that children were being hastily shuttled to the United States without proper safeguards or that the Vietnamese were being deprived of future generations, all for propaganda purposes.

Opponents of Operation Babylift deconstructed government narratives that claimed the policy was representative of an "American commitment to provide humanitarian aid to the helpless civilian refugees." They charged the administration instead with "cynicism" in its usage of children for "political ploy."[12] Tragically, the first orphan airlift crashed on April 4, 1975, killing an estimated 190 passengers, the vast majority of them children.[13] When the very same child survivors were put onto different planes the next day and additional onboard deaths from dehydration, sepsis, pneumonia, or prematurity were reported on subsequent flights, the public raised questions about the conditions of the operation and interests of the children involved.[14] A full-blown scandal erupted when observers in "immigration rooms" noted many of the children were not in fact deprived orphans of Vietnam, but were the sons and daughters of elite Vietnamese who were being flown to join extended relatives in the United States.[15] In several instances, entire families had gotten seats on emergency flights with the children posing as poor orphans and their parents as their adult "escorts."[16] Bureaucratic mismanagement accompanied the handling of even real children in need, many of whom were "accompanied by only the spottiest documentation."[17] Several Vietnamese-speaking interviewers discovered that some children were not orphans at all but had at least one living parent in South Vietnam; their mothers and fathers were perhaps unaware that their children had been airlifted out of the country.[18]

Communist accusations of a massive "kidnapping" were quickly picked up in both domestic and international circles. The Red Cross declared the adoptions a violation of a Geneva Convention requirement that war orphans, whenever possible, be educated within their own culture.[19] Caritas, the Vatican's relief organization, called the airlift "a deplorable and unjustified mistake" and instructed Roman Catholic agencies not to participate.[20] One Vietnamese American anthropologist claimed there were 22,000 daycare centers in North Vietnam and asked, "What is this terror Americans feel that my people will devour children?"[21] An Asia specialist with the United Methodist office at the United Nations had observed in late 1974 that in areas formerly under Saigon's control were beggars and youthful prostitutes rehabilitated, cared for, and educated under Vietcong

(142)   *The First Amerasians*

rule. The co-founder of Children's Medical Relief International and consultant to UNICEF in the north in 1973 concluded, "it is not necessary to rescue the children from the Communists."[22] In the United States, critics noted American chauvinism and xenophobia, pointing to "the ridiculousness of the belief that the communists would kill children at random and the equally ridiculous suspicion that even the best Vietnamese do not really love or know how to take care of their offspring."[23] Instead, they cited the north's good reputation for child care, which positioned the communists as the rightful protectors of South Vietnam's children rather than the US government.

In the face of intense criticism, proponents of Operation Babylift underscored the presence of Amerasian children among its precious cargo, countering debates about responsibility for Vietnamese orphans. In the process, reporters "greatly exaggerated" the number of mixed race orphans who were aboard the emergency flights and such children became the face of the effort—depicted as the majority of those rescued although really comprising just 20 percent of the total number.[24] One senator defended the government airlifts stating, "These children are innocent victims of a tragic war. They are a part of our involvement there and we are partly responsible for them." He added, "I'm chilled to think what the Viet Cong will do to these children, some of whom are obviously of mixed blood."[25] Moderates on the issue, such as American Friends Service Committee, a Quaker voluntary agency, agreed that just "two types of children should be flown out of South Vietnam—children of mixed GI heritage, or those who are physically handicapped and have no chance of survival in South Vietnam."[26] Others emphasized "that orphans fathered by American GIs—particularly Black ones—would face discrimination under a communist regime."[27]

Still, the most aggressive opponents maintained that "mixed race GI babies would not be discriminated against in the event of a communist victory."[28] Some even questioned the notion that mixed race Black and "Vietnamese orphans will get better treatment in the [United States]," pointing to domestic racial tensions and anti-Black racism.[29] Others were skeptical about the motivations surrounding the sudden "interest in the children of American fathers and Vietnamese mothers," pointing out that prior to the lifts "80 to 90 percent of the Vietnamese children adopted" were "pure Vietnamese" and Americans had, at that point, done little to help the mixed race individuals.[30] Some had even gone so far as to point to the domestic surplus of orphans to argue that these children were being adopted for the wrong reasons. While the debates over whether mixed race children might face discrimination in Vietnam seemed endless, a 1973 report on Vietnamese adoption conducted by Congressional Research Services had soberly investigated this matter. The study by US government officials, released almost two years before the controversial airlifts were even conceived of, argued that "in the absence of any evidence on this, the answer to such questions can only be a matter of speculation and if raised at this stage may not be to the best interest of any Vietnamese child of mixed parentage."[31]

In the midst of these discussions, perhaps the most fervent of proponents to weigh in on the issue were adoptive parents themselves. To advocate more rescues, families that had taken in recently airlifted children reprised arguments reminiscent of those made in the 1950s and 1960s about mixed race Koreans. Describing it as an urgent matter, they begged, "If we don't act now children are going to die."[32] Operation Babylift families found likely allies in the adoptive parents of mixed race Koreans, who supported such dramatic sentiments. These individuals pointed to their own children and testified that they too "might have died [had they] remained in Korea."[33] They gave accounts of the terrible conditions under which mixed race children in South Korea lived and suggested that Vietnamese children would meet similar fates if they were to be left behind to grow up in Southeast Asia. Together these adoptive families urged the nation to back the airlifts, silence their criticism, and insisted upon unconditional support "from the community as a whole" so that good American families could properly tend to the very special needs of these innocent war-torn children.[34]

But the mounting controversy stopped Operation Babylift right in its tracks. As weeks went by, attempts to expand the initiative in Congress were overturned, and ongoing lifts were even halted.[35] First, the Saigon government temporarily banned the emergency flights on April 7, 1975. Then, on April 16, 1975, federal immigration authorities discovered the orphan status of certain Cambodian children could not be confirmed and blocked any further airlifts for them.[36] By the time the Immigration and Naturalization Service granted permission to resume the flights a few days later, it seemed that the entire effort had been publicly humiliated. When the very last airlift brought the final group of Vietnamese children to the United States on April 26, the event made no major headlines and was not even documented in the national press, a stark contrast to the reporting around the first orphan rescues.[37] Just days later, on April 30, controversy around the orphan airlift erupted once more when a human rights group filed a class-action suit on behalf of the children transported by Operation Babylift.[38] After weeks of polarizing debates, the government initiative had ended but the failure to construct the airlifts as a humanitarian rescue

(144)   *The First Amerasians*

represented yet another chapter in a prolonged story about American failures, embarrassments, and defeat in Vietnam.

In the United States, the orphan rescue would soon become a "consensual amnesia" much like Vietnam itself, as the nation struggled to grapple with the war's meaning and losses.[39] In parallel ways, Vietnamese Amerasians also served as painful "reminders of all the good we failed to do" and faded from the national consciousness.[40] No major efforts would be made to bring these individuals "home" or back into public limelight until mixed race Koreans re-catalyzed interest in the Amerasian in the late 1970s.

In total, some 2,700 children had been evacuated to the United States (and approximately 1,300 more were flown to other Western nations).[41] Estimates of the number of mixed race children left behind varied. A report from 1973 put the number of mixed race children in Vietnamese orphanages at approximately 1,000 but taking into account "the number of these children seen on the streets . . . estimates of 5,000 to 10,000 are reasonable."[42] By the 1980s a figure upward of 25,000 would be frequently cited in news and government documents.[43] The various estimates are perhaps less an indication of the actual number of Amerasians in Vietnam at the time than they are a barometer of US interest in the matter. For years, the number of mixed race Koreans was also inflated by humanitarian and voluntary agencies to create a sense of urgency and garner more funds and support from the American public.

The question about what would become of these Amerasians left behind loomed large, but Americans expressed their curiosity in indirect ways so as to not reopen the controversial orphan rescue issue. On a practical level, information about Vietnamese children was extremely limited. After the fall of Saigon in 1975, diplomatic relations were severed, and the mass exodus of tens of thousands of US military and government personnel, journalists, voluntary aid workers, and other civilians left the happenings inside a now communist Vietnam largely unknowable. Searching for clues, American journalists reentered the camptown communities around US military bases in South Korea to investigate what had become of an older generation of children born into similar circumstances.

Mixed race Koreans had all but faded from public attention when US involvement in Vietnam was at its highest point in the late 1960s, and it was Southeast Asia that seized national consciousness rather than the Far East. While most of these children had been rescued during the 1950s and 1960s via emergency airlifts and adoptions, in the late 1970s American journalists found a cohort of 5,000 "abandoned" individuals who had been bypassed for placements into American families.[44] They reportedly lived

THE SECOND RESCUE   (145)

marginal existences in "the honky-tonk towns on the outskirts of the dwindling American military bases" and were described as "bitter," "half breeds," living "like hell," and longing "to escape from Korea."[45] Reporters claimed that mixed race individuals were "the last hired" and "first fired," that the men became pimps, gangsters, and beggars, and the women turned to prostitution like their mothers.[46] Journalists attributed their difficulties to "reasons grounded in Asian culture," such as homogeneity and Confucian patriarchal traditions that relegated those without fathers to "half-persons."[47] Reports even vilified Korean mothers, claiming that women who initially found their children "cute as babies" eventually "turned against them as they have grown up" and "became more and more of an embarrassment."[48] But journalists also made the argument that the American people, ranging from reckless GIs, to the US government, to the broader public, shared in some of the blame, as they had ignored and rejected these children for decades and had not provided a direct path out of their miserable circumstances. These narratives produced were not new, but rather reworkings of those that leading reformers such as Pearl S. Buck and the Holts had first crafted in the 1950s and 1960s about deprived mixed race children, a racist Korean society, and cold hardened mothers who did not even love their own kin.

In the years following Operation Babylift, Father Alfred Keane would take advantage of the renewed public interest in mixed race Koreans and build on these well-established tropes to garner public support for an Amerasian immigration bill. Having housed and placed hundreds of children for adoption through his orphanage in Incheon, the Maryknoll priest became a self-anointed spokesperson for mixed race Koreans in the late 1970s and early 1980s. Hyperbolic claims that Amerasians were "sold as slaves" in South Korea and that his work for these individuals was done "in the name of Jesus Christ" resembled older strategies employed by his predecessors and heightened the already dramatic journalistic portrayals of the situation in camptowns.[49] There was also a dark side to the seemingly good, humanitarian, and religious work he was doing for mixed race Koreans. Among the cohort of individuals who lived at St. Vincent's Home for Amerasians, Father Keane was known as a child-molester. He abused many young boys and girls who came into his custody in the 1970s and 1980s, while at the same time advocating for their legal rights in America. One mixed race woman detailed this later in an anthology:

> Growing up I was used to people sleeping in one room together. I wasn't surprised when I saw that boys were sleeping in Father Keane's room. I thought they were the ones that he liked the most, his favorites. I figured they must be

special to be chosen to sleep in the priest's room. When I first arrived though, some of the Korean women who worked there told me not to stay in Father Keane's room for too long. I didn't understand why. I learned later if the children wanted to do anything special, they had to go to Father Keane in his bedroom and get permission from him. I wanted to visit my eldest brother, so I went to Father Keane's room to ask if I could go see him. He asked me to give him a hug. I went to him, and when I got close I could smell alcohol on his breath. He put his arms around me to hug me and then he started to touch and kiss me. It felt like forever standing there with his hands all over me, not knowing what to do and how to get away. I wondered if I had said something that made him misunderstand what I wanted. After that first incident, each time I went to his room to ask him something he would abuse me. Sometimes he would cry while he groped and kissed me. I knew it wasn't right for him to do this to me, but I didn't know how to stop it. Each time I had to enter his room, I thought about how I could approach him differently so that he wouldn't touch me. The last time I was in his room, he told me to "get ready," and he asked me to make the bed. I told him I would be right back, but I ran away and never went back to his room.[50]

Few other, if any, mixed race Koreans who stayed at St. Vincent's Home have talked or written about their experiences there publicly.[51] Instead, they discuss in private "how the boys would all sleep in one room and lock legs and hold hands so when father came into the room he couldn't tear one from the group."[52] "Sometimes it worked," one man explained tearfully, "Sometimes it didn't."[53] When Father Keane died in 2007, those aware of the priest's abuse debated whether they should attend his funeral:

We had a sense that he helped us in some ways and that we should be grateful, that we owed him something. But I realized we owed Father Keane nothing. He knew the situations we were coming from, he knew how dire things were for us in Korea. We were traumatized children who thought we were going to a haven. We had been separated from our mothers; some of us were just small children or babies, others, like me, were older. All of us had been thrust into an unfamiliar environment into a way of life we had no knowledge of, with people who were strangers. Instead of the sanctuary we were promised, we were forced to live in a place where a man in power used our bodies for his own pleasure. I realize now that what he did to me is one of the causes of my PTSD. It is the major reason why I could never trust adults. Even after I arrived in America to live with my adoptive family, in a safe but chaotic environment with ten other adopted children, I still could not trust anyone.[54]

Figure 5.2 A young child at St. Vincent's Home for Amerasians in Incheon. Courtesy of National Archives, photo no. 330-CFD-DF-ST-82-07351.

In 1977, 1978, and later in 1980, Father Keane would spend months touring the United States, giving lectures, offering commentary to various media outlets, and agitating the public to lobby Congress for an Amerasian immigration bill.[55] Although Keane, like Pearl S. Buck and Harry Holt, championed mixed race Koreans specifically, he appealed to a broader national community by drawing connections between the children living at St. Vincent's Home and those born from the Vietnam War. Similarly, journalists writing about Amerasians in the 1980s continued to focus on mixed race Koreans, oftentimes opening with an anecdote about one of these individuals before segueing into a broader discussion of mixed race

(148) The First Amerasians

persons in Southeast Asia or elsewhere. An article in *Time*, for example, introduced Americans to Cha Mi Sun, a twenty-seven-year-old "half-breed" acupuncturist whose "patients loathed being touched by him because of his 'outlandish' looks."[56] In *GEO* magazine they learned of Sung-gu, living out of a "shack" and acknowledged by no one on his commute to work, as he was viewed by his countrymen a "cipher" and "a pariah, beneath notice."[57] In newspapers, Americans would read about five "children who were beaten by their peers because they did not fit Korean culture . . . were sick because no one would care for them," and were "caught in the gray between the black and white of American foreign policy" before they were adopted in the States by an American family.[58] Another story presented Rosemary who, as a young child, "was beaten frequently because she had her father's American face" and was "raised to believe that she was inferior because of her mixed-blood heritage."[59] By the time John Keller told his story in Congress in 1981, Father Keane and his allies had generated enough public interest in the issue that the proposed bill already had 140 cosponsors.[60] Throughout the various congressional hearings on Amerasian immigration, Keane would appear as witness to give expert testimony. He would be joined later by John Shade as a representative of both the Pearl S. Buck Foundation and Holt International Children's Service. From them, US lawmakers would learn how "half-Americans" were murdered and "sterilized" first in South Korea, a Confucian nation where "the problem is probably at its ugliest," but in other parts of "the racially pure society of Southeast Asia" as well.[61]

Curated testimony given by mixed race Koreans would also provide invaluable human perspective and strengthen arguments for an Amerasian rescue. Dozens of mixed race Koreans confirmed their marginal existence and pled directly to lawmakers "to pass the legislation that will enable us, abandoned Amerasians, in the Orient to come to the land of our fathers, our true country."[62] Their statements about South Korea also helped legislators to imagine the circumstances surrounding the roughly 100,000 mixed race individuals left behind in other Asian countries, including Thailand, the Philippines, Taiwan, Okinawa, Japan, Vietnam, Laos, and Cambodia. Individuals like Sung Woo Hong, born in 1959, claimed, "I will not be able to get a good job because I am not a pure blood, and I have a different face. . . . I cannot have a good marriage because a good Korean family would not let me into their family."[63] Eddie Choi, born in 1955, confirmed "there are many Black Amerasians in Korea. They have a very hard time. Koreans think of Black people as slaves."[64] Thus, at a time when Americans had shied away from addressing the Amerasian's plight in Vietnam, mixed race Koreans played a crucial role in bringing the issue back to the attention of the public and helping shape a policy solution for these individuals.

Although the US government had begun welcoming Vietnamese refugees into the country through the Orderly Departure Program (ODP) convened by the United Nations High Commissioner for Refugees in 1979, the policy had no special provisions for the resettlement of Amerasians. This was due in part to communist objections to the categorizing of Amerasians as refugees ("the Vietnamese reject this term because it implies official persecution in Vietnam") and to the US government's delay in settling the matter.[65] Although by 1982, a total of seventy-three Amerasians had entered the United States through the program, these were individuals whose births had been legitimated before the fall of Saigon through legal marriages between their American fathers and Vietnamese mothers.[66] Neither the Vietnamese nor American governments objected to the migration of such children because documentation could be provided to prove they were US citizens. The vast majority of Amerasians left behind in Vietnam, however, were the illegitimate or abandoned children of US servicemen, much like their Korean predecessors, and therefore had no documentary proof of their American paternity or citizenship. Recognizing this, in 1979, Stewart B. McKinney, a representative in Congress from the state of Connecticut, introduced the first Amerasian bill.[67] His bill, however, did not make it very far in Congress, perhaps a reflection of more pressing refugee concerns at the time. And yet, with severed diplomatic relations between Vietnam and the United States, Amerasians had also lost access to intercountry adoption.[68] Thus, in the aftermath of Saigon's fall, mixed race children were almost completely cut off from any path of entry into the United States. The immigration bills of the early 1980s represented the first major response to this issue since the controversial orphan airlifts of 1975.

In many ways, the Amerasian immigration hearings provided another opportunity for postwar redemption. In one statement, Walter Martindale, an official with the US State Department, testified that the communists "will not let [Amerasians] forget who they are and the sins of their fathers."[69] He added that "because of their failures as a government and system, the regime cannot feed them and/or will not educate them."[70] By stressing Vietnamese mistreatment of children and the insufficiencies of communism as a political system, US lawmakers and other witnesses reprised the justifications of Operation Babylift. The hearings also allowed Americans to assert that the United States was a multicultural nation that would welcome children of different racial and cultural backgrounds, refuting earlier claims by airlift skeptics that Black Amerasian children might fare better off in communist Vietnam given domestic US anti-Black racism. One adoptive mother of several Korean children argued, "America is in a better position to accept children of mixed parentage than are the homogenous societies in Asia. In America there are many minority groups where individuals can derive a sense of identity."[71] She continued, "Culturally, financially and practically we have the ability to help the Amerasian children and young people."[72] The juxtaposition of a prosperous, democratic, and multicultural United States against a "burdened," communist, and racist Vietnam (that viewed such children as the "dust of life," and "bad elements") enabled Americans to recast themselves as the rightful and able paternal protectors of mixed race individuals rather than a nation that had failed its own children and lost a war.[73]

Saving the Amerasian was framed in congressional testimony as a Cold War imperative and a matter of American prestige. Father Keane would warn legislators that, if nothing was to be done about the Amerasian child, "countries unfriendly to the United States" might "exploit the children for any gain or propaganda against the interests of the United States."[74] He claimed that the "passage of [an Amerasian] bill is of the utmost importance to us as a nation . . . because it allows us to be free from the one criticism that does so much damage to us in the countries of Asia."[75] Members of Congress expressed similar concerns that the presence of abandoned mixed race Asians scattered across US outposts in the Pacific prevented Americans from winning friends in the East and ultimately tarnished the image of American democracy in the world. Keane would bluntly assert that saving Amerasians was a question of the nation's morality: "Are we a decent and honorable people, a truly great nation?"[76] Or are we "a country of barbarians who would abandon even its own flesh and blood?"[77]

Legislators concerned about national prestige invoked the treatment of Eurasians from earlier colonial contexts and how those individuals had been dealt with by European imperial powers. William Lehman, state representative from Florida noted that "other nations, including the English, the French, and the Dutch, have taken responsibility for the offspring of their servicemen while in Asia."[78] He added, "Only the United States has turned its back on these children."[79] Troubled that "the military people abroad . . . do whatever they want" and "pay nothing for it," Pat Schroeder, a House representative from Colorado remarked, "It is like Imperial America."[80] Although a State Department official had coined the term Amerasian to distance "half-Americans" from Eurasians ("they were and are the children of American men, and they are born not of imperial rulers but of liberators"), the parallels could no longer be ignored.[81] Champions of the Amerasian argued that, because "other great countries which have been active in Southeast Asia, such as France, took these children back with them

THE SECOND RESCUE   (151)

when they returned home, gave them citizenship, and supported them until they completed their education" a "remedial precedent . . . which is both timely and Asian specifically" already existed.[82] Indeed, if the French could embrace 25,000 Eurasian children, certainly the United States was just as benevolent, egalitarian, and powerful and could do the same for its mixed race progeny.[83]

Although few argued against the need to pass such an imperative piece of legislation, the details of who constituted Amerasians and what kinds of privileges might be provided remained up for debate. With the nation experiencing economic recession, rising unemployment rates, and growing concerns about the influx of refugees from Southeast Asia, popular anti-immigrant sentiment ran high at the very moment that US lawmakers were deciding the fate of the Amerasian immigration bill. But since there was consensus that something must be done for these individuals, US lawmakers spent a greater portion of the hearings discussing how to convince their constituents that inviting more refugees into the country (albeit in the form of "half-Americans") would not strain the US economy.

Once again, mixed race Koreans proved critical in quelling American anxieties around these issues. Beginning in the 1970s, Father Keane's orphanage had operated a study abroad scholarship program with Gonzaga University in Spokane, Washington. In the congressional hearings, faculty from the Roman Catholic university spoke to the success and achievements of their mixed race students. Priests who had worked in "very close association with these young people" confirmed that "these young students are not delinquents, but industrious scholars and outstanding people."[84] Mixed race Koreans were further described as "practicing Christians," hard working, "loyal," better "than any other foreign group on campus," and "exemplary Americans."[85] Regarding national concerns "that Amerasians may become dependents on taxpayers," it was argued that "these students do not wish to accept charity of public assistance"; instead "they came, asking for employment."[86] Many Amerasian men expressed an innate devotion to the nation, emphasizing their US paternity and patriotism.[87] One such individual named Jonny Chung, born in 1961, was already a great patriot. He testified: "I would be so proud to be in the United States military. It is my dream."[88] In many ways, the Gonzaga University program served as a Petri dish, allowing US lawmakers to see how adult Amerasians might fit into American society before they arrived in larger numbers. This gave members of Congress the ammunition necessary to proceed with the bill despite national anxieties around immigration and economic recession.

When the Amerasian Immigration Act of 1982 was enacted, it was not an open immigration policy. The law would allow Amerasians to qualify

Figure 5.3 Mixed race Koreans at Gonzaga University. Courtesy of Gonzaga University Library.

under the first and fourth preference categories of US immigration law (unmarried sons and daughters of US citizens or married sons and daughters, respectively). This meant they were not given separate non-quota status and their migrations had to occur within the already established annual quota of 20,000 per country. Additionally, in order to qualify for the benefits of the law, Amerasians were required to have "received an acceptable guarantee of legal custody and financial responsibility" from a US citizen over the age of twenty-one.[89] This period of sponsorship was supposed to last for at least five years or until the child's twenty-first birthday, whichever time was longer. For children under the age of eighteen, placement into American families required a written irrevocable release on part of the mother or guardian. For determination of eligible Amerasian status, the law did not require an official admission of paternity on part of an American citizen. Immigration officials were instead to take into consideration "the physical appearance of the alien and evidence provided by the petitioner, including birth and baptismal certificates, local civil records, photographs of, and letters or proof of financial support from a putative father who is a citizen of the United States."[90] American consular offices and private voluntary aid organizations in the Amerasian's country of origin were instructed to facilitate this process and make a legal determination.

THE SECOND RESCUE   (153)

Although the requirements were strict, the law provided the first immigration pathway, beyond adoption, for mixed race individuals illegitimately fathered by US servicemen in Asia. This would be most critical for Amerasians over the legal adoptable age of fourteen. Further, because this solution allowed mixed race individuals to migrate under already existing immigration quotas and attached them to financial sponsors in the United States, legislators were able to present the act as a solution that would not burden the American taxpayer or increase the number of refugees in the United States. While this allowed the bill to avoid intense public and media scrutiny, the law's strict requirements severely curtailed the proclaimed goals of the act to welcome Amerasians home.

Moreover, the Amerasian Immigration Act extended special immigration provisions only to "certain" Asian children fathered by US citizens.[91] It restricted the geographic definition of the Amerasians to those born in Korea, Vietnam, Laos, Cambodia, or Thailand—notably leaving out mixed race individuals from Japan, the Philippines, and Taiwan. It also limited the Amerasian temporally. The year 1950 was chosen by US lawmakers "in recognition of the fact that our largest troop commitment to Korea occurred between the years of 1950-54" and clearly demarcated the start of the Amerasian at the onset of the Korean War. Furthermore, no mixed race individuals regardless of country of origin would be legally considered Amerasian if they were born after the date of the law's enactment (October 22, 1982).[92]

These requirements reinforced an official government position that not all mixed race Asians were equal and that only a select group was worthy of the nation's privileges.[93] The most vocal objection to this thinking came from the Philippine Heritage Federation in Washington, DC.[94] The Filipino American organization offered the following remarks during the congressional hearings:

> What is baffling about this section of the proposed law is the absence of any reference to Amerasians in the Philippines. It limits itself to Amerasian children born in Asian countries where the United States has been militarily involved in recent times. Although the Philippine Amerasian problem dates back to World War II and the post-liberation days, the problem is ongoing because of the continuing presence of the largest American military installations (Subic and Clark bases) outside the United States. During the Vietnam War, these bases were used as staging areas for US offensives in the Indochina theater.[95]

Although subject matter experts attested to the fact that US military operations in the Philippines had produced 5,000 "Vietnam War era

Amerasians," members of Congress were not interested in extending the legal rights of the Amerasian to these individuals.[96] Referencing the history of US colonial intervention in the Philippines dating back to the nineteenth century, one report, entered into the *Congressional Record*, gave some vague rationale for excluding Filipinos, arguing that "in some countries where an American presence has been tolerated for generations, Amerasians have attained a level of acceptance."[97] It continued: "Two of the most popular Filipino movie stars, Hilda Koronel and Elizabeth Oropesa, are daughters of American fathers. But in Korea, most Amerasian children and their mothers are still treated as outcasts."[98] Despite this belief that mixed race individuals in the Philippines did not constitute a stigmatized class of people, numerous proposals refuting this claim followed in attempts to extend the provisions of the Amerasian Immigration Act. In the most popular, Representative Lucien Blackwell of Pennsylvania proposed a 1993 bill to amend the Amerasian Immigration Act citing "30,000 Filipino Amerasians, mostly neglected and outcast children, living in squalor and poverty," following the withdrawal of the last US troops from Subic Bay.[99]

Mixed race Filipino individuals have repeatedly failed to receive comparable immigration status. In 1997 and again in 2001 other prominent bills to legally redefine the Amerasian so it would include aliens from the Philippines and Japan were also rejected.[100] Arguments prevailed that Filipino Amerasians were not victims of discrimination, that their mothers had been prostitutes (and therefore they were the product of illegal illicit encounters), and that these children had been born during peacetime.[101] Such grounds for excluding Filipinos from the rights and privileges of the Amerasian remain, to this day, unsatisfactory at best. Research on and testimonies from Filipino Amerasians have confirmed their low status within Philippine society. Earlier rescue narratives constructed for mixed race Koreans depended on depicting their mothers as prostitutes unable to care for their own children. And American bases in the Philippines have been central to US efforts in the Asia-Pacific region during times of war.

With its limited geographic and temporal boundaries, the Amerasian Immigration Act of 1982 appears to have been an ineffective piece of legislation. The law enabled the migrations of only eighty-seven Amerasians in the three years following its enactment, despite estimates of such individuals left behind in Asia being in the tens of thousands.[102] Of those eighty-seven successful migrants, most came from South Korea (and some from Thailand), but none from Vietnam, Cambodia, or Laos. However, these shortcomings should have been of no surprise to US lawmakers, as many experts had warned them in the congressional hearings that "the present lack of diplomatic relations" between the United States and its communist foes in Southeast Asia "appears to effectively limit the true and ultimate effect of such a remedy."[103] Indeed, without diplomatic offices or voluntary agencies on the ground, it was virtually impossible for mixed race individuals in Vietnam, Laos, and Cambodia to confirm American heritage and initiate immigration proceedings that would secure their entry into the United States. Furthermore, for those eligible mixed race Korean and Southeast Asian individuals immigrating to the United States as Amerasians, the law did not confer upon them automatic citizenship (and no law has to this day). US legislators were well aware of these issues, yet still proceeded with the act's passage.

Thus, rather than a sensible method to bring Amerasian individuals to the United States and secure for them US rights and privileges, the Amerasian Immigration Act of 1982 was a powerful and deliberate articulation of Cold War geopolitics. Its enactment in 1982 marked the first time that the federal government named and legally defined any of the nation's mixed race populations born from its many military incursions across the globe. Yet, the strict geographic and temporal boundaries of the Amerasian established that America's obligation and responsibility was limited to just "certain children of United States citizens," a position that has been repeatedly reaffirmed.[104] Indeed, mixed race Asians are not all the same, and in fact, some children fathered by US servicemen in Asia are not Amerasians after all. The Amerasian Immigration Act of 1982 confirmed that the category of Amerasian does not exist as an objective reality but remains a political and legal construction of the Cold War. As the orphan hearings surrounding mixed race Koreans in the 1950s first revealed, refugee identities are constitutive of the US government's foreign policy objectives. Mixed race individuals from the Philippines, Japan, and Taiwan were excluded from the Amerasian Immigration Act's provisions because these were not children of wars waged against communist aggressors— conflicts that were vastly unpopular among the American public for their brutality and ambivalent endings—and thus their rescues would have had relatively little symbolic value. The warm embrace of mixed race persons produced by relations during the Korean War and, later, the Vietnam War provided Americans with sentimental postwar victories, thus helping to justify US military intervention. The making of the Amerasian, then, was a Cold War matter of redeeming American prestige, reconciling defeat, and promoting dominant US ideologies at times when the nation needed this most.

By 1985 another immigration proposal was in the works to rectify the initial bill's practical shortcomings. In 1987, the Amerasian Homecoming Act was passed under the sponsorship of notable Vietnam War veterans and congressmen including Thomas Ridge, Robert Mrazek, and John McCain.[105] The law eliminated some of the strict sponsorship requirements and allowed Vietnamese Amerasians to immigrate to the United States with their relatives under the Orderly Departure program. Like refugees, these individuals would receive US government assistance including "housing for the first month as well as some cash for food, transportation, and other household expenses," medical examinations and treatment under Medicaid, school placements for children, assistance in locating jobs from resettlement agencies for adults, and financial assistance for those who were unable to work.[106] The bill did not extend these privileges to any other mixed race group nor broaden the definition of Amerasian in the 1982 law. Under the new 1987 act and its later extensions, over 75,000 Amerasians and their extended family members had entered into the United States by 1994, and that number was reported to be 100,000 by 2002.[107] Arguably, the largely pragmatic 1987 law could not have been enacted without the definitive 1982 act, which set the precedent that Americans were responsible for and obligated to assist "certain" mixed race children fathered in Asia. By extension, this incredible movement of tens of thousands of people could not have been achieved without mixed race Koreans, whose plight and rescue was built on with each successive generation until the Cold War construction of the Amerasian was complete.

Epilogue

Beyond Amerasian

My own parents met in a camptown during my father's military tour of South Korea in the 1980s. By then, US military policies had changed. Commanders were no longer preventing their soldiers from marrying Korean women (although they still discouraged them) and a number of children, my brother and I included, were receiving legal recognition through US-approved marriages that secured our immigration and status in America. In fact, social workers began noticing these changes as early as the mid-1960s when they entered the camptowns and observed "an increasing number of racially mixed children . . . being legitimated by marriage and going to the US with their mothers and fathers."[1] Back in the 1950s, when the first war bride migrations began, an average of just 200 Korean American couples a year received approval from the US military to marry, even though US troop populations were in the hundreds of thousands.[2] By the 1960s, that number was upwards of 1,000, and by the 1970s and 1980s it was more than 4,000 annually.[3] These statistics on marriages between Korean women and American men and insights from social workers at the time help to explain why, in the 1960s and 1970s, the population of mixed race children left behind was generally an older one and why the average age of those sent abroad for adoption seemed to climb each year.

The First Amerasians. Yuri W. Doolan, Oxford University Press. © Oxford University Press 2024.
DOI: 10.1093/oso/9780197534380.003.0007

(158)   *The First Amerasians*

I often think about how easy it was for my mother to immigrate to the United States relative to the women I write about in this book and how my own life might have been different had I been born thirty or even just twenty years earlier. Would I have remained in South Korea? Would I have been sent to the United States for adoption? As a historian, I recognize that it was a combination of sheer luck, interpersonal factors, and changes in US immigration law and military policies that allowed Korean American families like my own to move to the United States intact.[4]

The demise of the Amerasian has to do not only with these on-the-ground changes in military culture and US policy but also with the absence of outright war. By 1982, no more Amerasians would be born, according to the temporal boundaries set by the Amerasian Immigration Act—the same provisions that defined Koreans as the first Amerasians. Nonetheless, a massive and prolonged US military presence would remain installed in South Korea and elsewhere in Asia, and mixed race children would continue to be illegitimately fathered wherever US bases were. After bases closed, camptown neighborhoods often transformed into tourist destinations that served as sexual playgrounds for mostly Western men. A 2019 essay published in the *Guardian* discusses mixed race Filipino children born from sex tourism that thrives near a former installation in Manila that was shut down as part of a broader US military scale back at the end of the Cold War.[5] During my own travels to Chiang Mai, Thailand, in 2018—an R&R destination for American soldiers during the Vietnam War—I saw mixed race children and their mothers living on the streets of the night bazaar, begging for money from passersby. These mixed race children were likely the sons and daughters of Western male sex tourists, like those in Manila. Even today, an influx of Filipina migrant workers into South Korean camptowns has resulted in a substantial population of mixed race children. These individuals are not only the sons and daughters of US military men, but also of English language teachers and other Western tourists. Because all of these children have been born during "peacetime" they are not afforded the rights and privileges of the Amerasian.[6] Although voluntary agencies and religious groups continue to express their humanitarian concerns and reprise familiar arguments about Asian societies' mistreatment of these individuals, the lack of a massive military conflict has meant that there is little geopolitical or diplomatic incentive for US lawmakers to take legislative action. The Amerasian thus remains frozen in time and place between the years 1950 and 1982 in just South Korea and Southeast Asia, as defined by the Amerasian Immigration Act of 1982.

Figure 6.1 Mixed race Korean children pose on a US Army tank. Courtesy of Holt International, holtinternational.org.

In her 1966 travelogue, *For Spacious Skies*, Pearl S. Buck recalls her first encounters with mixed race children in Asia during the 1950s and 1960s and details the origins of the term Amerasian:

> I had seen them long ago in Asia, and they were called Eurasians. Then they had been the children of empire, their fathers English or European, their mothers Indian, Indo-Chinese, or Indonesian. But these now were not the children of empire. They were and are the children of American men, and they are born not of imperial rulers but of liberators. Let them be called Amerasians! You remember that was the name the man in the State Department suggested, when we went to Washington for advice.[7]

Indeed, the Amerasian, conceived of by American bureaucrats and popularized by American journalists, social workers, and humanitarians, was a Cold War construction utilized to obscure US empire in Asia and promote the image of US democracy in the world. The term is a reminder that as much as the Cold War was a series of protracted military conflicts it was also a war in which words had symbolic value and mattered immensely.[8] But for mixed race Koreans and their mothers, the Cold War construction

(160)   *The First Amerasians*

of the Amerasian was more than just an ideological concept. To them, it was a violent set of imperial practices and behaviors that profoundly shaped the trajectory of their lives. It began in South Korea with the destruction of Korean American families, continued with the subsequent separation of mixed race children from their birth mothers, and culminated in the ideological erasure of these individuals' Korean pasts after their migration to the United States. Yet the Amerasian's human consequences did not end once adoptions were finalized and mixed race children successfully assimilated into adoptive homes. Even now, mixed race Koreans and their mothers are still grappling with the "afterlives" of the first Amerasian rescue.[9]

During my field visits to camptowns in 2016, I regularly encountered elderly women who had once worked in the military sex industry and had, decades earlier, sent their mixed race children to the United States for adoption. A number of them approached me, as a mixed race Korean, and spoke about their sons and daughters. They would say things like, "You look like the son I once had, who I sent for adoption," and ask me to share with them details about my life in America.[10] I could sense that my presence gave them some temporary comfort, perhaps even validation, that their heartbreaking decisions made some fifty or sixty years earlier had been right all along. While some women announced that they were looking for their sons or daughters and expressed their hopes to one day be reunited with them, there were also those whom others whispered about—those women who once relinquished children but were too deeply saddened to talk about it anymore.[11] Many Korean mothers were never the same after they gave up their first children. They mourned their loss for years, fell into deep psychosis, tried to purge memories of their relinquished children, turned to drugs and alcohol for escape, and even tried to take their own lives. Other women did what they had to do to survive. They went to work in the camptowns, where they met new GI husbands, made new families, and immigrated to the United States, or they remained in South Korea sometimes becoming military hostesses, live-in girlfriends, and sex workers.

For elderly camptown women, the subject of lost mixed race children is a common topic in group therapy sessions.[12] These mothers lament to each other: "If I knew it would be like this, I wouldn't have sent them. I would have held onto them."[13] Some describe the experience of having their children taken away from them as more traumatic than any of the other indignities they experienced at the hands of the military personnel or health officials who violated their bodies:

EPILOGUE *(161)*

I have no joy and no pleasure. When I think about the past, there are only regrets and sad wounds. I feel like I should live the rest of my life well, but now I feel like I have nothing left in life but to grow old and die. Now I want to forget the past, but there is one thing I cannot forget even if I forget everything: my child's face, the child's last cry that I heard when we parted. . . . That's something I can never forget no matter how hard I try. If God asks me what my last wish is, I would ask to see my child's face just once while I am alive, no, even if I can't meet my child, if I could just hear of their news, whether they are dead or alive, I would have no regrets in life. . . . This is my last wish. Seeing the child at least once. I really wanted to say that I am sorry. That I wanted to meet you so much, but there was no way for me to contact you. I want to say those words. And not being able to hug her one last time has left me filled with *han* [sorrow]. If I am able to meet her, I want to hug her tightly.[14]

In the camptowns today, the legacies of the Amerasian are evident. The ghostly specter of the mixed race children who once walked the roads adjacent to US encampments alongside their mothers continues to haunt those who lost sons and daughters of their own, as well as those old enough to remember those years.[15]

On the other side of the Pacific Ocean, adult mixed race adoptees are also looking for their Korean mothers and for more information about where their lives began. However, for those sent to the United States in the 1950s and 1960s, before practices like proxy adoption were fully outlawed, this search for origins has been complicated by the fact that their adoptions into American families often took place with very limited documentation. While some states have laws in place mandating that social workers withhold identifying information about birth parents from adopted individuals, other agencies placed mixed race Koreans without completing their family histories or child study reports. Some deliberately provided adoptive parents with falsified, incomplete, and inaccurate documents. Consequently, many mixed race Koreans have never even seen the names of their biological parents in print. Others have searched for their birth families for decades, only to later discover that they were looking under a falsified or incorrect name. All of this has made it exceedingly difficult, if not impossible, for mixed race Koreans of this generation to trace their biological origins.

As this book has shown, individuals like Harry Holt and other humanitarian non-professionals went into the camptowns and operated as saviors, rather social welfare professionals, intent upon rescuing mixed race children from a racist and barbaric Korean society, and, to a lesser extent,

(162)   *The First Amerasians*

from their prostitute mothers, no matter what the costs. As such, they did not aim to keep biological families intact or to make it so that biological families were traceable to adopted individuals later on. Their sole focus was on removing as many children from South Korea as quickly as possible. This often included unethical and coercive "baby hunting" practices, the physical and forceful removal of children from Korean mothers, and sometimes even monetary bribes. In the United States, the process of legal and ideological erasure continued as mixed race children were placed into adoptive families. What little trace of their former lives that remained was eliminated through assimilationist policies promoted by social workers and adoptive parents. Consequently, mixed race individuals determined to find their origins have had to work against a system that was intent upon severing them from their Korean pasts. They have written to adoption agencies or social workers whose names are listed on their paperwork, taken out newspaper ads, filed missing persons reports, and gone on television shows in both South Korea and the United States. While these attempts to locate their birth families are sometimes successful, more often than not they reach dead ends. However, new technologies, combined with perseverance, have enabled this first generation of mixed race Korean adoptees to streamline their search and reunite with their birth families. The demise of the Amerasian, then, is just as much about the end of the Cold War in Asia as it is about mixed race subjectivity and efforts on the part of these individuals to confront the lasting legacies of this construct on their lives.

Since the late 1990s, the internet has played a crucial role in the development of Korean adoptee networks.[16] The formation of a distinct mixed race adoptee community followed in the 2010s.[17] One woman who has been at the center of this organizing is Katherine Kim, a mixed race Korean adoptee who was born in Incheon in 1957, relinquished by her mother in 1959, and placed into an adoptive home in the United States in 1961. Like most mixed race Koreans of her generation, Kim spent most of her childhood and young adult years largely isolated from other adoptees. But in 2012, while attending a screening of *Somewhere Between* (a documentary on intercountry adoption from China), Kim learned about the International Korean Adoptee Association (IKAA). Taking note of the organization's name during the film, she searched the internet for resources later that night, and was shocked to learn that there were hundreds of thousands of Korean adoptees just like her. Kim soon found a number of Korean adoptee (KAD) groups on Facebook. At the same time, she also learned that there had been much research on camptowns, and that this scholarship was growing. From these sources, she had an epiphany that her mother had "most likely been a military prostitute."[18] Wanting to further explore her origins and also create a venue for other mixed race Koreans to do the same, she created a Facebook group called "Koreans and Camptowns" in October of 2013. Slowly, she began carefully adding mixed race adoptees she met in the broader KAD groups to this Facebook group. But she encountered some pushback from those who were not so keen to confront their camptown pasts. So, that December, she also made a more general "Hapa" page for mixed race KADs.[19] Slowly, the Facebook groups attracted over 300 members each. These internet communities spawned a number of in-person gatherings where mixed race KADs would meet others like themselves. For many who encountered these groups in their late adulthood and responded to invitations to attend these informal gatherings, they reported that it was the first time in their lives they had ever seen another mixed race Korean, let alone an adoptee, in person. The burgeoning community of mixed race KADs that formed online eventually helped to make broader collective movements possible.

In 2014, another significant breakthrough occurred for mixed race KADs when the first "Hapa" homeland tour was organized by a nonprofit organization called Me and Korea. By that time, adult adoptees had become a discernible population and had long been making return migrations to South Korea, sometimes individually but also through heritage tours organized by post-adoption service professionals.[20] In 2014, Minyoung Kim, the director of Me and Korea, was in Boston organizing one of these trips. According to Katherine Kim, when the two met through a mutual acquaintance at that time, Minyoung was shocked to learn about mixed race Koreans ("You're adopted too? You're Korean?").[21] Although Minyoung had been working within adoptee spaces for years and was organizing KAD homeland tours of her own, she had no idea before meeting Katherine that the first wave of Korean adoptees had been largely those of mixed race background.[22] Katherine shared with Minyoung all she had learned from her research and from the discussions on her "Koreans and Camptowns" Facebook page. Compelled by their initial meeting, Minyoung Kim began organizing the first "Hapa" tour in South Korea later that year. Designed with mixed race Koreans in mind, the customized tour explored their past lives through visits to women's NGOs and former US military installations as well as by viewing historical and photographic exhibits on camptowns and adoption. The group spent time on Holt International's campus in Ilsan, and had a meeting with mixed race singer Insooni, among other activities. Katherine Kim would play an instrumental role in recruiting most of the twenty-five mixed race KADs who would take this first "Hapa" tour in the fall of 2014. It had been nearly sixty years since intercountry adoption from South Korea began. While Katherine has pointed out that "it would have only been natural for Holt to be hosting the tour," it took Minyoung Kim's relatively new

(164)   *The First Amerasians*

organization and the work of mixed race Koreans themselves to recover their Korean and camptown pasts and confront the lasting legacies of the Amerasian rescue on their lives.[23] Additional "Hapa" tours took place in 2015 and 2018.

From the "Hapa" tours came the first "Koreans and Camptowns" conference, organized by Me and Korea and documentary filmmaker Deann Borshay Liem (a KAD herself), and held in Berkeley, California, in September of 2015.[24] Through Facebook groups, other social media, and word of mouth, mixed race KADs from all over the country heard about the event and traveled to attend. There, they learned alongside academics, cultural producers, social workers, adoption professionals, and community organizers about the connections between camptowns and adoption. At that meeting Bella Siegel-Dalton gave a presentation about her work with Thomas Park Clement, a mixed race KAD philanthropist who had committed $1 million to fund a Global DNA Project for Korean Adoptees, Birthmothers and Korean War Veterans searching for lost relatives. Siegel-Dalton, a veteran of the US Coast Guard, had been recruited by Clement to administer the Korean War Veterans portion of the DNA project and had successfully reunited with her own birth family through DNA testing.

Adopted in 1966 at five years of age, Siegel-Dalton has very vague memories of her former life in South Korea ("I can remember a street with some small shops and a goat tied to a fence, that's it").[25] As a young adult, she had requested her non-identifying information from the state of California, written to both the Pearl S. Buck Foundation and Holt International to find out if she had ever lived at their institutions, and even visited a hypnotist to see if she could recover information about her biological parents and her past life in South Korea. Her efforts yielded few leads. When she was diagnosed with polycystic kidney disease in 2006, her health concerns reignited her search for her origins. She was interested in DNA testing to identify her biological parents, but at that time the technologies available to the public (both mitochondrial and Y-DNA test) were not yet advanced enough to secure matches beyond the sex-linked X and Y chromosomes and therefore could not provide information about her paternal line. Assuming that few, if any, Koreans would be interested in DNA testing, she decided that this would probably not yield any matches and was therefore not a worthwhile path for tracing her genealogy. But in 2012, there was a major breakthrough with autosomal DNA testing, and organizations like Ancestry, 23andMe, and Family Finder began offering genealogy kits widely. Immediately, she tested with Ancestry and received an instant third cousin match. After three years of genealogical and records research, she finally identified her father through that match.

Since reuniting with her paternal family, Bella Siegel-Dalton discovered that her biological father died of cancer in 2010. On his death bed, he had told her siblings about the child he left behind in South Korea and urged them to accept their half-brother or half-sister with open arms if and when his oldest child ever sought them out. From her meeting with her biological father's family, Siegel-Dalton finally learned about the circumstances of her birth. When her father requested an extension of his military tour upon learning about her mother's pregnancy in 1961, his commanding officer denied the request and immediately ordered that he return to the States. When her father "tried to stay anyway, he was arrested and put into the Brig," slang for a US military prison.[26] During that time he lost contact with her mother and after he returned to the States, he never heard from his wife again. After not even knowing her birth parents' names, Bella found, through a single DNA match, the story of her biological origins. She would later discover that her kidney problems were not from her father's side but inherited from her maternal line, making it all the more imperative to locate her mother before it was too late.

Katherine Kim was not only in the audience that day, but she and Bella Siegel-Dalton also shared a conference hotel room, along with three other mixed race women. The group of five were all connected to one another through the numerous Facebook groups, "Hapa" tours, and informal gatherings of mixed race KADs that had been organized since 2013. That night, after Bella's presentation, the group continued their earlier discussion about DNA and shared their personal experiences in locating their birth families. Bella recalls from that conversation:

> When we got to talking about how I found my father through DNA, the others were like, "Well we took the DNA test, but there's no information. There's no match." And I said, "No, if you took your DNA there's definitely information. Let me log in and have a look." So, then I logged on and I see a second cousin match for one of the women and I say, "Look here, look at this! You've got a second cousin match and she lives in Alabama. We can find out who your father is from this!" And so, we started talking and then someone says, "but most of us really just want to know who our mothers are." And then I paused for a moment, thought about it and said, "Well this would work to find out who your mothers are, if we were able to get Korean people into the database."[27]

From this was born the idea for 325KAMRA, the only organization dedicated to reuniting Korean adoptees with their biological families through DNA testing. The name of the organization, 325, was taken from the room number that five co-founders shared in Berkeley; KAMRA was the acronym for Korean American Mixed Race Association (today the name has changed to Korean Adoptees Making Reunions Attainable).

One month later, Katherine Kim began the process of filing for 325KAMRA's nonprofit status. She and the other co-founders also presented their idea to Thomas Park Clement and secured from him a donation of DNA kits to take to South Korea. In the process, Katherine Kim also located her biological father through a DNA match to a first cousin. Although she had first tested in 2011 and had matched to a very distant cousin at that time, this new match was much closer and had also completed a family tree. When Katherine logged on to view it, she saw the name "Gerald Krohn" and instantly knew that this was her father. Her whole life she had been searching for her father under "Jerry Crown," the name transliterated onto her child history report completed by ISS social workers in South Korea. Immediately, she recognized the power of DNA to reunite birth families and "to cut through the fictional or nonexistent paperwork."[28] Although mixed race KADs "have to work harder than those with intact biological families to find their origins," the work of activists like Katherine Kim and Bella Siegel-Dalton, as well as the efforts of their organization 325KAMRA, provides mixed race Koreans an effective way to do so.[29] By 2016, in addition to their American staff, 325KAMRA had a dedicated volunteer working to administer DNA testing in South Korea. The following year, the organization had earned enough through donations and memberships (secured mostly from mixed race Korean adoptees) to fund one salaried position in South Korea and was able to hire a second salaried worker in South Korea in 2018. The organization's entire staff in the United States are volunteers, mostly mixed race Koreans.

325KAMRA not only provides genealogical and records research for its clients to help them identify potential biological family members but it also facilitates family reunions and provides translation and interpretation services for those meeting their Korean matches. Within the first three and half years of its founding, 325KAMRA had already reunited more than 100 families through their casework and at least 200 more through automatic DNA matches. Such a figure represents at least 2 percent (or 1 in every 50) of mixed race Koreans sent to the United States for adoption between 1955 and 1969.[30] Ironically, organizations like Holt International, which gained international acclaim by separating children from their Korean mothers and sending them to the United States for adoption, are not forthcoming about their reunion statistics. Katherine Kim commented in 2019:

No one is talking about reunions. No one is telling me how many reunions occur each year, how they are facilitated, how they are found. No one wants to come

Figure 6.2 One mixed race Korean woman's search for origins is featured in Deann Borhsay Liem's 2019 documentary film *Geographies of Kinship*. Photograph by Allison Shelley. Courtesy of Mu Films.

forth with that information. I've asked the adoption agencies, I've asked Korean Adoption Services, I've asked Holt. So, say there are 300 reunions in three and a half years. It may not seem like a lot but when you consider what came before, it's at least something.[31]

While 325KAMRA has now turned its focus to DNA testing in South Korea to increase the volume of Korean DNA into the databases and facilitate matches that might yield family reunions, the organization also plans to ramp up its efforts with Korean American families. Among their cohort of matches, a small portion of Korean mothers were actually found to be residing in the United States. In several cases, they arrived in the country through marriages to US servicemen even before the adoptions of their mixed race children had been completed in South Korea.[32] While mixed race Korean adoptees have for years believed their mothers to still be in South Korea, the work of 325KAMRA has revealed that some of these women had spent decades in the United States. As for the fathers identified in the United States, 325KAMRA casework has demonstrated how many of them had formed second, third, and fourth families during their military tours of Japan, the Philippines, and Vietnam as well as South Korea.

In 2018, Katherine Kim and three Korean American writers published an anthology titled *Mixed Korean: Our Stories* through Thomas Park Clement's Truepeny Publishing Company. The volume brought together a diverse group of mixed race contributors whose prose, poetry, memoir, and oral history capture their diverse and complex identities in both the United States and South Korea. The collection's goals were to document and preserve the lived experiences of mixed race Koreans, from those with intact biological families to those affected by adoption, before those histories were lost. In 2020, 325KAMRA published a second anthology, *Together at*

Figure 6.3 An oil on canvas, used as the cover art for *Mixed Korean: Our Stories*. Courtesy of Jacky Lee.

Last: Stories of Adoption and Reunion in the Age of DNA, to showcase their DNA reunions.[33] In 2024, the organization is led by Linda Papi Rounds and continues to facilitate family reunions not just for mixed race individuals, but, given the strength of its ever-growing transnational database, for all Korean adoptees.[34]

The work of mixed race Koreans in the 2010s and 2020s marks the emergence of a distinct mixed race Korean subjectivity. One not so concerned with the Cold War construction of the Amerasian but, given its focus on actual people, is inevitably engaged in its upending. Through these efforts, mixed race Koreans have not only claimed their own identities beyond Amerasian but have also successfully undone the ideological erasure of their pasts. This book is written with the hope that one day mixed race Koreans might read it themselves and use it as yet another tool to uncover the secrets of their origins. Perhaps it will bring them closer to their beginnings and to their unanswered questions, and they might find within its many pages the spirits of their Korean mothers.

APPENDIX

Table A.1 US IMMIGRATION LAWS PERTAINING TO KOREAN AND JAPANESE WAR BRIDES

Date	Popular Title	Description
May 26, 1924	Immigration and Nationality Act	Barred "aliens ineligible to citizenship" from entry into the United States.
December 28, 1945	War Brides Act	Provided European spouses of US servicemen entry under existing quota system. Expired on December 28, 1948.
July 22, 1947	Public Law 213	Expanded the provisions of the War Brides Act to cover racially ineligible spouses.
August 19, 1950	Public Law 717	Revived the War Brides Act to provide for admission of Japanese and Korean spouses in particular. Originally scheduled to last only six months but extended for an additional six months.
June 27, 1952	McCarran-Walter Act	Ended racial exclusions in the former laws and provided non-quota status for all foreign spouses of US citizens.

(172)   *Appendix*

Table A.2 ASIAN IMMIGRANT WOMEN ADMITTED TO UNITED STATES
AS WIVES OF AMERICAN CITIZENS BY COUNTRY OF ORIGIN AND YEAR

Year	Korea	Japan
1947	0	14
1948	0	298
1949	0	445
1950	1	9
1951	11	125
1952	101	4,220
1953	96	2,042
1954	116	2,802
1955	184	2,843
1956	292	3,661
1957	288	5,003
1958	410	4,841
1959	488	4,412
1960	649	3,887
1961	405	3,176
1962	692	2,677
1963	1,350	2,745
1964	1,340	2,653
1965	1,281	2,350
1966	1,225	1,991
1967	1,389	1,821
1968	1,356	1,845
1969	1,954	1,842
1970	2,646	2,104
1971	3,033	2,023
1972	2,148	1,626
1973	2,134	2,077
1974	2,461	1,773
1975	2,155	1,376
1976	4,251	1,504
1977	3,454	1,125
Total	37,063	69,699

Source: US Commissioner of Immigration and Naturalization, Annual Reports, 1947–77, Table 6
(Washington, DC), reprinted in Bok-Lim Kim, *Women in Shadows: A Handbook for Service Providers Working
with Asian Wives of U.S. Military Personnel* (La Jolla, CA: National Committee Concerned with Asian Wives
of US Servicemen, 1981), 12.

Appendix (173)

Table A.3 US IMMIGRATION LAWS PERTAINING TO MIXED RACE KOREANS

Date	Popular Title	Description
August 7, 1953	Refugee Relief Act	Provided 4,000 non-quota immigrant visas for eligible orphans under 10 years old. Expired December 31, 1956.
September 11, 1957	Public Law 316	Extended the refugee orphan program for an unlimited number of eligible orphans under 14 years old. Expired June 30, 1959.
September 9, 1959	Public Law 253	Extended the refugee orphan program but required a home investigation made by Immigration and Naturalization Service and a social welfare agency. Expired June 30, 1960.
July 14, 1960	Public Law 648	Extended the refugee orphan program. Expired June 30, 1961.
September 26, 1961	Public Law 301	Amended the Immigration and Nationality Act to permanently provide an unlimited number of non-quota immigrant visas for children adopted abroad by US citizens or entering the United States to be adopted. Ended proxy adoption.

(174) Appendix

Table A.4 KOREAN CHILDREN SENT OVERSEAS FOR ADOPTION BY RACE AND YEAR

Year	Mixed Race	Non-Mixed	Total
1955	52	7	59
1956	618	53	671
1957	411	75	486
1958	623	307	930
1959	291	360	741
1960	245	393	638
1961	361	304	665
1962	158	96	254
1963	196	246	442
1964	232	230	462
1965	201	250	451
1966	249	245	494
1967	276	350	625
1968	317	632	949
1969	308	882	1,190
1970	361	1,517	1,932
Total	4,899	5,947	10,846

Source: Ministry of Health and Welfare, Statistical Yearbook on Welfare and Society, 1961 (Seoul, KR); Ministry of Health and Welfare, Statistics on Child Welfare, 1967 (Seoul, KR); Ministry of Health and Welfare, Statistical Yearbook on Welfare and Society, 1970 (Seoul, KR).

NOTES

PROLOGUE

1. The documents pertaining to Nicholas Rossow's marriage, dated June 6 to 17, 1949, can be found in United States Army Forces in Korea (USAFIK) Adjutant General, General Correspondence (Decimal Files) 1945–1949, National Archives at College Park (NARA), Records of General Headquarters, Far East Command, Supreme Commander of the Allied Powers, and United Nations Command (RG 554), Box 17.

2. While the Immigration Act of 1924 barred aliens racially ineligible for citizenship from entry into the United States, the ban on Asian naturalization was based on nationality laws from 1790 and 1870. Persons of Asian heritage who were born on US soil, however, were still entitled to US citizenship by birthright. For a fuller consideration of the Immigration Act of 1924, see Mae Ngai, *Impossible Subjects: Illegal Aliens and the Making of Modern America* (Princeton, NJ: Princeton University Press, 2004).

3. Public Law 213, approved by Congress on July 22, 1947, was amended as The War Brides Act of 1945 by a new section that read: "The alien spouse of an American citizen by a marriage occurring before thirty days after the enactment of this Act, shall not be considered as inadmissible because of race, if otherwise admissible under this Act." Under this law, Asian spouses of US servicemen would be eligible for entry into the United States if their marriages occurred within this brief time frame. An Act to Amend the Act Approved December 28, 1945 (Public Law 271, Seventy-ninth Congress), entitled "An Act to expedite the Admission to the United States of Alien Spouses and Alien Minor Children of Citizen Members of the United States Armed Forces," Public Law 213, *US Statutes at Large* 61 (1947): 401.

4. These 500 men would remain as part of the Korean Military Advisory Group: Bruce Cumings, *Korea's Place in the Sun: A Modern History* (New York: W. W. Norton), 212.

5. The use of the word "ruined" to describe Korean women who entertained or were involved romantically with US servicemen is very common. For an example of a camptown woman using the phrase to describe herself, see the oral history of "Ms. Noh" in Ji-Yeon Yuh, *Beyond the Shadow of Camptown: Korean Military Brides in America* (New York: New York University Press, 2002), 65.

6. Seungsook Moon's work examines the gendered nature of Korean nationality and family law. For a fuller consideration of these topics, see Seungsook Moon, "Begetting the Nation: The Androcentric Discourse of National History and Tradition in South Korea," in *Dangerous Women: Gender and Korean Nationalism*,

(176)   *Notes to pages xvii–1*

ed. Elaine Kim and Chungmoo Choi (New York: Routledge, 1998), 33–66; Seungsook Moon, *Militarized Modernity and Gendered Citizenship in South Korea*, (Durham, NC: Duke University Press, 2005).

7. In Occupied Germany and Britain, children born to foreign women and US servicemen were automatically conferred citizenship if their parents were married or if the father made a paternity claim. Historian Yukiko Koshiro even notes that this was the case in Occupied Japan. It does not seem to have been this easy in South Korea, where US military commanders continually refused to comply with such standard procedures present in other US occupation zones. For more, see Jenel Virden, *Good-bye, Piccadilly: British War Brides in America* (Urbana: University of Illinois Press, 1995); Yukiko Koshiro, *Trans-Pacific Racisms and the US Occupation of Japan* (New York: Columbia University Press, 1999); Heide Fehrenbach, *Race After Hitler: Black Occupation Children in Postwar Germany and America* (Princeton, NJ: Princeton University Press, 2005).

8. For more on the genealogy of Korea's ethnic nationalism, see Gi-Wook Shin, *Ethnic Nationalism in Korea: Genealogy, Politics, and Legacy* (Stanford, CA: Stanford University Press, 2006).

9. "Marriage of Enlisted Man to Korean National," June 16, 1949, USAFIK Adjutant General, Decimal Files 1945-1949, NARA, RG 554, Box 17.

10. Ibid.

11. Ibid.

12. "Marriage of Corporal Nicholas Rossow," June 13, 1949, USAFIK Adjutant General, Decimal Files 1945-1949, NARA, RG 554, Box 17.

13. "Marriage of Enlisted Man to Korean National," June 17, 1949, USAFIK Adjutant General, Decimal Files 1945-1949, NARA, RG 554, Box 17.

INTRODUCTION

1. Emma Jinha Teng, *Eurasians: Mixed Identities in the United States, China, and Hong Kong, 1842–1943* (Berkeley: University of California Press, 2013).

2. Nicholas Trajano Molnar, *American Mestizos, the Philippines, and the Malleability of Race, 1898–1961* (Columbia: University of Missouri Press, 2017).

3. US military presence in Korea began in September of 1945, when 72,000 American soldiers from the Twenty-Fourth Army Corps arrived to transfer power from the devastated Japanese imperial government: Seungsook Moon, "Regulating Desire, Managing Empire: US Military Prostitution in South Korea, 1945–1970," in *Over There: Living with the US Military Empire from World War Two to Present*, ed. Maria Höhn and Seungsook Moon (Durham, NC: Duke University Press, 2010), 41.

4. The year 1950, chosen "in recognition of the fact that our largest troop commitment to Korea occurred between the years of 1950–54," confirmed that mixed race Koreans were the first Amerasians. Those born on October 22, 1982 (the date of enactment), were the last: US Congress, Senate, Committee on Governmental Affairs, *Amerasian Immigration Proposals: Hearing Before the Subcommittee on Immigration and Refugee Policy of the Committee on the Judiciary*, 97th Cong., 2nd sess., June 21, 1983, 15; *An Act to Amend the Immigration and Nationality Act to Provide Preferential Treatment in the Admission of Certain Children of United States Citizens*, Public Law 359, *US Statutes at Large* 96 (1982): 1716–1717.

5. US Congress, *Amerasian Immigration Proposals*, 66 and 14.

6. Various congressmen have since proposed bills to broaden the definition of Amerasian. Some notable attempts occurred in 1985, 1991, 1993, 1997, and 2001.

7. Scholarly critiques about the Amerasian Immigration Act often center around the law's strict temporal and geographic boundaries as well as the fact that, to date, no provision confers upon mixed race individuals born illegitimately in Asia automatic rights of US citizenship. For some examples of these critiques, see Sue-Je Lee Gage, "The Amerasian Problem: Blood, Duty, and Race," *International Relations* 21, no. 1 (2007): 86–102; W. Taejin Hwang, "The 'Amerasian' Knot: Transpacific Crossings of 'GI Babies' from Korea to the United States," in *Race and Racism in Modern East Asia*, vol. 3, *Interactions, Nationalism, Gender and Lineage*, ed. Rotem Kowner and Walter Demel (Leiden, NL: Brill, 2015), 504–526; Sabrina Thomas, *Scars of War: The Politics of Paternity and Responsibility for the Amerasians of Vietnam* (Lincoln: University of Nebraska Press, 2021).

8. The verbiage "certain" mixed race children is taken from *An Act to Amend the Immigration and Nationality Act to Provide Preferential Treatment in the Admission of Certain Children of United States Citizens*, 1716.

9. In *Cold War Constructions*, Christian Appy and his contributors, seeking alternative interpretations beyond traditional diplomatic and military histories, explore "the ways in which US political culture has shaped specific foreign sites of Cold War conflict." Together, they demonstrate how "discourse has ideological resonance that extends well beyond conventional associations": Christian G. Appy, *Cold War Constructions: The Political Culture of United States Imperialism, 1945–1966* (Amherst: University of Massachusetts Press, 2000), 4.

10. Scholars have established that the ideology of American exceptionalism bolstered US military commitments in Korea and other parts of the world while simultaneously obscuring the violence and destruction brought about by those commitments. Some important works that situate themselves within such critical analyses of American exceptionalism include Amy Kaplan, "Left Alone with America: The Absence of Empire in the Study of American Culture," in *Cultures of United States Imperialism*, ed. Amy Kaplan and Donald Pease (Durham, NC: Duke University Press, 1993); Oscar Campomanes, "The New Empire's Forgetful and Forgotten Citizens: Unrepresentability and Unassimilability in Filipino-American Postcolonialities," *Critical Mass* 2, no. 2 (1995): 145–200; Julian Go and Anne F. Foster, *The American Colonial State in the Philippines: Global Perspectives* (Durham, NC: Duke University Press, 2003); Paul Kramer, *The Blood of Government: Race, Empire, the United States and the Philippines* (Chapel Hill: University of North Carolina Press, 2006); Sunaina Marr Maira, *Missing: Youth, Citizenship, and Empire after 9/11* (Durham, NC: Duke University Press, 2009); Jodi Kim, *Ends of Empire: Asian American Critique and the Cold War* (Minneapolis: University of Minnesota Press, 2010); Julian Go, *Patterns of Empire: The British and American Empires, 1688 to the Present* (Cambridge: Cambridge University Press, 2011).

11. The vast majority of Amerasians were brought to the United States via refugee law. The most obvious example is the Refugee Relief Act of 1953, which expired on December 31, 1956, but was renewed three times before permanent provisions for international adoption were made in US immigration law in 1961. Between 1953 and 1961, Americans adopted 2,601 mixed race Korean children under the category of "refugee orphan." Additionally, in 1987, when the Amerasian Homecoming Act was enacted, it allowed for Vietnamese Amerasians to immigrate to the United States through the Orderly Departure Program (ODP) convened by the United Nations High Commission for Refugees. Given the lack of diplomatic relations between the United States and the communist nations of Southeast Asia, Vietnamese Amerasians could not be processed for immigration

(178)   *Notes to pages 3–4*

through the Amerasian Immigration Act of 1982. The Amerasian Homecoming Act of 1987 would address this shortcoming by allowing Amerasians to immigrate through refugee law instead. From the Amerasian Homecoming Act, approximately 23,000 Vietnamese Amerasians and 67,000 of their relatives immigrated to the United States in the 1990s. This will be further explored in chapter 5, which engages more directly with the field of critical refugee studies and the following work: Yen Le Espiritu, *Body Counts: The Vietnam War and Militarized Refugees* (Oakland: University of California Press, 2014).

12. US Congress, *Amerasian Immigration Proposals: Hearing Before the Subcommittee on Immigration and Refugee Policy of the Committee on the Judiciary*, 78.

13. "Report of Inspection of the Administration of the Refugee Relief Act of 1953, as Amended, and Related Problems in the Countries of Southeast Asia and North Asia," on July 27, 1956, 84th Congress, 2nd sess., *Congressional Record 102*, pt. 11: 15283.

14. Caroline Chung Simpson, *An Absent Presence: Japanese Americans in Postwar American Culture, 1945–1960* (Durham, NC: Duke University Press, 2001); Ji-Yeon Yuh, *Beyond the Shadow of Camptown: Korean Military Brides in America* (New York: New York University Press, 2002); Christina Klein, *Cold War Orientalism: Asia in the Middlebrow Imagination, 1945–1961* (Berkeley: University of California Press, 2003); David L. Eng, "Transnational Adoption and Queer Diasporas," *Social Text* 21, no. 3 (Fall 2003): 1–37; Naoko Shibusawa, *America's Geisha Ally: Reimagining the Japanese Enemy* (Cambridge, MA: Harvard University Press, 2006); Susan Zeiger, *Entangling Alliances: Foreign War Brides and American Soldiers in the Twentieth Century* (New York: New York University Press, 2010); Susie Woo, *Framed by War: Korean Children and Women at the Crossroads of US Empire* (New York: New York University Press, 2019).

15. Penny Von Eschen, *Race Against Empire: Black Americans and Anticolonialism, 1937–1957* (Ithaca, NY: Cornell University Press, 1997); Mary Dudziak, *Cold War, Civil Rights: Race and the Image of American Democracy* (Princeton, NJ: Princeton University Press, 2000); Cindy I-Fen Cheng, *Citizens of Asian America: Democracy and Race during the Cold War* (New York: New York University Press, 2013).

16. I use the term "anti-Asian violence" to make clear the ways that US militarism and empire depend upon a structural devaluation of Asian lives and humanity or this idea that Asian lives are somehow "expendable in order to safeguard the freedoms promised by the nation-state." This also helps to connect transnational forms of violence (e.g., waging war, bombing and murdering civilians, taking children from birth mothers and giving them to adoptive American families, the discursive denial of all this as violence, etc.) to US-based domestic racism (e.g., hate crimes, racial violence, civil rights violations, structural inequality, etc.). I agree with historian Simeon Man when he argues that "anti-Asian violence is a part of the violence of the United States itself, that is, US imperialism." See Simeon Man, "Anti-Asian Violence and US Imperialism," *Race and Class* 62, no. 2 (2020): 24–33.

17. In just three years of combat, The Korean War ended with more than 5 million casualties, 3 million refugees, 10 million separated families, and 2 million children orphaned and displaced making the conflict vastly unpopular to international and domestic audiences alike. Most of the destruction and devastation wrought on the Korean peninsula was from US actions during the war. The US Air Force dropped some 635,000 tons of bombs and 32,557 tons of napalm leaving every village and city destroyed and leveling nearly every standing building in northern and central Korea. South Korean atrocities were also notable including

Notes to pages 4–6 *(179)*

the regular procurement of enemy and destitute girls for "comfort stations" (brothels) for Allied troops, the racketeering and blackmail of innocent civilians, and massive political killings. International correspondents reported on these American and South Korean misdeeds until censorship preventing criticism of the Allied forces rendered the war largely unknowable—"forgotten" to Americans before it was even over. Images of General MacArthur slaughtering innocent Korean women and children circulated in communist propaganda mirroring some of the civilian massacres that Americans engaged in, the most infamous of which is the harrowing tale of the bridge at No Gun Ri. For a fuller consideration of the Korean War, see Bruce Cumings, *The Korean War: A History* (New York: Modern Library, 2011).

18. Klein, *Cold War Orientalism*, 17.

19. US Congress, House, Committee on Un-American Activities, *The Kremlin's Espionage and Terror Organizations (Testimony of Petr S. Deriabin Former Officer of the USSR's Committee of State Security (KGB): Hearing Before the Committee on Un-American Activities*, 86th Cong., 1st sess., March 17, 1959, 1627–1629.

20. Penny Von Eschen, "Who's the Real Ambassador? Exploding Cold War Racial Ideology," in *Cold War Constructions: The Political Culture of United States Imperialism, 1945–1966* (Amherst: University of Massachusetts Press, 2000, ed. Christian Appy, 112.

21. Ann Stoler, *Carnal Knowledge and Imperial Power: Race and the Intimate in Colonial Rule* (Berkeley: University of California Press, 2002); Durba Ghosh, *Sex and Family in Colonial India: The Making of Empire* (Cambridge: Cambridge University Press, 2006); David Pomfret, *Youth and Empire: Trans-Colonial Childhoods in British and French Asia* (Stanford, CA: Stanford University Press, 2015).

22. Satoshi Mizutani, *The Meaning of White: Race, Class, and the 'Domiciled Community' in British India 1858–1930* (Oxford: Oxford University Press, 2011), 34.

23. Pomfret, *Youth and Empire*, 258.

24. Ann Stoler, "Sexual Affronts and Racial Frontiers: European Identities and the Cultural Politics of Exclusion in Colonial Southeast Asia," *Comparative Studies in Society and History* 34, no. 3 (July 1992), 525.

25. Ibid., 519.

26. Pomfret, *Youth and Empire*, 246.

27. Ibid.; "South Korea: Confucius' Outcasts," *Time*, December 10, 1965.

28. Pomfret, *Youth and Empire*, 258.

29. In January 1947, a circular from the headquarters of United States Army Forces in Korea instructed all male personnel "to refrain from association with Korean women," forbidding relations with local girls, "other than through the lowest form of prostitution": "Association with Korean Women," January 25, 1947, USAFIK, Decimal Files 1945–1949, NARA, RG 554, Box 50; Peggy Pascoe's insight that interracial intimacy has been historically constructed as illicit in the United States is helpful to understand this reaction: Peggy Pascoe, *What Comes Naturally: Miscegenation Law and the Making of Race in America* (New York: Oxford University Press, 2009).

30. Despite Public Law 213's amendment to the War Brides Act of 1945, which allowed the entry of Asian brides who married US servicemen during a brief thirty-day window during the summer of 1947, no Korean women immigrated under these provisions. It seems that this had to do with local military policy since, comparatively, immigration statistics record the entry of 757 Japanese brides of US citizens in the 1940s. For the full figures, see Table A.2 in the Appendix.

(180)   *Notes to pages 6–7*

31. Public Law 717, enacted August 19, 1950, revived the War Brides Act of 1945 (which had expired on December 28, 1948) while removing racial restrictions for Japanese and Korean women. Initially, the law was applicable only for those whose marriages occurred within "six months after enactment," but was later extended another six months. The McCarran-Walter Act (also known as the Immigration and Nationality Act of 1952) granted all spouses of US citizens (regardless of race) non-quota immigration status. The law also lifted racial restrictions on naturalization and re-designated what was previously the "Asiatic Barred Zone" as an "Asia-Pacific Triangle," for which quotas, rather than exclusion, applied. *An Act to Permit the Admission of Alien Spouses and Minor Children of Citizen Members of the United States Armed Forces*, Public Law 717, *US Statutes at Large 64* (1950): 464–465.

32. For instance, according to immigration statistics, in the 1950s approximately 30,000 Japanese brides immigrated to the United States as wives of US citizens while only 2,000 Korean women are recorded, despite comparable troop populations.

33. See Deborah Cohen's chapter on the British Nabob family's secret: Deborah Cohen, *Family Secrets: Shame and Privacy in Modern Britain* (New York: Oxford University Press, 2013), 13–46.

34. These longer-term bonds have largely been overlooked in studies of camptowns, which tend to focus on the issue of prostitution around US military bases. See Katharine Moon, *Sex Among Allies* (New York: Columbia University Press, 1997); Moon, "Regulating Desire, Managing Empire," 39–77; Na Young Lee, "The Construction of US Camptown Prostitution in South Korea: Trans/formation and Resistance" (PhD diss., University of Maryland, College Park, 2006); Na Young Lee, "The Construction of Military Prostitution in South Korea during the US Military Rule, 1945–1948," *Feminist Studies* 33, no. 3 (Fall 2007): 453–481; Sealing Cheng, *On the Move for Love: Migrant Entertainers and the US Military in South Korea* (Philadelphia: University of Pennsylvania Press, 2013); Jeong-Mi Park, " A Historical Sociology of the Korean Government's Policies on Military Prostitution in US Camptowns, 1953–1995: Biopolitics, State of Exception, and the Paradox of Sovereignty under the Cold War," *Korean Journal of Sociology* 49, no. 2 (April 2014), 1–33; Na-Young Lee, "Un/forgettable Histories of US Camptown Prostitution in South Korea: Women's Experiences of Sexual Labor and Government Policies," *Sexualities* 21, no. 5–6 (2018): 751–775; Jeong-Mi Park, "Liberation or Purification? Prostitution, Women's Movement and Nation Building in South Korea Under US Military Occupation, 1945–1948," *Sexualities* 22, no. 7–8 (2019): 1053–1070.

35. Voluntary agencies, press reports, and prospective adoptive parents referred to mixed race children by a variety of names at first. Examples such as "Eurasian," "Korean-American orphan," "little Korean outcasts," "Korean war orphan," "GI refugee children," can be found here: Senator Wayne Morse, Increase in Number of Visas to Be Issued to Orphans Under the Refugee Relief Act of 1953, on July 26, 1956, 84th Cong., 2nd sess., *Congressional Record* 102, pt. 11:14742–14743.

36. The origin story for the term "Amerasian" can be found in the following books: Peter Conn, *Pearl S. Buck: A Cultural Biography* (Cambridge: Cambridge University Press, 1996), 313; Pearl S. Buck and Theodore F. Harris, *For Spacious Skies* (New York: John Day, 1966), 54.

37. Teng, *Eurasians*, 6.

38. Ibid.

Notes to pages 7–8 (181)

39. Melvyn Leffler, *A Preponderance of Power: National Security, the Truman Administration, and the Cold War* (Stanford, CA: Stanford University Press, 1992).

40. Henry Luce, *The American Century* (New York: Farrar and Rinehart, 1941).

41. Melani McAlister, *Epic Encounters: Culture, Media, and US Interests in the Middle East Since 1945* (Berkeley: University of California Press, 2005), 235–265.

42. Christina Klein, "Family Ties and Political Obligation: The Discourse of Adoption and the Cold War Commitment to Asia," in *Cold War Constructions: The Political Culture of United States Imperialism, 1945–1966* (Amherst: University of Massachusetts Press, 2000), ed. Christian Appy, 35.

43. Laura Briggs, *Somebody's Children: The Politics of Transnational and Transracial Adoption* (Durham, NC: Duke University Press, 2012).

44. Although the field of critical adoption studies has turned scholarly focus away from the adoptive family and instead toward the experiences and cultures of adoptees themselves, it can be said that the search for birth mothers is still under way. One exception to this is Hosu Kim's ethnography of Korean birth mothers. See Hosu Kim, *Birth Mothers and Transnational Adoption Practice in South Korea: Virtual Mothering* (New York: Palgrave Macmillan, 2016.

45. Other important works in critical adoption studies that may or may not mention mixed race Koreans (but if so, do not center their lived historical experiences) include Eleana Kim, *Adopted Territory: Transnational Korean Adoptees and the Politics of Belonging* (Durham, NC: Duke University Press, 2010); Catherine Ceniza Choy, *Global Families: A History of Asian International Adoption in America* (New York: New York University Press, 2013); Soojin Pate, *From Orphan to Adoptee: US Empire and Genealogies of Korean Adoption* (Minneapolis: University of Minnesota Press, 2014); Arissa Oh, *To Save the Children of Korea: The Cold War Origins of International Adoption* (Stanford, CA: Stanford University Press, 2015); Kim Park Nelson, *Invisible Asians: Korean American Adoptees, Asian American Experiences, and Racial Exceptionalism* (New Brunswick, NJ: Rutgers University Press, 2016); Kimberly D. McKee, *Disrupting Kinship: Transnational Politics of Korean Adoption in the United States* (Champaign: University of Illinois Press, 2019); Kori Graves, *A War Born Family: African American Adoption in the Wake of the Korean War* (New York: New York University Press, 2020).

46. There is, however, a small body of work outside critical adoption studies that explores mixed race Koreans' lived historical experiences and position within broader South Korean society. See Margo Okazawa-Rey, "Amerasian Children of GI Town: A Legacy of US Militarism in South Korea," *Asian Journal of Women's Studies* 3 (1997): 71–102; Sue-Je Lee Gage, "Pure Mixed Blood: The Multiple Identities of Amerasians in South Korea" (PhD diss., Indiana University, 2007); Mary Lee, "Mixed Race Peoples in the Korean National Imaginary and Family," *Korean Studies* 32 (2008): 56–85; Yuri Doolan, "Being Amerasian in South Korea: Purebloodness, Multiculturalism, and Living Alongside the US Military Empire" (Honors thesis, Ohio State University, 2012).

47. Adoption professionals dealing with mixed race Koreans often did not conduct home studies or background checks of prospective adoptive parents, instead placing children by "proxy." This meant an American couple could avoid institutional red tape and quickly adopt remotely, through a power of attorney. "Proxy" adoptions represented an unconventional departure from what was considered the ethical social welfare practices of the time, and social welfare professionals hotly debated whether such an expedited method could be justified in the case of mixed race children, who were uniformly viewed as a vulnerable population. In

(182) Notes to pages 8–9

addition to the home studies and background checks, in typical adoptions, children remained in the custody of the state for a period of about one year, even as they lived with their prospective adoptive parents. During this time, social workers would regularly visit the adoptive family, making assessments about the home environment and the child's adjustment, until a final recommendation for adoption could be made. The "proxy" method did not involve local welfare institutions and instead skipped all of these safety measures intended to protect the child. Children from Korean orphanages were simply handed over to adoptive parents without any sort of follow up afterward.

48. This resonates with what Soojin Pate has called "militarized humanitarianism." For more, see introduction and chapter 1 of Pate, *From Orphan to Adoptee.*

49. There are other works in Korean American studies that also explore centrally these connections between US militarism, camptowns, and adoption. See Patti Duncan, "Genealogies of Unbelonging: Amerasians and Transnational Adoptees as Legacies of US Militarism in South Korea," in *Militarized Currents: Toward a Decolonized Future in Asia and the Pacific,* ed. Setsu Shigematsu and Keith L. Camacho (Minneapolis: University of Minnesota Press, 2010); Hosu Kim and Grace M. Cho, "The Kinship of Violence," in *Mothering in East Asian Communities: Politics and Practices,* ed. Patty Duncan and Gina Wong (Bradford, ON: Demeter Press, 2014), 31–52.

50. Edward Said first defined Orientalism as a Western mode of perceiving, understanding, and representing the East. This system of knowledge emerged as Occidental imperial powers engaged in colonization. Based on the material reality of unequal power relations, Orientalism is an essentializing and overexaggerating of difference in which the East serves as a contrasting and inferior image that helps to define the West. For instance, if the East is backward, irrational, childlike, and feminine then the West is progressive, rational, adult, and masculine. Since his seminal work, there have been a number of important studies on American Orientalism. See Edward W. Said, *Orientalism* (New York: Vintage Books, 1978); John Kuo Wei Tchen, *New York Before Chinatown: Orientalism and the Shaping of American Culture, 1776–1882* (Baltimore: Johns Hopkins University Press 2001); Klein, *Cold War Orientalism,* Mari Yoshihara, *Embracing the East: White Women and American Orientalism* (New York: Oxford University Press, 2003); Karen J. Leong, *The China Mystique: Pearl S. Buck, Anna May Wong, Mayling Soong, and the Transformation of American Orientalism* (Berkeley: University of California Press, 2005); Judy Tzu-Chun Wu, *Radicals on the Road: Internationalism, Orientalism, and Feminism during the Vietnam Era* (Ithaca, NY: Cornell University Press, 2013).

51. Yukiko Koshiro, *Trans-Pacific Racisms and the US Occupation of Japan* (New York: Columbia University Press, 1999), 159–200; Robert A. Fish, "The Heiress and the Love Children: Sawada Miki and the Elizabeth Saunders Home for Mixed-Blood Orphans in Postwar Japan" (PhD diss., University of Hawai'i, 2002); Lily Ann Yumi Welty, "Advantage Through Crisis: Multiracial American Japanese in Post–World War II Japan, Okinawa and America 1945–1972" (PhD diss., University of California Santa Barbara, 2012).

52. Donna Alvah, *Unofficial Ambassadors: American Military Families Overseas and the Cold War 1946–1965* (New York: New York University Press, 2007); Michael Cullen Green, *Black Yanks in the Pacific: Race in the Making of American Military Empire After World War II* (Ithaca, NY: Cornell University Press, 2010), 30–59.

53. Susan T. Petiss, "Effect of Adoption of Foreign Children on US Adoption Standards and Practices," *Child Welfare* 37 (1958): 27–32.

54. Kimberly D. McKee, "Monetary Flows and the Movements of Children: The Transnational Adoption Industrial Complex," *Journal of Korean Studies* 21, no. 1 (Spring 2016): 137.

55. This was a common request among white prospective adoptive parents interested in Korean War orphans during the years of 1954–1966.

56. This anecdote comes from International Social Service Case Records from 1956, found in Box 63, Folder 41310 at the Social Welfare History Archives held at the University of Minnesota.

57. These figures are from 2002: Kay Johnson, "Children of the Dust," *Time*, May 13, 2002.

58. Examples of this can be found in US Congress, Senate, Committee on the Judiciary, *Immigration Reform: Hearing Before the Subcommittee on Immigration, Refugees and International Law*, 97th Cong., 1st sess., October 14, 15, 21, 26, 28, November 12, 17, and 19, 1982; US Congress, *Amerasian Immigration Proposals*.

59. For important sources on Amerasians, see Thomas A. Bass, *Vietnamerica: The War Comes Home* (New York: Soho Press, 1996), Steven DeBonis, *Children of the Enemy: Oral Histories of Vietnamese Amerasians and Their Mothers* (Jefferson, NC: McFarland, 1995); Linda Kerber, "The Stateless as the Citizen's Other: A View from the United States," *American Historical Review* 112, no. 1 (2007): 1–34; Jana Lipman, "'The Face Is the Road Map': Vietnamese Amerasians in U.S. Political and Popular Culture, 1980–1988," *Journal of Asian American Studies* 14, no. 1 (2011): 33–68; Jana Lipman, "Mixed Voices, Mixed Policy: Vietnamese Amerasians in Vietnam and the United States" (Senior thesis, Brown University, 1997); Dana Sachs, *The Life We Were Given: Operation Babylift, International Adoption, and the Children of War in Vietnam* (Boston, MA: Beacon Press, 2010); Sabrina Thomas, "The Value of Dust: Policy, Citizenship and Vietnam's Amerasian Children" (PhD diss., Arizona State University, 2015); Sabrina Thomas, "Blood Politics: Reproducing the Children of 'Others' in the 1982 Amerasian Immigration Act," *Journal of American-East Asian Relations* 26, no. 1 (2019): 51–84; Thomas, *Scars of War*; Kieu-Lin Caroline Valverde, "From Dust to Gold: The Vietnamese Amerasian Experience," in *Racially Mixed People in America*, ed. Maria P. Root (Newbury Park, CA: Sage, 1992), 144–161; Allison Varzally, *Children of Reunion: Vietnamese Adoptions and the Politics of Family Migrations* (Chapel Hill: University of North Carolina Press 2017); Trin Yarborough, *Surviving Twice: Amerasian Children of the Vietnam War* (Washington, DC: Potomac Books 2005).

60. Sociologist Yen Le Espiritu argues that in the absence of a liberated Vietnam and people, the figure of the freed and reformed Vietnamese refugee became central to the "(re)cuperation of American identities and the shoring up of US militarism in the post-Vietnam War era." Given the analogous argument this study makes about the first Amerasians, one might suggest that mixed race Koreans are, in fact, Espiritu's "good refugee" predecessor by several decades: Espiritu, *Body Counts*, 2.

61. Bruce Cumings explains that the Korean War is both "a forgotten war and a never-known war." Forgotten because it is wedged between two global conflicts which hold a much more indelible position within collective historical memory (after all Korea's stalemate ending was ambivalent, while the good war was an outright victory and Vietnam "tore the United States apart"). Never-known because censorship and a culture of repression rendered the happenings in Korea unknowable even before it was over: Cumings, *The Korean War*, 62–63.

62. "The bridge at No Gun Ri" is the name of an incident in which US soldiers opened fire and air assault on Korean civilians in late July 1950, massacring

(184)   *Notes to pages 11–17*

hundreds—the majority of which were women and children. The harrowing tale was largely unknown and officially denied until a team of Associated Press investigative reporters broke the story in 1999 and published their findings later in a book: Charles J. Hanley, Martha Mendoza, and Sang-hun Choe, *The Bridge at No Gun Ri: A Hidden Nightmare from the Korean War* (New York: Holt Paperbacks, 2002).

63. Grace M. Cho, *Haunting the Korean Diaspora: Shame, Secrecy, and the Forgotten War* (Minneapolis: University of Minnesota Press, 2008), 50–88.

64. Cumings further notes: "It was the Korean War, not Greece or Turkey or the Marshall Plan or Vietnam, that inaugurated big defense budgets and the national security state, that transformed a limited containment doctrine into a global crusade, that ignited McCarthyism just as it seemed to fizzle, and thereby gave the Cold War its long run": Bruce Cumings, *War and Television* (New York: Verso, 1992), 148.

65. I take the lead from scholars who have furthered arguments about Korea's primacy to post–World War II modernity. In addition to the aforementioned works, another example of this can be found in Monica Kim, *The Interrogation Rooms of the Korean War: The Untold Story* (Princeton, NJ: Princeton University Press, 2019).

66. This book is, in many ways, also about "the United States in its entirety and its place in the world" as well as "society and the human condition broadly." It is informed by the field of Third World studies, described in Gary Okihiro, *Third World Studies: Theorizing Liberation* (Durham, NC: Duke University Press, 2016), 2.

67. These sources come from the military records of the Supreme Commander for Allied Powers, Far East Asia Command, Eighth US Army, US Army Military Government in Korea, US Forces Korea, the War Department, and the Adjutant General.

68. US Congress, Senate, Committee on the Judiciary, *Relating to General Immigration Matters: Hearing Held Before Subcommittee on Immigration and Naturalization of the Committee on the Judiciary— S. 116, 504, 925, 952, 954, 1196, 1280, 1468, 1523, 1532, 1610, 1919, 1996, 1974*, 86th Cong., 1st sess., vol. 1, May 20, 1959, 52.

69. US Congress, Senate, Committee on the Judiciary, *Indochina Evacuation and Refugee Problems (Part I: Operation Babylift & Humanitarian Needs): Hearing Before the Subcommittee to Investigate Problems Connected with Refugees and Escapees*, 94th Cong., 1st sess., April 8, 1975, 86–89.

CHAPTER 1

1. Crawford F. Sams, *Medic: The Mission of an American Military Doctor in Occupied Japan and Wartorn Korea* (Armonk, NY: M. E. Sharpe, 1998), 108.

2. Ibid.

3. For more on "comfort women," see Yoshimi Yoshiaki, *Comfort Women: Sexual Slavery in the Japanese Military During World War II* (New York: Columbia University Press, 2002); C. Sarah Soh, *The Comfort Women: Sexual Violence and Postcolonial Memory in Korea and Japan* (Chicago: University of Chicago Press, 2008).

4. This article, published in a leading African American newspaper, focused on the perspectives of Black personnel: Milton Smith, "GIs Spurn Korean Gals, Wait for Jap Lassies," *Chicago Defender*, December 16, 1950.

5. Ibid.

6. Ibid.

7. Ibid.

8. Ibid.

Notes to pages 17–19   *(185)*

9. Ibid.
10. Ibid.
11. I borrow the phrase "shack up" from a US military document: "Venereal Rate and Discipline," April 14, 1948, United States Army Forces in Korea (USAFIK) Adjutant General, General Correspondence (Decimal Files) 1945–1949, National Archives at College Park (NARA), Records of General Headquarters, Far East Command, Supreme Commander of the Allied Powers, and United Nations Command (RG 554), Box 147.
12. Seungsook Moon, "Regulating Desire, Managing Empire: US Military Prostitution in South Korea, 1945–1970," in *Over There: Living with the US Military Empire from World War Two to Present*, ed. Maria Höhn and Seungsook Moon (Durham, NC: Duke University Press, 2010), 41.
13. Taejin Hwang, "Militarized Landscapes of Yongsan: From Japanese Imperial to Little Americas in Early Cold War Korea," *Korea Journal* 58, no. 1 (Spring 2018): 127.
14. Won-sang Han, "The Japanese Armed Forces at War and their System of Sexual Slavery" in *Forced Prostitution in Times of War and Peace*, ed. Barbara Drinck and Chung-noh Gross (Bielefeld, DE: Kleine Verlag, 2007), 211–213.
15. Bruce Cumings, "Silent but Deadly: Sexual Subordination in the US-Korea Relationship," in *Let the Good Times Roll: Prostitution and the US Military in Asia*, ed. Saundra Pollack and Brenda Stoltzfus (New York: New Press, 1992): 174.
16. Tongŭn Pak, "Special Issue: South Korea and the US, Yanggongju and Mixed-Blood Children," *Shindonga* (September 1966): 277.
17. "Association with Korean Women," January 25, 1947, USAFIK, Decimal Files, NARA, RG 554, Box 50.
18. In the three years of its rule from 1945 to 1948, the United States declared itself the sole governing body south of the 38th parallel, overthrew the Korea People's Republic established by Korean independence activists just days prior to US arrival, and promoted pro-American anti-Communist Korean leadership including collaborators from the Japanese colonial era. As a result, southern Korea's three years under USAMGIK rule were marked by civilian uprisings, peasant rebellions, and violent political oppression—the worst of which occurred on Jeju on April 3, 1948, when an insurgency against the US/UN elections was labeled "communist" and up to 60,000 islanders were massacred by Korean military and police forces. By 1948 Syngman Rhee had been elected in the South with Kim Il Sung taking leadership of the North. By summer 1949, the US military withdrew with just 500 officers in the form of a military advisory group remaining to train the South Korean army. One year later, the Korean War would break. For a fuller consideration of the occupation era, see Bruce Cumings, *The Korean War: A History* (New York: Modern Library, 2011), 101–146.
19. "Association with Korean Women."
20. Ibid.
21. "Message from the Commanding General," January 17, 1947, USAFIK, Decimal Files, NARA, RG 554, Box 50.
22. Seungsook Moon, "Begetting the Nation: The Androcentric Discourse of National History and Tradition in South Korea," in *Dangerous Women: Gender and Korean Nationalism*, ed. Elaine Kim and Chungmoo Choi (New York: Routledge, 1998), 33–66.
23. My translation: "Special Product of 10 Years of Liberation: The Yanggongju," *Donga Daily*, August 18, 1955.

(186)   *Notes to pages 19–22*

24. My translation: Pak, "Special Issue," 277.
25. "Association with Korean Women."
26. In 1966, it was said that such pejoratives were the most severe insult any Korean women could receive: Pak, "Special Issue," 277.
27. "Venereal Control Program in South Korea," July 27, 1948, USAFIK, Decimal Files, NARA, RG 554, Box 147.
28. Ibid.
29. Dong-Won Shin, "Public Health and People's Health: Contrasting the Paths of Healthcare Systems in South and North Korea, 1945–60," in *Public Health and National Reconstruction in Post-War Asia: International Influences, Local Transformations*, ed. Liping Bu and Ka-Che Yip (New York: Routledge, 2015): 93.
30. Sams, *Medic*, 108.
31. Edward Grant Meade, *American Military Government in Korea* (New York: King's Crown Press, 1951): 220.
32. Jeong-Mi Park, "A Historical Sociology of the Korean Government's Policies on Military Prostitution in US Camptowns, 1953–1995: Biopolitics, State of Exception, and the Paradox of Sovereignty under the Cold War," *Korean Journal of Sociology* 49, no. 2 (April 2014): 8.
33. Katharine Moon, *Sex Among Allies* (New York: Columbia University Press, 1997), 156.
34. "Venereal Disease Council Meeting," April 5, 1948, USAFIK, Decimal Files, NARA, RG 554, Box 147.
35. Sams, *Medic*, 108.
36. Ibid.
37. "Venereal Disease Lecture," undated 1948, Adjutant General's Section Operations Division, Decimal Files, NARA, RG 554, Box 280.
38. Meade, *American Military Government in Korea*, 221.
39. Ibid., 221, 261.
40. "VD Council Meeting," January 7, 1948, USAFIK, Decimal Files, NARA, RG 554, Box 147.
41. "Venereal Control Program in South Korea."
42. Ibid.; "VD Control Program in South Korea," August 23, 1948, USAFIK, Decimal Files, NARA, RG 554, Box 147.
43. Ibid.
44. Sams, *Medic*, 107; "Venereal Control Program in South Korea."
45. "Venereal Control Program in South Korea."
46. Ibid.
47. Ibid.
48. Ibid.
49. Ibid.
50. Ibid.
51. In Japan, the US Occupation Forces had outlawed public prostitution two years prior on January 21, 1946. US military doctor Crawford Sams explains, "Holding human beings in bondage for any purpose could not be reconciled with our attempts to establish the basic premise of democracy, which is worth of the individual in the eyes of the law": Sams, *Medic*, 107.
52. "Venereal Control Program in South Korea."
53. Ibid.

Notes to pages 22–26 (187)

54. I borrow the term "circulation" from US documents, reflecting the military's view of Korean women as mere commodities.
55. "Venereal Disease Control," April 19, 1948, USAFIK, Decimal Files, NARA, RG 554, Box 147.
56. "Venereal Disease Council Meeting," April 5, 1948.
57. "Venereal Disease Council Meeting," September 30, 1948, USAFIK, Decimal Files, NARA, RG 554, Box 147.
58. This method was also utilized in Occupied Japan. See Sams, *Medic*, 106–107.
59. "Report: VD Control Council, 15 February–15 March 1948," April 11, 1948, USAFIK, Decimal Files, NARA, RG 554, Box 147.
60. "Report of Meeting of Venereal Disease Council," April 19, 1948, USAFIK, Decimal Files, NARA, RG 554, Box 147.
61. Ibid.
62. "Venereal Disease Council Meeting," May 11, 1948, USAFIK, Decimal Files, NARA, RG 554, Box 147.
63. "Major General Orlando Ward to Commanding General John R. Hodge, September 30, 1948," USAFIK, Decimal Files, NARA, RG 554, Box 147.
64. Ibid.
65. Ibid.
66. Ibid.
67. The VD Rehabilitation Center, housing about 200 "trainees" at a time, opened November 4, 1947, and closed September 15, 1948.
68. "Venereal Disease Rehabilitation Center," August 14, 1948, USAFIK, Decimal Files, NARA, RG 554, Box 147.
69. "Venereal Disease Rehabilitation Training Center," October 24, 1947, USAFIK, Decimal Files, NARA, RG 554, Box 147; "Visit to Venereal Disease Rehabilitation Center," December 15, 1947, USAFIK, Decimal Files, NARA, RG 554, Box 147; "Visit to USAFIK Venereal Disease Rehabilitation Training Center, Chinhae, Korea," January 20, 1948, USAFIK, Decimal Files, NARA, RG 554, Box 147.
70. "Venereal Disease Control," April 17, 1948, USAFIK, Decimal Files, NARA, RG 554, Box 147.
71. "Summary of Venereal Disease for Four Week Period Ending 24 September 1948," October 4, 1948, USAFIK, Decimal Files, NARA, RG 554, Box 147.
72. It is not completely clear how the US military categorized these women. However, "solicitors" might refer to "streetwalker"; "prostitutes" might refer to "kisaeng" and those working in "houses of prostitution" that had remained undetected and in operation; and "pickups" might refer to camptown locals: "Summary of Venereal Disease for Four Week Period Ending 24 September 1948."
73. "Venereal Disease Lecture."
74. Ibid.
75. Ibid.
76. "Minutes of Monthly Meeting, Character Guidance Control," January 22, 1948, USAFIK, Decimal Files, NARA, RG 554, Box 147.
77. "Venereal Disease Lecture."
78. "Venereal Rate and Discipline."
79. Ibid.
80. "Venereal Disease Council Meeting."
81. "Increase in Venereal Disease," August 17, 1947, USAFIK, Decimal Files, NARA, RG 554, Box 147.

(188) *Notes to pages 26–33*

82. "Personal Conduct," August 27, 1948, USAFIK, NARA, RG 554, Box 50.
83. "Meeting of the Venereal Disease Control Council," October 5, 1948, USAFIK, NARA, RG 554, Box 50; "Major General Orlando Ward to Commanding General John R. Hodge, May 21, 1948," USAFIK, Decimal Files, NARA, RG 554, Box 147.
84. "Meeting of the Venereal Disease Control Council," October 5, 1948, USAFIK, NARA, RG 554, Box 50; "Major General Orlando Ward to Commanding General John R. Hodge, May 21, 1948," USAFIK, Decimal Files, NARA, RG 554, Box 147.
85. Moon, "Regulating Desire, Managing Empire," 73.
86. "Colonel M. B. Bell to Commanding General John R. Hodge, November 20, 1948," USAFIK, Decimal Files, NARA, RG 554, Box 147.
87. "Meeting of the Venereal Disease Control Council," September 2, 1948, USAFIK, Decimal Files, NARA, RG 554, Box 147.
88. "Venereal Disease Council Meeting," September 30, 1948.
89. "Venereal Disease Council," November 20, 1948, USAFIK, Decimal Files, NARA, RG 554, Box 147.
90. "Colonel M. B. Bell to Commanding General John R. Hodge, November 20, 1948."
91. "Factors Influencing Venereal Disease Rates in this Command," undated 1949, USAFIK, Decimal Files, NARA, RG 554, Box 147.
92. Ibid.
93. Ralph Loren, "The Historic Role of Military Preventative Medicine and Public Health in US Armies of Occupation and Military Government," in *Military Preventative Medicine: Mobilization and Deployment*, vol. 1, ed. Patrick Kelley (Washington, DC: Office of the Surgeon General at TMM Publications, 2003), 71.
94. For more on military prostitution in Japan, see Michiko Takeuchi, "'Pan-Pan Girls' Performing and Resisting Neocolonialism(s) in the Pacific Theater: US Military Prostitution in Occupied Japan, 1945–1952," in *Over There: Living with the US Military Empire from World War Two to Present*, ed. Maria Höhn and Seungsook Moon (Durham, NC: Duke University Press, 2010), 78–108; Robert Kramm, *Sanitized Sex: Regulating Prostitution, Venereal Disease, and Intimacy in Occupied Japan, 1945–1952* (Oakland: University of California Press, 2017).
95. The phrase "workshop of democracy" to refer to postwar Japan is used in Takeuchi, "'Pan-Pan Girls' Performing and Resisting Neocolonialism(s) in the Pacific Theater."
96. Hwang, "Militarized Landscapes of Yongsan," 126.
97. Ibid.
98. Ibid.
99. "General Headquarters Far East Command Character Guidelines," Feb 9, 1949, Adjutant General's Section Operations Division, NARA, RG 554, Box 168.
100. Ibid.
101. Ibid.
102. At one point the "the colored rate was 15 times as great as the white rate." "Discipline and Venereal Disease," March 24, 1947, USAFIK, Decimal Files, NARA, RG 554, Box 147.
103. Michael Cullen Green, *Black Yanks in the Pacific: Race in the Making of American Military Empire After World War II* (Ithaca, NY: Cornell University Press, 2010), 30–59.
104. *An Act to Expedite the Admission to the United States of Alien Spouses and Alien Minor Children of Citizen Members of the United States Armed Forces*, Public Law 271, *US Statutes at Large* 59 (1945): 659; *An Act to Limit the Immigration of Aliens*

into the United States, and for Other Purposes, Public No. 139, *US Statutes at Large* 43 (1924): 159.

105. See chapter 1 in Masako Nakamura, "Families Precede Nation and Race?: Marriage, Migration, and Integration of Japanese War Brides after World War II" (PhD diss., University of Minnesota, 2010), 23–74.

106. *An Act to Amend the Act Approved December 28, 1945 (Public Law 271, Seventy-ninth Congress), Entitled "An Act to Expedite the Admission to the United States of Alien Spouses and Alien Minor Children of Citizen Members of the United States Armed Forces,"* Public Law 213, *US Statutes at Large* 61 (1947): 401.

107. US Congress, Senate, Committee on the Judiciary, *Amending the Act to Expedite the Admission to the United States of Alien Spouses and Alien Minor Children of Citizen Members of the United States Armed Forces*, 80th Cong., 1st sess., July 11, 1947.

108. *Joint Resolution to Authorize the Completion of the Processing of Visa Cases, and Admission into the United States, of Certain Alien Fiancés, and Fiancées of Members, or of Former Members, of the Armed Forces of the United States, as was Provided in the so-called GI Fiancées Act (60 Stat. 339), as Amended*, Public Law 51, *US Statutes at Large* 63 (1949): 56–57.

109. "Asian Women Immigrants Admitted to US as Wives of American Citizens by Country of Origin and Year," US Commissioner of Immigration and Naturalization, Annual Reports, 1947–77, Table 6 (Washington, DC), reprinted in Bok-Lim Kim, *Women in Shadows: A Handbook for Service Providers Working with Asian Wives of US Military Personnel* (La Jolla, CA: National Committee Concerned with Asian Wives of US Servicemen, 1981), 12.

110. "Privileges of Japanese Married to US Citizens," October 3, 1946, Eighth US Army (EUSA) 1944–56, Adjutant General Section, Decimal Files, NARA, Records of US Army Operational, Tactical, and Support Organizations World War II and Thereafter (RG 338), Box 163.

111. "Marriage of Military and Civilian Personnel," June 26, 1948, EUSA, Decimal Files, NARA, RG 338, Box 361.

112. "Eligibility for Dependent Housing for Personnel Marrying in Japan," October 1, 1947, EUSA, Decimal Files, NARA, RG 338, Box 361.

113. "Permission to Marry," April 1, 1948, USAFIK, Decimal Files, NARA, RG 554, Box 52.

114. Ibid.

115. "Marriage of American Occupation Personnel to Japanese Nationals," April 21, 1947, EUSA, Decimal Files, NARA, RG 338, Box 672.

116. "Colonel J. W. Donnell to Mr. Harelson M. Alling, August 19, 1948," EUSA, Decimal Files, NARA, RG 338, Box 361.

117. "Sergeant Louis Broaddus to Senator Paul H. Douglas, August 9, 1956," EUSA, Decimal Files, NARA, RG 338, Box 645.

118. "Marriage of Military and War Department Civilian Personnel," January 13, 1947, EUSA, Decimal Files, NARA, RG 338, Box 320.

119. "Reconsideration on Application for Permission to Marry," September 14, 1948, EUSA, Decimal Files, NARA, RG 338, Box 361.

120. Ibid.

121. Ibid.

122. "Marriage of Japanese Nationals," December 27, 1948, EUSA, Decimal Files, NARA, RG 338, Box 672.

(190)   *Notes to pages 36–38*

123. "Permission to Marry," August 3, 1948, EUSA, Decimal Files, NARA, RG 338, Box 672.
124. Ibid.
125. Ibid.
126. "Marriage of US Citizen to Japanese National," July 27, 1948, EUSA, Decimal Files, NARA, RG 338, Box 672.
127. "Marriage of Japanese Nationals."
128. "Application for Permission to Marry," February 20, 1948, "Marriage of Japanese Nationals," December 27, 1948, EUSA, Decimal Files, NARA, RG 338, Box 672.
129. Examples of some of these monthly reports, titled "Report of Pregnant Japanese National Wives of Department of Army Civilian Employees and Military Personnel," can be found in EUSA, Decimal Files, NARA, RG 338, Box 361.
130. The difference in suitable living conditions for military spouses in Occupied Japan versus Korea is evident in the following note: "Because of the unsuitability of available quarters, other than dependent housing, for the care of mother and child during the early post-natal period, it is essential that pregnant women be removed from Korea sufficiently far in advance to withstand the hazards of travel with safety. In addition to the safety factor, the time required in which to arrange suitable passage operates to require early action in such cases." This document, showcasing the US military's careful treatment of pregnant military spouses, can be found here: "Pregnancy," November 7, 1948, "Marriage of Japanese Nationals," December 27, 1948, EUSA, Decimal Files, NARA, RG 338, Box 645.
131. Despite this, Korean and US newspaper records made note of a few marriages occurring in the summer of 1947 and the presence of Korean military brides in Hawai'i, respectively. Some incomplete records of approved marriages from 1948 are also present in USAFIK, Decimal Files, NARA, RG 554, Box 52. This all seems to suggest that some servicemen succeeded in getting their wives to Hawai'i. Because Hawai'i did not achieve statehood until 1959, immigration statistics suggest that no Korean military brides entered the US in the 1940s. The comparative figure for Japanese brides entering the mainland United States is 757.
132. "Request for Marriage," January 27, 1949, USAFIK, Decimal Files, NARA, RG 554, Box 17.
133. "Application for Permission to Marry," February 12, 1949, USAFIK, Decimal Files, NARA, RG 554, Box 17.
134. "Application to Marry," March 28, 1949, USAFIK, Decimal Files, NARA, RG 554, Box 17.
135. "Request for Permission to Marry," April 12, 1949, USAFIK, Decimal Files, NARA, RG 554, Box 17.
136. "Untitled Disposition Form," April 1, 1949, USAFIK, Decimal Files, NARA, RG 554, Box 17.
137. "Infraction of Orders," April 18, 1949, USAFIK, Decimal Files, NARA, RG 554, Box 17.
138. "Request for Permission to Marry," April 11, 1949, USAFIK, Decimal Files, NARA, RG 554, Box 17.
139. "Marriage of Corporal Nicholas Rossow," June 7, 1949, USAFIK, Decimal Files, NARA, RG 554, Box 17.
140. "Marriage of Corporal Nicholas Rossow," June 13, 1949, USAFIK, Decimal Files, NARA, RG 554, Box 17.

Notes to pages 38–40 (191)

141. Ibid.

142. In the postwar era, the Japanese American Citizens League would be instrumental in lobbying the US Congress to repeal racial restrictions in US immigration and naturalization laws. In 1950, Public Law 717, which would allow Nisei serving in Occupied Japan to bring their Japanese wives and children stateside, was viewed as a compromise before more widespread legislation was passed in the form of the McCarran Walter Act of 1952. For more on this, see chapter 1 in "Families Precede Nation and Race? Marriage, Migration, and Integration of Japanese War Brides after World War II," 23–74. Furthermore, US servicemen themselves were also keen to point out the contradictions of US branded democracy. Frustrated because "chaplains of many units of the Armed Forces [were] orienting American soldiers so as to stop the increasing rate of intermarriage of white Americans to colored Orientals," a soldier of enlisted rank argued that "American foreign policy cannot win friends in the Far East no matter how much money we spend as long as [we] continue to destroy the practical precepts of human equality." Arguments such as this highlighted how US citizens often utilized marriages between servicemen and Asian brides to espouse the imperatives of racial pluralism and Cold War liberalism: "Re: Alleged Segregation on Okinawa," Army Adjutant General, Decimal File 1953–54, NARA, The War Department and the Army Records (RG 407), Box 129. One of the best examples of this Cold War narrative can be found in "A War Bride Named 'Blue' Comes Home," *Life*, November 5, 1951: 40–41.

143. *An Act to Permit the Admission of Alien Spouses and Minor Children of Citizen Members of the United States Armed Forces*, Public Law 717, US Statutes at Large 64 (1950): 464–465.

144. *An Act to Revise the Laws Relating to Immigration, Naturalization, and Nationality; and for Other Purposes*, Public Law 414, US Statutes at Large 66 (1952): 163–281.

145. For the full figures, see Table A.2 in the Appendix.

146. Colonel Joseph H. McNinch, "Venereal Disease Problems, US Army Forces, Far East 1950–53," *Medical Science Publication* 4, vol. 2 (April 1954): 145.

147. The reestablishment of the "comfort women" system during the Korean War reflects how the US military reinstated many Japanese collaborators (due to their anti-communist and pro-American sensibilities) into the South Korean government and military leadership following so-called liberation.

148. Headquarters of the Republic of Korea (ROK) Army, *War History on the Homefront: Volume on Personnel Affairs* (Seoul, KR: Headquarters of the ROK Army, 1956), 148; Moon, "Regulating Desire, Managing Empire," 51.

149. My translation of Sumin Pak's oral history in Sunlit Sisters' Center, *Oral Histories of the Sunlit Sisters' Center's Grandmothers: Part IV* (Pyongtaek, KR: Sunlit Sisters' Center, 2013), 19.

150. Moon, "Regulating Desire, Managing Empire," 52.

151. Bruce Cumings, *North Korea: Another Country* (New York: New Press, 2003), 35.

152. Moon, "Regulating Desire, Managing Empire," 52.

153. ROK Army, *War History on the Homefront*, 150.

154. Ibid.

155. Ibid., 148.

156. Ibid.

157. "United Nations Civil Affairs Activities in Korea: United Nations Command Monthly Summary," November 1952, Military Historian's Office, Organizational History Files, Records of United States Army, Pacific (RG 550), Box 75, 49.

(192) Notes to pages 40–44

158. "Civil Affairs Activities in Korea," April 1953, Military Historian's Office, Organizational History Files, RG 550, Box 76, 51.

159. ROK Army, *War History on the Homefront*, 149.

160. In the same year, the South Korean government passed the "Act on the Prevention of Infectious Diseases," under the pressures of the US military, which provided, for the first time, a legal basis for VD screening in camptowns. Under the guise of public health and sanitation, the law required that women working in service sector jobs handling consumable goods be required to regularly undergo sexual health examinations. Around permanent US military installations the South Korean government built VD clinics, dispatched health officials, and the US military provided medics and penicillin: Jeong-Mi Park, "A Historical Sociology of the Korean Government's Policies on Military Prostitution in US Camptowns, 1953–1995: Biopolitics, State of Exception, and the Paradox of Sovereignty under the Cold War," *Korean Journal of Sociology* 49, no. 2 (April 2014): 10.

161. "Marriage Applications," September 11, 1951, EUSA, Decimal Files, NARA, RG 338, Box 491.

162. Ibid.

163. "Application for Permission to Marry," March 16, 1956, EUSA, Decimal Files, NARA, RG 338, Box 644.

164. "PFC Garry Choat," March 3, 1956, EUSA, Decimal Files, NARA, RG 338, Box 644.

165. "Certificate from Headquarters Metropolitan Police Bureau (Seoul, Korea)—Chung Sang Soon," March 14, 1956, EUSA, Decimal Files, NARA, RG 338, Box 644.

166. Ruth Keller, interview by author.

167. Moon, *Sex Among Allies*, 27.

168. Park, "A Historical Sociology of the Korean Government's Policies on Military Prostitution in US Camptowns," 10.

169. "Major General John J. Binns to Mr. Carl W. Strom, April 30, 1956," EUSA, Decimal Files, NARA, RG 338, Box 645.

170. According to immigration statistics, in the 1960s Japanese wives (24,987) of US citizens more than doubled that of Korean women (11,641). For the full figures, see Table A.2 of the Appendix.

171. This verbiage is borrowed from the title of a magazine article covering the adoption of a Korean war waif by a US serviceman: "A New American Comes 'Home,'" *Life*, November 30, 1953.

172. "Visit to Korea: November 21st–30th, 1956," Box 35, Folder 38, International Social Service, United States of America Branch (ISS-USA) Papers, Social Welfare History Archives at the University of Minnesota (SWHA).

173. "A New American Comes 'Home.'"

CHAPTER 2

1. All names in this document have been changed to protect the identities of the individuals involved.

2. The historical records of the International Social Service, United States of America Branch, Inc. (ISS-USA, located in Baltimore, MD) on which this study is based are held by the Social Welfare History Archives at the University of Minnesota (SWHA, in Minneapolis, MN). Permission for their use in this research project was granted by ISS-USA. For more information, see http://www.

iss-usa.org and http://special.lib.umn.edu/swha. Further, points of view in this book are those of the author and do not necessarily represent the official position or polices of ISS-USA: "Lee Soon Ja to Anderson," December 28, 1959, Case No. 591535, Box 115, ISS-USA Case Records, SWHA.

3. "Emilie T. Strauss (ISS-USA, Supervisor) to Eileen Marshall (Anchorage Department of Public Welfare, District Representative), January 21, 1960," Case No. 591535, Box 115, ISS-USA Case Records, SWHA.

4. "Dove M. Kull (Alaska Department of Public Welfare, Child Welfare Worker) to Suzanne M. Tierney (ISS-USA, Case Consultant), January 12, 1960," Case No. 591535, Box 115, ISS-USA Case Records, SWHA.

5. "The problem of the mixed blood child" was an expression commonly used by adoption advocates and other American humanitarians during the 1950s and 1960s. This verbiage appears in numerous social work documents cited throughout this chapter. Despite the phrase's problematic conflation of blood with race, "the problem of the mixed blood child" was an idea employed to advocate the removal of thousands of mixed race children from South Korean camptowns. It is therefore useful in our consideration of the Amerasian as a social, cultural, and political construction—not a biological reality.

6. Anne Norman, "Babies GIs Left Behind Are Tragic Aftermath of Wars: War Baby Tragedy," *Los Angeles Times*, October 23, 1957; "Holt Press Release," October 14, 1955, private collection of Molly Holt (chairperson of Holt Children's Services, Ilsan, South Korea), cited in Susie Woo, "A New American Comes 'Home'": Race, Nation, and the Immigration of Korean War Adoptees, 'GI Babies,' and Brides" (PhD diss., Yale University, 2010), 136.

7. Norman, "Babies GIs Left Behind Are Tragic Aftermath of Wars."

8. "Brown Babies Under Hardship in Orient," *Philadelphia Tribune*, February 1, 1955.

9. Inez Robb, "A Fairy Story Come True," *Boston Globe*, December 24, 1955; William Hilliard, "Children Die in Holt's Korean Orphanage While Congress Holds Up Relief Legislation," *The Oregonian*, July 7, 1957.

10. "Child Study, August 31, 1959," Case No. 591535, Box 115, ISS-USA Case Records, SWHA.

11. "Suzanne M. Tierney (ISS-USA, Case Consultant) to Eileen Marshall (Anchorage Department of Public Welfare, District Representative), October 8, 1959," Case No. 591535, Box 115, ISS-USA Case Records, SWHA.

12. "Suzanne M. Tierney (ISS-USA, Case Consultant) to Eileen Marshall (Anchorage Department of Public Welfare, District Representative), September 9, 1959," Case No. 591535, Box 115, ISS-USA Case Records, SWHA.

13. "Suzanne M. Tierney (ISS-USA, Case Consultant) to Eileen Marshall (Anchorage Department of Public Welfare, District Representative), October 8, 1959."

14. "Emilie T. Strauss (ISS-USA, Supervisor) to Eileen Marshall (Anchorage Department of Public Welfare, District Representative), January 21, 1960."

15. For a full set of figures on Korean children sent overseas for adoption by race and year, see Table A.4 in the Appendix.

16. "Notes on Field Visit-ISS Korea Staff, July 12, 1962," Box 35, Folder 26, ISS-USA Papers, SWHA.

17. "Bachelor Father: Korean Boy Adopted by GI Comes to US," *Los Angeles Times*, November 23, 1953.

18. Ibid.

19. Ibid.

(194)   *Notes to pages 48–51*

20. ISS field studies in camptowns reveal that US military commanders were quite brazen about such prejudicial behavior, even well into the 1960s: "Visit to Korea, June 23 to July 6, 1965," Box 35, Folder 2, ISS-USA Papers, SWHA; "Notes on Field Visit-ISS Korea Staff, July 12, 1962."

21. For this example, see "Report of Visit to Korea, June 18 to July 13, 1962," Box 35, Folder 26, ISS-USA Papers, SWHA.

22. William Hilliard, "Mothers of Mixed Bloods Have Hard Life in Korea," *The Oregonian*, December 18, 1956.

23. Ibid.

24. American GIs marrying Korean women during this era could hear phrases like this from their loved ones and military superiors, many who aggressively opposed their plans to bring their Korean brides and families stateside. In some cases, GIs were introduced to "decent American girls" in an attempt to persuade their disengagement from their families left behind in South Korea following sudden reassignments or red tape delays. Other times they were told they would be disowned by parents and other family members if they were to go back to South Korea for their Korean wives and children. Such behavior on part of Americans encouraged the abandonment of Korean wives and children and resembled earlier European practices of leaving illegitimate families behind in colonial possessions while maintaining legitimate families in the metropole.

25. Examples of this pipeline to prostitution can be found in the following field studies: Anne Davison, "The Mixed Racial Child," undated 1961, Box 34, Folder 22, ISS-USA Papers, SWHA; "Report of Visit to Korea, June 18 to July 13, 1962."

26. Tongǔn Pak, "Special Issue: South Korea and the US, Yanggongju and Mixed-Blood Children," *Shindonga* (September 1966): 276–298.

27. Margaret A. Valk, "Adjustment of Korean-American Children in Their American Adoptive Homes," undated 1957, Box 10, Folder 2, ISS-USA Papers, SWHA.

28. "Visit to Korea: November 21st–30th, 1956," Box 35, Folder 28, ISS-USA Papers, SWHA.

29. Ibid.

30. "First Korean War Baby Brought Here by Nurse," *Los Angeles Times*, December 21, 1953.

31. Ibid.

32. Ibid.

33. Arissa Oh, *To Save the Children of Korea: The Cold War Origins of International Adoption* (Stanford, CA: Stanford University Press, 2015), 53.

34. "Seoul Sanitarium and Hospital Orphanage," *The Record: Southwestern Union Conference of Seventh Day Adventists* 53, no. 4 (January 27, 1954): 1.

35. Eleana Kim, *Adopted Territory: Transnational Korean Adoptees and the Politics of Belonging* (Durham, NC: Duke University Press, 2010), 60–61; Oh, *To Save the Children of Korea*, 55.

36. In their outreach to the American public, humanitarians spearheading South Korea's postwar recovery were keen to describe their efforts in the language of the Cold War, positioning Korean women and children, in particular, as helpless victims of communist aggression and worthy beneficiaries of US aid. This provided a sturdy foundation for imagining mixed race Koreans in similar Cold War terms later on. For example, to entice Americans to donate their money to Korea's postwar recovery, Leonard Mayo, then director of the Association for the Aid of Crippled Children and member of the Rusk Mission to Korea, argued that "the children of South Korea are a symbol of Korea's plight and by the same token

they offer the free world a receptive soil for a fruitful demonstration of democracy." Pleas for US dollars like this one generally used the figure of the war waif or orphan to help US citizens understand the geopolitical significance of South Korea in a broader Cold War project of containment. This made clear that while military conflict had ended, the war was far from over on ideological grounds. Furthermore, because the Korean War was vastly unpopular and, in particular, the brutality of the US military in that conflict had tarnished the image of Americans as benevolent liberators, a successful postwar recovery campaign served as an alternative entry point for imagining US relations with Asian people and helped to absolve US violence: Leonard W. Mayo, "2,000 Reasons to Help South Korea," *New York Times Sunday Magazine*, August 2, 1953; Dr. J Calvitt Clarke, "Am I My Brother's Keeper?" *New York Times*, November 9, 1952.

Additionally, popular television programs at the time, like *The Loretta Young Show*, also made similar arguments about children and the importance of donating US dollars to the postwar recovery of South Korea. See *The Loretta Young Show*, "Dateline Korea," episode no. 5430, National Broadcasting Company, March 13, 1955.

37. Bob Stein, "Two Hundred and Forty Korean Children Have Arrived in the States via Orphan Airlift—Idea Was Conceived by Oregon Farmer Who Adopted Eight War Orphans Himself—He Has Since Built Orphanage in Seoul to Coordinate Mass Adoption Program," *Post Dispatch*, February 26, 1957.

38. Because many of the organizations participating in the postwar recovery of South Korea had religious affiliations, the cultural work surrounding these efforts often positioned Christianity at odds with godless communist tyranny. Such narratives connected religious persecution with US Cold War efforts in South Korea and appealed to Christian constituents making monetary contributions. For example, in 1951, a Christian Children's Fund advertisement asking Americans to symbolically "adopt" a homeless Korean child for $10 a month, argued that many "newly created orphans" had parents who were "slaughtered by the Reds because they were Christians." The video showed to the Holts reprised this martyrdom. See Dr. J. Calvitt Clarke, "In Korea: 'Operation Kiddie Car,'" *New York Herald Tribune*, September 2, 1951.

39. Oh, *To Save the Children of Korea*, 90.

40. Stein, "Two Hundred and Forty Korean Children Have Arrived in the States Via Orphan Airlift."

41. Bertha Holt, *Bring My Sons from Afar: The Unfolding of Harry Holt's Dream* (Eugene, OR: Holt International Children's Services, 1986), 2–3.

42. Rev. H. P. Sconce, "Operation Babylift," *Guideposts Magazine* 11, no. 7 (September 1956).

43. Stein, "Two Hundred and Forty Korean Children Have Arrived in the States Via Orphan Airlift."

44. Sconce, "Operation Babylift."

45. Ibid.

46. Oh, *To Save the Children of Korea*, 92.

47. "Families Welcome 12 Korean Orphans," *Baltimore Sun*, October 15, 1955; "Oregonian Takes 8 Seoul Orphans: Farmer, Aided by an Act of Congress, Is Flying Them Here from Korea," *New York Times*, October 2, 1955.

48. A so-called eligible orphan was, according to the Refugee Relief Act, a child under the age of ten years old whose parents had either died or disappeared, or abandoned, deserted, or irrevocably released them. While all eight Holt children could

(196) *Notes to pages 53–55*

have technically entered through the McCarran Walter Act of 1952, adopted children of American citizens were entitled to fourth preference status, which, at the time, was "heavily oversubscribed, resulting in over a 2-year wait." As a result, a private bill in addition to the Refugee Relief Act's eligible orphan provisions was the most efficient way to expedite the immigration of all eight Holt children: US Congress, Senate, Committee on the Judiciary, *Certain Korean War Orphans: Report to Accompany S. 2312*, 84th Cong., 1st sess., 1955, S. Rep. 1216, 3.

49. *An Act for the Relief of Certain Korean War Orphans*, Public Law 475, *US Statutes at Large* 69 (1955): A161; "'Pied Piper' Corrals 12 Korean Babies, Flies Them to America for Adoption," *Washington Post and Times Herald*, October 14, 1955.

50. Oh, *To Save the Children of Korea*, 92.

51. "Oregonian Takes 8 Seoul Orphans"; Senator Richard L. Neuberger, speaking on "Mr. and Mrs. Harry Holt of Creswell, Oregon and Eight Korean War Orphans," on July 30, 1955, 84th Congress, 1st sess., *Congressional Record* 101, pt. 10: 10706.

52. Oh, *To Save the Children of Korea*, 92.

53. "'Stork' Plane Brings 12 Korean Foundlings," *Washington Post and Times Herald*, October 15, 1955.

54. Oh, *To Save the Children of Korea*, 92.

55. Stein, "Two Hundred and Forty Korean Children Have Arrived in the States via Orphan Airlift."

56. "'Pied Piper' Corrals 12 Korean Babies."

57. "8 Korean Waifs at Family Table," *The Sun*, November 25, 1955.

58. Although the term "Operation Babylift" is more likely to invoke images of the orphan airlift in South Vietnam upon the collapse of the Saigon government in 1975, it was first used to describe the efforts of Harry Holt toward mixed race Koreans: Kenneth Ishii, "Victims of War: Soft Hearted Farmer Helps in Widespread Adoptions," *Atlanta Daily World*, April 7, 1956.

59. "Parents of 6 Fill Home with Korean Orphans," *Daily Boston Globe*, April 18, 1957.

60. William Hilliard, "Holt Pushes Waif Airlift—Creswell Farmer Races Against Time, Government Redtape in Mercy Plan," *The Oregonian*, December 15, 1956.

61. Ibid; US Congress, Senate, Committee on the Judiciary, *Amendments to Refugee Relief Act 1953: Hearing Before the Subcommittee of the Committee on the Judiciary United States Senate Eighty-Fourth Congress Second Session on S. 3570, S. 3571, S. 3372, S. 3573. S. 3574, and S. 3606 Bills to Amend the Refugee Relief Act of 1953, So as to Increase the Number of Orphan Visas and Raise the Age; Extend the Life of the Act; Permit Issuance of Visas to Persons Afflicted with Tuberculosis; Permit the Giving of Assurances by Recognized Voluntary Agencies: Provide for the Reallocation of Visas, and Change the Conditions Under Which Visas May Be Issued to Refugees in the Far East*, 84th Cong., 2nd sess., May 3, 1956, 14.

62. Jack Brown, "Child Census in Korea Ordered—Holt Gains Rhee's Help in Waif Job," *Register Guard*, April 9, 1956.

63. "Oregon Farmer Brings 12 More Orphans from Korea for New Homes in America," *Oregonian*, April 8, 1956; "Adopter of 8 Koreans Off to Get 200 More," *New York Times*, March 26, 1956.

64. Brown, "Child Census in Korea Ordered."

65. Stein, "Two Hundred and Forty Korean Children Have Arrived in the States Via Orphan Airlift."

66. Hilliard, "Mothers of Mixed Bloods Have Hard Life in Korea."

67. "Visit to Korea: November 21st–30th, 1956."

Notes to pages 55–59 (197)

68. William Hilliard, "GIs Welcome at Orphan Homes in Korea—Some Servicemen Adopt Forgotten Waifs," *The Oregonian*, December 27, 1956.
69. "Oregon Farmer Brings 12 More Orphans from Korea."
70. Hilliard, "GIs Welcome at Orphan Homes in Korea."
71. By April 1956, Holt had already "received 1,500 applications from parents who want to adopt the mixed-blood children": Brown, "Child Census in Korea Ordered"; By June that same year, thousands more applications from prospective adoptive parents poured into the Holts' home. Overwhelmed and facing expiring legislation, they stopped processing the applications: "Harry Holt to Prospective Adoptive Parents," undated 1956, Box 10, Folder 30, ISS-USA Papers, SWHA.
72. US Congress, *Amendments to Refugee Relief Act 1953*, 13.
73. Ibid., 12.
74. Molly Holt, letter regarding "Needed Revision of the McCarran-Walter Act," on July 23, 1956, 84th Congress, 2nd sess., *Congressional Record* 102, pt. 10: 13982.
75. Senator Wayne Morse, speaking on "Needed Revision of the McCarran-Walter Act," on July 23, 1956, 84th Congress, 2nd sess., *Congressional Record* 102, pt. 10: 13982.
76. Ibid.
77. Mrs. C. O. Alford, letter regarding "Needed Revision of the McCarran-Walter Act," on July 23, 1956, 84th Congress, 2nd sess., *Congressional Record* 102, pt. 10: 13982.
78. Mr. and Mrs. Luke Knowlton, letter regarding "Needed Revision of the McCarran-Walter Act," on July 23, 1956, 84th Congress, 2nd sess., *Congressional Record* 102, pt. 10: 13982; Berta Burch Babb, letter regarding "Increase in Number of Visas to Be Issued to Orphans Under the Refugee Relief Act of 1953," on July 26, 1956, 84th Congress, 2nd sess., *Congressional Record* 102, pt. 11: 14742.
79. Senator Wayne Morse, speaking on "Increase in Number of Visas to Be Issued to Orphans Under the Refugee Relief Act of 1953," on July 26, 1956, 84th Congress, 2nd sess., *Congressional Record* 102, pt. 11: 14741.
80. Mrs. Edith Waddington, Mrs. Sylvia N. Gould, et al., Mr. and Mrs. Vernon Polson, Mr. and Mrs. William A. K. Lammert, Mr. and Mrs. V. J. Graff, letters regarding "Increase in Number of Visas to Be Issued to Orphans Under the Refugee Relief Act of 1953," on July 26, 1956, 84th Congress, 2nd sess., *Congressional Record* 102, pt. 11: 14742–14743.
81. "Report of Inspection of the Administration of the Refugee Relief Act of 1953, as Amended, and Related Problems in the Countries of Southeast Asia and North Asia," on July 27, 1956, 84th Congress, 2nd sess., *Congressional Record 102*, pt. 11: 15283.
82. Ibid., 15285.
83. Ibid., 15283.
84. Ibid., 15285.
85. US Congress, Senate, Committee on the Judiciary, *Final Report of the Administrator of the Refugee Relief Act of 1953, as Amended*, 85th Congress, 1st sess., November 15, 1957, 65.
86. Ibid., 61.
87. Ibid., 135; Oh, *To Save the Children of Korea*, 80; The Holts stopped actively processing prospective parents' applications in June 1956: "Harry Holt to Prospective Adoptive Parents."

(198)   *Notes to pages 59–62*

88. For a chart with the full breakdown of Refugee Relief Act orphans entering the United States (by year and country of origin), see US Congress, *Final Report of the Administrator of the Refugee Relief Act of 1953*, 135.
89. Hilliard, "Holt's Korean Orphanage."
90. This statistic first spread in South Korean camptowns in 1956 before finding its way into US newspaper reports ("It has been said—on what basis I do not know—that 90 percent of the mixed-blood babies perish"): "Visit to Korea: November 21st–30th, 1956"; "Plight of Korean Homeless: Orphans Not Wanted," *New York Herald Tribune*, October 23, 1957; Norman, "Babies GIs Left Behind Are Tragic Aftermath of Wars." OK
91. Senator Richard L. Neuberger, letter regarding "Admission of 10,000 Refugee Orphans to the United States," on January 25, 1957, 85th Congress, 1st sess., *Congressional Record* 103, pt. 1: 964.
92. Senator Richard L. Neuberger, speaking on "Private Relief Legislation," on July 16, 1957, 85th Congress, 1st sess., *Congressional Record* 103, pt. 9: 11827.
93. Mrs. Hadyn Waddington, letter regarding "Private Relief Legislation," on July 16, 1957, 85th Congress, 1st sess., *Congressional Record* 103, pt. 9: 11827.
94. Hilliard, "Children Die in Holt's Korean Orphanage.
95. Sconce, "Operation Babylift."
96. My translation: Kim Jung Ja, "My Work Report: The Mother of 17 Children," *Tonga Ilbo*, October 10, 1955.
97. Ibid.
98. Some mixed race Koreans of this generation remember being treated well, if not favorably by Korean orphanage staff. Their memories are confirmed in press reports from that time. For another example of what one reporter describes as "a paradise for mixed race children" at a time when the lack of pertinent legislation prevented the immigration of mixed race Koreans, see (my translation): "Orphans Who Were Raised in a Family Full of Love," *Chosŏn Ilbo*, November 28, 1954.
99. Harry Holt, letter regarding "Private Relief Legislation," on July 16, 1957, 85th Congress, 1st sess., *Congressional Record* 103, pt. 9: 11828--1829.
100. Ibid.
101. Pearl S. Buck, "Letters to the Times: Entry for Orphans Urged Delay in Action on Bills Admitting Mixed-Blood Children Queried," *New York Times*, June 9, 1957.
102. Buck, "Letters to the Times."
103. Ibid.
104. Ibid.
105. Ibid.
106. See the work of David Pomfret, Ann Stoler, and Paul Kramer for more on colonial subjects in French Indochina, the Dutch East Indies, and the American Philippines, respectively: David Pomfret, *Youth and Empire: Trans-Colonial Childhoods in British and French Asia* (Stanford, CA: Stanford University Press, 2015); Ann Stoler, *Carnal Knowledge and Imperial Power: Race and the Intimate in Colonial Rule* (Berkeley: University of California Press, 2002); Paul Kramer, *The Blood of Government: Race, Empire, the United States & the Philippines* (Chapel Hill: University of North Carolina Press, 2006).
107. Pearl S. Buck, "Should White Parents Adopt Brown Babies?" *Ebony*, June 1958, 29.
108. During this era, US social workers refused to place children across color lines, preferring to pair "Korean-Caucasian children . . . with Caucasian Americans,

and the Korean-Negro children with Negro Americans." See Valk, "Adjustment of Korean-American Children in their American Adoptive Homes."

109. "More Brown Babies Being Helped By: Welcome House," *Baltimore Afro-American*, March 22, 1958.

110. Ibid.; Such Cold War pleas to adopt Black Korean children did not seem to resonate with Black families as deeply as they did white Americans. This is partially because while there was a shortage of adoptable white babies in the United States, there was a surplus of Black orphans. In one article claiming that "the greatest tragedies confronting social agencies and orphanages in this country is the plight of hundreds of Negro children in orphanages and institutions," clarification that "these children are not mixed German or Korean" was needed, given the dominant image of the abandoned orphan being that of a GI baby abroad. Part of the reason that "suitable adoption homes" for Black children were so "difficult to find" was because many Black families did not meet the financial requirements set by adoption agencies or were discriminated against by white social workers who were more willing to work with white families: "Need of Homes for Orphans," *Chicago Defender*, June 21, 1958.

111. "Visit to Korea: November 21st–30th, 1956."

112. James Lattie, "Baby Lift Brings Tots," *The Oregonian*, May 25, 1961.

113. My translation: Sunlit Sisters' Center, *Oral Histories of the Sunlit Sisters' Center's Grandmothers: Part III* (Pyongtaek, KR: Sunlit Sisters' Center, 2012), 39.

114. Senator Richard L. Neuberger, speaking on "Private Relief Legislation," on July 16, 1957, 85th Congress, 1st sess., *Congressional Record* 103, pt. 9: 11827.

115. Ibid.

116. In a 1956 letter to prospective parents, the Holts describe their child placement methods: "Our procedure is adoption by proxy, that is, you give us your power of attorney and we adopt the child to you under Korean law, and he or she enters the country as your son or daughter. He doesn't have to be adopted again under state law. This saves the extra legal cost of about $300." See "Harry Holt to Prospective Adoptive Parents."

117. Even journalists helped to construct these professional norms as unnecessary hassles (note the title of the following article): "Thieves Further Delay Korean Baby Airlift, Already Harassed by Redtape," *The Oregonian*, December 16, 1956.

118. "Susan T. Pettiss (ISS-USA, Assistant Director) to Christine C. Reynolds (Tennessee Department of Public Welfare, Commissioner), June 30, 1958," Box 10, Folder 31, ISS-USA Papers.

119. Monroe Woollard, "A Study of the Adoption Records from the Holt Adoption Program Between 1956–1968 with Special Attention to Adoption Replacements," August 1968, Box 10, Folder 33, ISS-USA Papers, SWHA, 2.

120. Ibid., 9.

121. Ibid.

122. Ibid.

123. Ibid.

124. Ibid., 6.

125. "Wilmer H. Tole (St. Joseph County Department of Welfare, Director) to Lucille De Voe (Indiana Department of Public Welfare Children's Division, Director), April 9, 1958," Box 10, Folder 31, ISS-USA Papers, SWHA.

126. Ibid.

127. Ibid.

128. Ibid.

(200)   *Notes to pages 64–68*

129. Ibid.
130. Ibid.
131. "Charge Foster Mother Killed Korea Orphan," *Chicago Daily Tribune*, July 24, 1957.
132. Oh, *To Save the Children of Korea*, 115.
133. Visit to Korea: November 21st–30th, 1956."
134. Ibid.
135. "Susan T. Pettiss to Christine C. Reynolds, June 30, 1958."
136. The Holt family poured a significant amount of their personal savings into absorbing costs for prospective adoptive parents who could not afford their already heavily discounted fees. In their initial years of operation, the Holts charged just half the amount of other adoption agencies. In 1956, the expenses included $300 for travel costs, a $50 adoption fee, and $15 for a "home study" (credit check). The Holts often waived the $50 adoption fee for families who could not afford to pay and would refund the credit check for anyone whose home was disapproved: "Harry Holt to Prospective Adoptive Parents."
     This of course was in addition to the money they spent in building and maintaining the World Vision Reception Center for mixed race children and their own orphanage. By February of 1957, the Holts had already "spent more than $50,000 of their own funds" toward solving "the problem of the mixed blood child." Stein, "Two Hundred and Forty Korean Children Have Arrived in the States via Orphan Airlift."
     Part of the reason the Holts were so willing to pour their personal money into the program was because they truly believed they were doing "God's work." For more on this and the relationship between religious missions and Korean adoption, see chapter 3 in Oh, *To Save the Children of Korea*, 79–111.
137. One ISS representative observed the media fanfare surrounding the Holt planes: "There were cameras everywhere, and most families were polite and allowed their picture to be taken either by complete strangers or perhaps members of their extended family. The child was utterly bewildered by all this posing and the flickering of flashbulbs." See Arnold Lyslo, "A Few Impressions on Meeting the Harry Holt Plane the 'Flying Tiger,' Which Arrived in Portland, Oregon, December 27, 1958 Carrying 107 Korean Children Who Were Adopted Through the Holt Proxy Adoption Program by Families in the United States," Box 10, Folder 31, ISS-USA Papers, SWHA.
138. "Susan Pettiss to Files, June 6, 1958," Box 34, Folder 21, ISS-USA Papers, SWHA.
139. Lyslo, "A Few Impressions on Meeting the Harry Holt Plane, the 'Flying Tiger'".
140. Lyslo, "A Few Impressions on Meeting the Harry Holt Plane, the 'Flying Tiger'"; "Korean Orphan Dies En Route to New Parents, " *Daily Boston Globe*, July 17, 1959.
141. "Susan Pettiss to Files, June 6, 1958."
142. In this case "Miss Holt" refers to one of the Holts' daughters (most likely Molly Holt), Mrs. Rhee is a Korean ISS staff member, and names of birth mothers and children are pseudonyms to protect their identities: "ISS Korea to ISS New York, March 28, 1958," Case No. 36608, Box 17, ISS-USA Case Records, SWHA.
143. Anne Davison's report, titled "The Mixed Racial Child," was published in Korean Child Welfare Committee, *Handicapped Children's Survey Report, Korea, 1961* (Seoul, KR: Ministry of Health and Social Affairs, 1961).
144. Davison, "The Mixed Racial Child."
145. Ibid.

Notes to pages 69–73 *(201)*

146. Ibid.
147. Similarly, earlier efforts of the Holts (albeit unsuccessful) to change the label of GI babies to "U.N. orphans" also sought to minimize the role of American actors in creating the problem of mixed race Koreans: "Oregon Farmer Brings 12 More Orphans from Korea for New Homes in America."
148. "ISS Korea to ISS New York, June 2, 1958."
149. Ibid.
150. Ibid.
151. Ibid.
152. Ibid.
153. According to a professional welfare spokesman in 1959, nearly 800,000 more American families wished to adopt than there were adoptable children. This is echoed in "An Analysis of the United Presbyterian Position on Orphans in Korea," May 1961, Box 35, Folder 16, ISS-USA Papers, SWHA. Of course, this statement really applied only to white children and similarly Korean white children. While there was a shortage of adoptable white children both in the United States and South Korean camptowns, the same could not be said for Black or Korean Black children, respectively. For a fuller consideration of Black families, adoption, and Korean children, see Kori Graves, *A War Born Family: African American Adoption in the Wake of the Korean War* (New York: New York University Press, 2020).
154. Sue-Je Lee Gage, "Pure Mixed Blood: The Multiple Identities of Amerasians in South Korea" (PhD diss., Indiana University, 2007), 72, 98.
155. Oral History 23.
156. My translation of Misuk Pak's oral history in Sunlit Sisters' Center, *Oral Histories of the Sunlit Sisters' Center's Grandmothers: Part III* (Pyongtaek, KR: Sunlit Sisters' Center, 2012), 68.
157. "ISS Korea to ISS New York, June 2, 1958."
158. Oral History 19.
159. Ibid.
160. Oral History 11.
161. Ibid.
162. One mother commented to an ISS-Korea worker, "I know you'll take special care to place my child in a good family, because if you don't your own children will suffer." The implication was that "bad luck will be visited upon her children" if she did not: "Notes on Field Visit-ISS Korea Staff, July 12, 1962."
163. Hyun Sook Han, *Many Lives Intertwined* (St. Paul, MN: Yeong and Yeong, 2004), 99–100.
164. My translation of Talsun Ch'oe's oral history in Sunlit Sisters' Center, *Oral Histories of the Sunlit Sisters' Center's Grandmothers: Part II* (Pyongtaek, KR: Sunlit Sisters' Center, 2011), 84–85.
165. Valk, "Adjustment of Korean-American Children in Their American Adoptive Homes."
166. Ibid.
167. "Report of Visit to Korea, June 18 to July 13, 1962."
168. For example, by June 30, 1958, just one year following Public Law 316's enactment, a total 2,040 orphan immigrants had entered the United States; 915 of the 2,040 were Korean children, 369 Japanese, 282 Greek, and 171 Italian, while "the remaining children had come from twenty other countries in Europe or Asia." See US Congress, Senate, Committee on the Judiciary, *Relating to*

(202)   *Notes to pages 73–76*

General Immigration Matters: Hearing Held Before Subcommittee on Immigration and Naturalization of the Committee on the Judiciary – S. 116, 504, 925, 952, 954, 1196, 1280, 1468, 1523, 1532, 1610, 1919, 1996, 1974, 86th Cong., 1st sess., vol. 1, May 20, 1959, 51.

169. This remark by Senator Neuberger, which comes from the July 17, 1959, *Congressional Record*, is an echo of a statement made in *Amendments to Refugee Relief Act 1953*: "When I had to listen to Mr. Holt, and the Reverend Bob Pierce, and other people tell me of the desperate plight of these orphans in Korea, for example, I do not see how they could be any worse off in this country, no matter what the situation, and that 9 times out of 10 they would be better off."

170. Senator Richard L. Neuberger, speaking on "Extension of Orphan Immigration Program," on July 17, 1959, 86th Congress, 2nd sess., *Congressional Record* 105, pt. 11: 13670.

171. Jay Racusin, "Pearl Buck Pleads for Orphans: 'Half-Americans Dying in Korea,'" *New York Herald Tribune*, January 7, 1959.

172. Some form of this rumor also circulated in adoption circles three years prior when the Refugee Relief Act's expiration loomed. For example, an ISS report in 1956 noted that "the President, Mr. Syngman Rhee, is said to have stated at a Cabinet Meeting that he did not care what happened so long as the children were got out of the country—and quickly." See "Visit to Korea: November 21st–30th, 1956."

173. You Chan Yang, "Aiding Korean Waifs: General Lot of Orphans, Rhee's Attitude Defended," *New York Times*, January 27, 1959.

174. Ibid.

175. The Korean ambassador's claims that conditions in South Korea were improving for "mixed blood" orphans had also been corroborated by reports made by both American journalists and ISS social workers. See Yang, "Aiding Korean Waifs"; William Hilliard, "Ocean Flight Gets Lonely—Writer Warned of Korean Cold," *The Oregonian*, December 12, 1956; "ISS Korea to ISS New York, June 2, 1958," in "Enclosures to Mrs. Weber's Memorandum of March 25, 1958," Box 34, Folder 21, ISS-USA Papers, SWHA.

176. US Congress, Senate, Committee on the Judiciary, *Relating to Admission to United States of Alien Orphan Children: Hearing Held Before Subcommittee on Immigration and Naturalization of the Committee on the Judiciary – S. 1498, S. 1532, S. 1610, S. 2004*, 86th Congress, 1st sess., vol. 1, June 23, 1959, 70.

177. Ibid.

178. US Congress, *Relating to General Immigration Matters*, 52.

179. For example, between September 9, 1959, and December 31, 1960, of the 924 proxy adoptions that had occurred, 726 were of Korean children. In considering the total of all refugee orphan visas processed in this period (proxy or otherwise), the total for Korean children is 815. The second highest number from any country of origin comes from Italy, at 363, less than half the number of Korean children. For the full chart, see "Orphan Petitions Approved Under the Act of Sept. 11, 1957, as Amended by Act of Sept. 9, 1959, by Type of Adoption and Country or Region of Birth: Sept. 9, 1959–Dec. 31, 1960," on July 23, 1956, 84th Congress, 2nd sess., *Congressional Record* 102, pt. 10: 7041.

180. These numbers are based on the official figures provided by the Ministry of Health and Welfare and can be found in Table A.4 of the Appendix. The hope for domestic solutions is expressed by Korean mothers in the following report: "Notes on Field Visit-ISS Korea Staff, July 12, 1962."

Notes to pages 76–80 (203)

181. These percentages are based on the statistics compiled in the following report: "An Analysis of the United Presbyterian Position on Orphans in Korea." The rest of the children had been mostly placed by missionary groups like the Seventh Day Adventist Mission.

CHAPTER 3

1. "An Analysis of the United Presbyterian Position on Orphans in Korea," May 1961, Box 35, Folder 16, ISS-USA Papers, SWHA.
2. Ibid.
3. Ibid.
4. Ibid.
5. Ibid.
6. Ibid.
7. Ibid.
8. For an example of American social workers making these observations, see "ISS Korea to ISS New York," June 2, 1958 in "Enclosures to Mrs. Weber's Memorandum of March 25, 1958," Box 34, Folder 21, ISS-USA Papers, SWHA.
9. "Report of Visit to Korea, June 18 to July 13, 1962," Box 35, Folder 26, ISS-USA Papers, SWHA.
10. Gi-Wook Shin has written about South Korean ethnic nationalism, while Eleana Kim and Arissa Oh have researched the origins of intercountry adoption. Kim has argued that sending mixed race Koreans abroad for adoption is an example of state racism on part of the South Korean government. Oh shares a similar understanding of adoption as a race-based evacuation but also acknowledges that South Korea's desires for a racially pure nation aligned well with US interests to rescue these children. Other scholars, myself included, have also emphasized "pure blood" ideology in considering the lived historical experiences of mixed race Koreans. Little, if anything, has been said to complicate such a narrative. For the former literature, see Gi-Wook Shin, *Ethnic Nationalism in Korea: Genealogy, Politics, and Legacy* (Stanford, CA: Stanford University Press, 2006); Eleana Kim, *Adopted Territory: Transnational Korean Adoptees and the Politics of Belonging* (Durham, NC: Duke University Press, 2010); Arissa Oh, *To Save the Children of Korea: The Cold War Origins of International Adoption* (Stanford, CA: Stanford University Press, 2015); Yuri Doolan, "Being Amerasian in South Korea: Purebloodness, Multiculturalism, and Living Alongside the US Military Empire" (Honors thesis, Ohio State University, 2012); Margo Okazawa-Rey, "Amerasian Children of GI Town: A Legacy of US Militarism in South Korea," *Asian Journal of Women's Studies* 3 (1997): 71–102; Mary Lee, "Mixed Race Peoples in the Korean National Imaginary and Family," *Korean Studies* 32 (2008): 56–85.
11. For if South Korea's rejection of mixed race persons was mostly based on Confucian principles or political ideologies seeking to reunite the nation on the basis of a singular ethnic identity, then why did North Korea, with a shared history and desire in the postwar era, fail to excise a similar population in the aftermath of the Korean War?
12. The phrase "Confucius' Outcasts" is borrowed from a popular *Time* magazine feature on Korean Amerasians. See "South Korea: Confucius' Outcasts," *Time*, December 10, 1965.
13. "Report of Visit to Korea, June 18 to July 13, 1962."

(204)   *Notes to pages 81–84*

14. "Notes on Field Visit-ISS Korea Staff, July 12, 1962," Box 35, Folder 26, ISS-USA Papers, SWHA.
15. Oral History 27.
16. See Anne Davison, "The Mixed Racial Child," undated 1961, Box 34, Folder 22, ISS-USA Papers, SWHA; also published in Korean Child Welfare Committee, *Handicapped Children's Survey Report, Korea, 1961* (Seoul, KR: Ministry of Health and Social Affairs, 1961).
17. Oral History 27.
18. "Report of Visit to Korea, June 18 to July 13, 1962."
19. Oral History 26.
20. Oral History 22.
21. This experience is reminiscent of Natasha Driscoll's (now Natasha Pruss) before she was "discovered" by American photojournalist Nick Smolan and adopted to the United States. When Smolan found her, she was a confident and self-assured eleven-year-old, who appeared to be insulated from prejudice and a leader among the village children. Nonetheless, she was depicted as having experienced extreme hardship, ridicule, and pain prior to her adoption and was used in 1980s media reporting as an exemplar of the American dream.
22. Oral History 22.
23. For more on Eurasians, see Ann Stoler, *Carnal Knowledge and Imperial Power: Race and the Intimate in Colonial Rule* (Berkeley: University of California Press, 2002); Durba Ghosh, *Sex and Family in Colonial India: The Making of Empire* (Cambridge: Cambridge University Press, 2006); David Pomfret, *Youth and Empire: Trans-Colonial Childhoods in British and French Asia* (Stanford, CA: Stanford University Press, 2015).
24. Lily Lee Lu, "Growing Up in Korea," in *Mixed Korean: Our Stories, An Anthology*, ed. Cerissa Kim et al. (Bloomfield, IN: Truepeny, 2018), 61.
25. Ibid., 56.
26. Although, by the author's half-sister's account, their father loved his Korean family more than he ever loved his American family: Ibid., 60.
27. There was a point in the narrator's late teenage years when her mother did consider giving her up for adoption. At that time she was too old to be adopted (children had to be under the age of fourteen to qualify as eligible for intercountry placement). This was in the 1970s when the social and economic conditions in camptowns had drastically declined. These broader changes in the camptowns are discussed at the end of this chapter: Ibid., 60, 62.
28. Oral History 26.
29. *Kŏmdungi* is a Korean pejorative that translates directly to "darky." It was aimed at this oral history narrator because she is part Black.
30. Oral History 22.
31. Oral History 27.
32. Ibid.
33. "Report of Visit to Korea, June 18 to July 13, 1962."
34. Oral History 27.
35. "Notes on Field Visit-ISS Korea Staff, July 12, 1962."
36. Ibid.
37. Ibid.
38. Davison, "The Mixed Racial Child."
39. Oral History 12.

40. My translation: Jeong Ja Kim, *The Hidden Truth of the US Military Comfort Women* (Seoul, KR: Hanul Academy, 2013), 120.
41. "Notes on Field Visit-ISS Korea Staff, July 12, 1962."
42. Ibid.
43. "Visit to Korea, June 23 to July 6, 1965," Box 35, Folder 2, ISS-USA Papers, SWHA.
44. Ibid.
45. Dong-Myeon Shin, *Social and Economic Policies in Korea: Ideas, Networks and Linkages* (London: Routledge Curzon, 2003), 49–50.
46. Hosu Kim, *Birth Mothers and Transnational Adoption Practice in South Korea: Virtual Mothering* (New York: Palgrave Macmillan, 2016), 41.
47. At this time social welfare was only 2.5 percent of the national budget, with mere fractions of that percentage going toward women's and children's welfare. Overburdened by postwar recovery, economic development, and the military expenditure necessary to keep the nation war-ready, the South Korean government's reliance on foreign aid was convenient but also a product of the powers that had divided the nation in the first place and left the Koreas locked in a perpetual state of Cold War standoff: Oh, *To Save the Children of Korea*, 196.
48. "Visit to Korea, June 23 to July 6, 1965."
49. Ibid.
50. Ibid.
51. In 1961, the following agencies were operating an intercountry adoption program in South Korea: ISS, Child Placement Service (CPS), Holt Adoption Program, National Catholic Welfare Committee, the Seventh Day Adventist Mission, American Soul Clinic, and Welcome House. Of these, only one organization was Korean (CPS): "An Analysis of the United Presbyterian Position on Orphans in Korea."
52. "Visit to Korea, June 23 to July 6, 1965."
53. Ibid.
54. Ibid.
55. Ibid.
56. Ibid.
57. Ibid.
58. Ibid.
59. "The KAVA Resolution on Children with Racially Mixed Parentage, Adopted on January 22, 1964," Box 35, Folder 2, ISS-USA Papers, SWHA.
60. Ibid.
61. Ibid.
62. Ibid.
63. "Visit to Korea, June 23 to July 6, 1965."
64. *T'wigi* is a Korean pejorative used to refer to mixed race people. It loosely translates to "mule" or "half-breed," although some say that the term is closer to "devil's child" in meaning: Oral History 16.
65. Jan Kim, "Umma's Dreams Fulfilled," in *Mixed Korean: Our Stories, An Anthology*, ed. Cerissa Kim et al. (Bloomfield, IN: Truepeny, 2018), 49.
66. It is important to note that such a policy would have also affected the enrollment of "pure blood" Korean children being raised by single mothers. Such exclusion from grade school was based less on a child's racial difference than it was on a child's illegitimacy and precarious legal status.
67. Being born to a Korean mother did not confer automatic citizenship onto mixed race Koreans at the time. South Korean citizenship was granted by paternal *jus*

(206) *Notes to pages 89–94*

sanguinis, or entry onto any male head of household's family register. The male head of household could even be a male orphanage director. This means that mixed race Koreans were not always "stateless babies" like the former literature on the topic has overwhelmingly suggested. Furthermore, children found abandoned in the territory of South Korea automatically gained citizenship in accordance with South Korean nationality law (although it is unclear whether Korean mothers were aware of this and whether it factored into their decisions to relinquish their children).

68. My translation of Sŏnhwa Yun's oral history in Sunlit Sisters' Center, *Oral Histories of the Sunlit Sisters' Center's Grandmothers: Part I* (Pyongtaek, KR: Sunlit Sisters' Center, 2008), 54–55.

69. Ibid.

70. Oral History 26.

71. Oral History 22.

72. "Visit to Korea, June 23 to July 6, 1965."

73. Ibid.

74. Ibid.

75. Oh, *To Save the Children of Korea*, 56.

76. "Visit to Korea, June 23 to July 6, 1965."

77. Ibid.

78. Elizabeth Ford, "She Aids Little Outcasts: A Project for Asian Children," *Washington Post*, May 29, 1964.

79. "Report on Activities of Pearl Buck Foundation," undated 1965, Box 17, Folder 2, ISS-USA Papers, SWHA.

80. Margo Miller, "Soldier's Offspring: US-Korean Children Aided by Pearl Buck," *Boston Globe*, June 12, 1964.

81. Ibid.

82. Matt Weinstock, "Foundation Is Helping Those GI 'Orphans,'" *Los Angeles Times*, February 22, 1965; "Buck Foundation Seeks to Aid Waifs from Asia," *Chicago Tribune*, April 24, 1965; Ford, "She Aids Little Outcasts."

83. Miller, "Soldier's Offspring"; "Buck Foundation Seeks to Aid Waifs from Asia."

84. "Report on Activities of Pearl Buck Foundation."

85. "Buck Foundation Seeks to Aid Waifs from Asia."

86. Ibid.

87. Harry Golden, "Only In America: Children for Adoption," *Chicago Daily Defender*, May 3, 1965.

88. "Confucius' Outcasts."

89. Ibid.

90. Pearl S. Buck also authored "an admirable book" on the topic: Pearl S. Buck, *Children for Adoption* (New York: Random House, 1964) cited in Golden, "Only in America."

91. This account can be found in "Report on Activities of Pearl Buck Foundation"; and "Girl Tells Mixed-Blood Plight," *Chicago Tribune*, December 6, 1965.

92. Weinstock, "Foundation Is Helping Those GI 'Orphans'"; "Asian Kids Homeless," *Chicago Daily Defender*, May 3, 1965.

93. "Report on Activities of the Pearl Buck Foundation"; Weinstock, "Foundation Is Helping Those GI 'Orphans.'"

94. "Visit to Korea, June 23 to July 6, 1965."

95. "Report on Activities of the Pearl Buck Foundation."

96. "Gardner M. Munro (ISS Korea, Director) to Edna Weber (Headquarters ISS Geneva, Executive Director), December 11, 1965," Box 35, Folder 2, ISS-USA Papers, SWHA.
97. Ibid.
98. Ibid.
99. Ibid.
100. Ibid.
101. Ibid.
102. Ibid.
103. "Report on Activities of Pearl Buck Foundation."
104. Golden, "Only in America."
105. Miller, "Soldier's Offspring."
106. Examples include the following articles (some of which were explored in the previous chapter): Pearl S. Buck, "Letters to the *Times*: Entry for Orphans Urged Delay in Action on Bills Admitting Mixed-Blood Children Queried," *New York Times*, June 9, 1957; Jay Racusin, "Pearl Buck Pleads for Orphans: 'Half-Americans Dying in Korea,'" *New York Herald Tribune*, January 7, 1959.
107. Ruth Keller, interview by author.
108. Ibid.
109. Dorothy McCardle, "Pearl S. Buck Heading East," *Washington Post*, June 5, 1965; "Report on Activities of Pearl Buck Foundation."
110. "Report on Activities of Pearl Buck Foundation."
111. Ibid.
112. Ibid.
113. Ibid.
114. Ibid.
115. Ibid.
116. Ibid.
117. Ibid.
118. Ibid.
119. Ibid.
120. Ibid.
121. Ibid.
122. Ibid.
123. Ibid.
124. Child Placement Service, "Report on ECLAIR Program," undated June 1971, Box 35, Folder 5, ISS-USA Papers, SWHA.
125. Ibid.
126. "Youn Taek Tahk (Director, CPS) to Patricia Nye (ISS-Hong Kong, Director), February 19, 1968," Box 35, Folder 4, ISS-USA Papers, SWHA.
127. "James L. Pullman to Gloria C. Matthews (Inter-Office FPP Communication), February 21, 1968," Box 35, Folder 4, ISS-USA Papers, SWHA; "James L. Pullman to Advisory Board of ECLAIR Program, January 25, 1968," Box 35, Folder 4, ISS-USA Papers, SWHA.
128. "James L. Pullman to Advisory Board of ECLAIR Program, January 25, 1968.
129. "Youn Taek Tahk to James L. Pullman, February 16, 1968," Box 35, Folder 4, ISS-USA Papers, SWHA.
130. "James L. Pullman to Advisory Board of ECLAIR Program, January 25, 1968"; "Youn Taek Tahk to James L. Pullman, February 16, 1968."

(208) Notes to pages 98–104

131. "James L. Pullman to Gloria C. Matthews (Inter-Office FPP Communication), February 21, 1968."
132. "Report on Visit to Korea—June 24 to July 2, 1968," Box 34, Folder 17, ISS-USA Papers, SWHA.
133. Ibid.
134. Ibid.
135. Ibid.
136. Child Placement Service, "Report on ECLAIR Program."
137. Youn Taek Tahk, "Measures for the Welfare of Mixed-Blood Children in Korea," August 8, 1967, report prepared for the 19th Social Work Summer School, Central Theological Seminary (Seoul, Korea), Box 35, Folder 7, ISS-USA Papers, SWHA.
138. Ibid.
139. Ibid.
140. Despite criticism on the part of Korean social workers that these institutions hampered mixed race children's integration, they were widely praised by the broader child welfare community in South Korea for the quality of their staff, facilities, and programming: Ibid.
141. "Pearl Buck Foundation: Mixed-Blood Boys Kill Neighbor," *Korea Times*, July 13, 1971.
142. Child Placement Service, "Report on ECLAIR Program."
143. Historian Ji-Yeon Yuh also uses this phrase to describe a general sense of fascination with all things American that swept through South Korea in the latter half of the twentieth century. This inclination toward America prompted many South Koreans to explore the US-oriented culture of the camptowns. The Itaewon neighborhood in Seoul is one famous example of this. For some women, these camptown encounters resulted in a relationship with an American GI through which marriage and migration to the United States also occurred. See chapter 2 in Ji-Yeon Yuh, *Beyond the Shadow of Camptown: Korean Military Brides in America* (New York: New York University Press, 2002), 42–83.
144. Oral History 27.
145. Ibid.
146. Child Placement Service, "Report on ECLAIR Program."
147. Oral History 15.
148. Child Placement Service, "Report on ECLAIR Program."
149. Ibid.
150. "Youn Taek Tahk to Patricia Nye, December 11, 1970," Box 35, Folder 5, ISS-USA Papers, SWHA.
151. In 1970, another major initiative began under the direction of Maryknoll priest, Father Alfred V. Keane, whose lobbying for Amerasian immigration reform is discussed in chapter 5. The Catholic Maryknoll order established St. Vincent's Home for Amerasians, promoted intercountry adoption for mixed race Koreans, and operated a scholarship and study abroad program at Gonzaga University in Spokane, Washington, during the 1970s.
152. For a fuller consideration of the camptown's transformation during these years, see chapter 4 in Katharine Moon, *Sex Among Allies: Military Prostitution in US-Korea Relations* (New York: Columbia University Press, 1997).
153. Moon, *Sex Among Allies*, 67–68.
154. Oral History 12.
155. "Notes on Field Visit-ISS Korea Staff, July 12, 1962."

Notes to pages 104–112 (*209*)

156. Oral History 12.
157. Ibid.
158. Many mixed race Koreans who grew up in the camptowns during the 1970s recall seeing few if any other children like them. This drastically differed from the previous decade. For a firsthand account of camptowns in the 1960s, see the diary entry cited in Bruce Cumings, "Silent but Deadly: Sexual Subordination in the US-Korea Relationship," in *Let the Good Times Roll: Prostitution and the US Military in Asia*, ed. Saundra Pollock Sturdevant and Brenda Stoltzfus (New York: New Press, 1992), 171.
159. Oral History 16.
160. Oral History 12.
161. Bella Siegel-Dalton, "Chosun One," in *Mixed Korean: Our Stories, An Anthology*, ed. Cerissa Kim et al. (Bloomfield, IN: Truepeny, 2018), 94.

CHAPTER 4

1. All names in this document have been changed to protect the identities of the individuals involved.
2. "Mary Jim Stephens (Texas Department of Public Welfare, Regional Adoption Worker) to Margaret A. Valk (ISS-USA, Case Consultant)," August 10, 1956, Case No. 41310, Box 63, ISS-USA Case Records, SWHA.
3. Ralph D. Millard, "Oriental Peregrinations," *Plastic and Reconstructive Surgery* 16, no. 5 (1955): 319.
4. Ibid, 319–332.
5. Ibid, 334.
6. Ibid, 331.
7. "Mary Jim Stephens to Margaret A. Valk," November 14, 1956, Case No. 41310, Box 63, ISS-USA Case Records, SWHA.
8. Adoptee memoirs by mixed race Koreans include Thomas Park Clement, *Dust of the Streets: The Journey of a Biracial Orphan of the Korean War* (Bloomfield, IN: Truepeny Publishing, 2012); Joel L.A. Peterson, *Dreams of My Mothers: A Story of Love Transcendent* (Minneapolis: Huff Publishing, 2015).
9. To be clear, this also happened to fully Korean children, like documentary film maker Deann Borshay Liem, who also reports having had a cosmetic surgical procedure done to her as a young child: *First Person Plural*, directed by Deann Borshay Liem (San Francisco, CA: Center for Asian American Media, 2000).
10. The years 1952 and 1968 mark the passage of the McCarran Walter Act and the enactment of the Immigration and Nationality Act of 1965. The former law, which has been discussed at great length in earlier chapters, allowed for the non-quota entry of dependents of US citizens which in combination with various refugee orphan programs facilitated the entry of mixed race Koreans. It also established strict racial quotas for other Asian migration, and this was not normalized until the latter law was passed in 1965 but enacted in 1968.
11. The arrival of mixed race Koreans in their new adoptive homes made headlines in local, regional, and national newspapers in the 1950s and 1960s. These articles, many of which were clipped and saved by the adoptive parents of my oral history narrators, produce similar, celebratory narratives of a new kind of Cold War, American, and multicultural family. Kim Park Nelson, both an adoptee and scholar, discusses these newspaper clippings, including one of her own adoption, and notes that Korean children are often represented in these documents as an exception, or a bright spot, in US race relations. For more, see Kim Park

(210)   *Notes to pages 112–116*

Nelson, *Invisible Asians: Korean American Adoptees, Asian American Experiences, and Racial Exceptionalism* (New Brunswick, NJ: Rutgers University Press, 2016).

12. Margaret A. Valk, "Adjustment of Korean-American Children in Their American Adoptive Homes," undated 1957, Box 10, Folder 2, ISS-USA Papers, SWHA.

13. Ibid.

14. Ibid.

15. Ibid.

16. Ibid.

17. Very few "full Korean" children are represented in the early years of ISS adoption casework. This is also reflected in the Ministry of Health and Welfare's official adoption statistics. For example, in 1955, the first year that intercountry adoption from Korea really took off, only seven were those of "full Korean" parentage; the rest were mixed race. In 1956 that number would increase to fifty-three, but that only constituted a mere 8 percent of a total of 671 children placed that year. For the full figures, see Table A.4 of the Appendix.

18. For an example of this, see Case No. 631628, Box 180, ISS-USA Case Records, SWHA.

19. Valk, "Adjustment of Korean-American Children in their American Adoptive Homes."

20. "An Analysis of the United Presbyterian Position on Orphans in Korea," May 1961, Box 35, Folder 16, ISS-USA Papers, SWHA.

21. "Need of Homes for Orphans," *Chicago Defender*, June 21, 1958.

22. The phrase "to the land of their fathers" was often used by humanitarians and adoption advocates: "Report of Meeting with Dr. Pierce of World Vision," March 13, 1956, Box 10, Folder 29, ISS-USA Papers, SWHA.

23. "Mary Jim Stephens (Texas Department of Public Welfare, Regional Adoption Worker) to Margaret A. Valk (ISS-USA, Case Consultant)," August 10, 1956, Case No. 41310, Box 63, ISS-USA Case Records, SWHA.

24. Historian Elaine Tyler May has written about how the formation of white middle-class domesticity was central to the US state's broader Cold War politics and foreign policy agenda. See Elaine Tyler May, *Homeward Bound: American Families in the Cold War Era* (New York: Basic Books, 2008).

25. Valk, "Adjustment of Korean-American Children in Their American Adoptive Homes."

26. Oral History 21.

27. Oral History 16.

28. Oral History 28.

29. Oral History 30.

30. Oral History 23.

31. Ibid.

32. One mixed race Korean adoptee writes about his memories of oatmeal in the following piece: Joel L.A. Peterson, "Mom's Love in a Breakfast Bowl," in Cerissa Kim et al., *Mixed Korean: Our Stories, An Anthology* (Bloomfield, IN: Truepeny Publishing 2018),

33. Oral History 23.

34. Ibid.

35. Ibid.

36. Oral History 14.

37. Valk, "Adjustment of Korean-American Children in Their American Adoptive Homes."

38. Ibid.
39. Oral History 27.
40. Oral History 30.
41. Oral History 24.
42. "Notes on Field Visit-ISS Korea Staff, July 12, 1962," Box 35, Folder 26, ISS-USA Papers, SWHA.
43. For a harrowing account of what this day was like from the perspective of a Korean mother, see chapter 7 in Jeong Ja Kim, *The Hidden Truth of the US Military Comfort Women* (Seoul, KR: Hanul Academy, 2013).
44. Jan Kim, "Umma's Dreams Fulfilled," in Cerissa Kim et al., *Mixed Korean: Our Stories, An Anthology* (Bloomfield, IN: Truepeny Publishing, 2018), 50.
45. Oral History 14.
46. Oral History 24.
47. Valk, "Adjustment of Korean-American Children in Their American Adoptive Homes."
48. "Report on Visit to Korea—June 24 to July 2, 1968," Box 34, Folder 17, ISS-USA Papers, SWHA.
49. Valk, "Adjustment of Korean-American Children in Their American Adoptive Homes."
50. Ibid.
51. Oral History 13.
52. Oral History 28.
53. Oral History 4.
54. Oral History 23.
55. Oral History 24.
56. Oral History 21.
57. Oral History 8.
58. There are some exceptions, of course. One mixed race Korean woman who was placed into an American family in Berkeley, California, at age five, recalls that her adoptive mother always kept a jar of kimchi for her in their refrigerator. Oral History 3.
59. For an example of this, see "Helen Chandler (California Department of Social Welfare, Child Welfare Worker) to Helen Day (Church World Service, Assistant Director of Immigration Services)," October 8, 1954, Case No. 36716, Box 63, ISS-USA Case Records, SWHA.
60. Oral History 1.
61. Soojin Chung, *Adopting for God: The Mission to Change America Through Transnational Adoption* (New York: New York University Press, 2021), 62.
62. Oral History 4.
63. Michael Cullen Green, *Black Yanks in the Pacific: Race in the Making of American Military Empire after World War II* (Ithaca, NY: Cornell University Press, 2010), 89; Kori Graves, *A War Born Family: African American Adoption in the Wake of the Korean War* (New York: New York University Press, 2020), 5.
64. Oral History 1.
65. Oral History 24.
66. Oral History 24; Oral History 30.
67. Eugenia Kim, "Cross-pollination: An Interview with the Honorable Judge Judy Preddy Draper," in Cerissa Kim et al., *Mixed Korean: Our Stories, An Anthology* (Bloomfield, IN: Truepeny Publishing, 2018), 105–106.

Notes to pages 124–131

68. Kim Einhorn, "The Yellow Bus," in Cerissa Kim et al., *Mixed Korean: Our Stories, An Anthology* (Bloomfield, IN: Truepeny Publishing, 2018), 230.
69. Oral History 9.
70. Oral History 2.
71. Oral History 21.
72. Ibid.
73. Ibid.
74. Ibid.
75. Oral History 12.
76. Oral History 1.
77. Oral History 21.
78. Oral History 22.
79. Oral History 1.
80. Oral History 27; Oral History 26.
81. Oral History 14.
82. Oral History 17.
83. Bella Siegel-Dalton, "Chosun One," in Cerissa Kim et al., *Mixed Korean: Our Stories, An Anthology* (Bloomfield, IN: Truepeny Publishing, 2018), 94.
84. Valk, "Adjustment of Korean-American Children in Their American Adoptive Homes."
85. Ibid.
86. Oral History 24.
87. I borrow the term "camptown shadow" from Ji-Yeon Yuh, *Beyond the Shadow of Camptown* (New York: New York University Press, 2002).
88. Oral History 21.
89. Oral History 4.
90. Oral History 25.
91. Oral History 1.
92. Oral History 21.
93. Oral History 1; Oral History 21; Oral History 22.
94. Oral History 29.
95. I use the term "hypersexualization," building on Celine Parreñas Shimizu's contention that "Asian/American women's hypersexuality, as 'naturally' excessive and extreme against a white female norm, directly attaches to a specific race and gender ontology." I agree with Shimizu when she says that the notion of "the Asian woman" as "culturally prone to sexual adventure and exotic difference, emerges from the colonial encounter of war." For more on this, see Celine Parreñas Shimizu, *The Hypersexuality of Race: Performing Asian/American Women on Screen and Scene* (Durham, NC: Duke University Press, 2007), 143.
96. Oral History 1.
97. Incidents of childhood sexual abuse are recounted in other oral history collections documenting the lived historical experiences of Korean adoptees. This excerpt is narrated by a mixed race woman born in 1957 and adopted to an African American family in 1963. Coded as NY5763, her interview is part of the *Side By Side Project*. All 100 interviews have been made available to the public by the documentary filmmakers and can be accessed at Glenn Morey and Julie Morey, "Side By Side Project," *Side By Side Project*, 2018, https://sidebysideproject.com.
98. Oral History 7.
99. Oral History 21.
100. Oral History 1.
101. Oral History 16.

Notes to pages 131–141 *(213)*

102. Oral History 21.
103. Oral History 24.
104. Oral History 23.
105. Ibid.
106. Ibid.
107. Oral History 12.
108. Oral History 1.
109. Oral History 6.
110. Oral History 9.
111. Oral History 4.
112. Oral History 18.
113. This number is based on the official figures provided by the Ministry of Health and Welfare. For the full figures, see Table A.4 in the Appendix.

CHAPTER 5

1. US Congress, House, Committee on the Judiciary, *Immigration Reform: Hearing Before the Subcommittee on Immigration, Refugees and International Law*, 97th Cong., 1st sess., October 14, 15, 21, 26, 28, November 12, 17, and 19, 1982, 925–928.
2. US Congress, Senate, Committee on the Judiciary, *Amerasian Immigration Proposals: Hearing Before the Subcommittee on Immigration and Refugee Policy*, 97th Cong., 2nd sess., June 21, 1982, 21.
3. As Christian Appy writes, "With the possible exception of the Civil War, no event in US history has demanded more soul-searching than the war in Vietnam. The false pretexts used to justify our intervention, the indiscriminate brutality of our warfare, the stubborn refusal of elected leaders to withdraw despite public opposition, and the stunning failure to achieve our stated objective." See Christian G. Appy, *American Reckoning: The Vietnam War and Our National Identity* (New York: Penguin Books, 2016), x.
4. Yen Le Espiritu, *Body Counts: The Vietnam War and Militarized Refugees* (Oakland: University of California Press, 2014), 1.
5. "Press Conference No. 12 of the President of the United States," April 3, 1975, White House Press Releases, the Gerald R. Ford Presidential Library, Box 9, 1.
6. US Congress, Senate, Committee on the Judiciary, *Indochina Evacuation and Refugee Problems (Part I: Operation Babylift & Humanitarian Needs): Hearing Before the Subcommittee to Investigate Problems Connected with Refugees and Escapees*, 94th Cong., 1st sess., April 8, 1975, 99.
7. "The Orphans: Saved or Lost?," *Time*, April 21, 1975.
8. "Pool Report One, San Diego to Palm Springs," April 3, 1975, White House Press Releases, the Gerald R. Ford Presidential Library, 1.
9. *Indochina Evacuation and Refugee Problems*, 91; "The Orphans."
10. This verbiage appears in numerous presidential statements, including: "Statement by the President," April 4, 1975, White House Press Releases, the Gerald R. Ford Presidential Library, Box 9, 1; "San Francisco Bay Area Council," April 4, 1975, President's Speeches and Statements: Reading Copies, the Gerald R. Ford Presidential Library, Box 7 26b; "National Association of Broadcasters, Las Vegas, Nevada," April 7, 1975, Presidential Speeches and Statements: Reading Copies, the Gerald R. Ford Presidential Library, Box 7, 47.
11. Such sentiments reflected an emerging discourse in the American cultural and political psyche post-Vietnam to restore American masculinity: Susan Jeffords, *The*

Remasculinization of America: Gender and the Vietnam War (Bloomington: Indiana University Press, 1989); "National Association of Broadcasters," 43–44.

12. "National Association of Broadcasters," 42; *Indochina Evacuation and Refugee Problems*, 89.

13. "Point Paper for the Special assistant to the Secretary and Deputy Secretary of Defense: Orphan Evacuation Program—Vietnam/Cambodia," April 16, 1975, Indochina Refugees—Orphan Airlift, Theodore C. Marrs Files, the Gerald R. Ford Presidential Library, Box 10, 1.

14. Ibid., 2; "The Orphans."

15. "Clouds over the Airlift," *Time*, April 28, 1975.

16. Ibid.

17. Ibid.

18. Ibid.

19. "The Orphans."

20. *Indochina Evacuation and Refugee Problems*, 85.

21. "The Orphans."

22. *Indochina Evacuation and Refugee Problems*, 92.

23. Ibid.

24. "'Operation Babylift' Is Criticized," *Baltimore Afro-American*, April 12, 1975.

25. Greg Waskul, "Influx of South Vietnamese Waifs Stirs Concern for American Orphans," *Los Angeles Times*, April 12, 1975.

26. Ibid.

27. "The Orphans."

28. "'Operation Babylift' Is Criticized."

29. Arthur Siddon, "Rally Hears Other Side—Babylift Guilt Trip: Viet Women," *Chicago Tribune*, April 8, 1975.

30. Ibid.

31. US Library of Congress, Congressional Research Service, *Vietnamese Adoption and Child Care*, by Jean Yavis Jones, HV 741 (1973), 14.

32. Ibid.

33. Patricia Carter, "She Too Adopted an Orphan from Asia, Long Before the Babylift," *Los Angeles Times*, April 15, 1975.

34. Ibid.

35. Stephen Wermiel, "Opposition Surfaces to Orphans Airlift," *Boston Globe*, April 8, 1975; Siddon, "Rally Hears Other Side."

36. United Press International, "'Babylift' Resumed Under Pressure," *Los Angeles Times*, April 7, 1975; Bill Richards and Elizabeth Becker, "Airlifting of Babies Ordered Suspended," *Washington Post*, April 17, 1975; "'Irregularities' Eyed: End to 'Babylift' Ban Seen," *Washington Post*, April 18, 1975.

37. While I could find no major newspaper record recording the details of the final orphan airlift from Saigon, the following interview sheds light on the event: Allison Martin, "An Interview with Cherie Clark," *ComeUnity*, 2000, https://www.comeunity.com/apv/babylift-clark.htm.

38. While these children were already in adoptive homes in the United States, they were not yet legally adopted. In the United States, when a child is placed into a home there is a period of adjustment that occurs under the supervision of a professional social welfare agency before an adoptive family can finalize the adoption of a child. This lawsuit moved to halt the process for hundreds of children (because allegedly they were not orphans) until permission and consent could be obtained from their parents back in Vietnam: "Suit Seeks to Block Adoptions of

Notes to pages 143–148 *(215)*

Many Vietnamese Children," *New York Times*, May 1, 1975; *Indochina Evacuation and Refugee Problems*, 88.

39. Although the Vietnam War looms large in American popular culture and memory today, this was not always the case. As the nation struggled to grapple with the war's meaning, journalist Martha Gellhorn argued that "consensual amnesia was the American reaction, an almost instant reaction, to the Vietnam War." Bruce Cumings also points out that the moniker "forgotten war" (now much more commonly associated with the Korean War) was applied by some journalists in the immediate aftermath years of Vietnam. See Martha Gellhorn, *The Face of War* (New York: Atlantic Monthly Press, 1988), 274; Bruce Cumings, *The Korean War: A History* (New York: Modern Library, 2010), 63.

40. The Broadway musical *Miss Saigon* opens its second act with a chorus of men, portraying Vietnam War veterans, singing to the gut-wrenching melodies of "Bui Doi." The song's title is taken from a Vietnamese language term that roughly translates to "the dust of life," a pejorative used to describe mixed race GI children. The scene portrays the plight of Amerasian children left behind in Vietnam and casts these individuals as a tragic metaphor for the good intentions but failed outcomes of the American government and its people during the Vietnam War.

41. Janet P. Gardner, *Precious Cargo* (San Francisco, CA: Independent Television Service, 2001).

42. Jones, *Vietnamese Adoption and Child Care*, 21.

43. Bernard Weinraub, "A Priest's Obsession: These Are Our Children," *New York Times*, April 9, 1982; *Amerasian Immigration Proposals*, 24.

44. Kenneth Paik, "Korean War 'Half-Breeds' Victims of Bias," *Chicago Tribune*, March 13, 1977.

45. Ibid.; Leon Daniel, "Mixed Race Children: Legacies of War," *Los Angeles Times*, December 3, 1976; Richard Halloran, "Now-Grown Children of G.I.'s in Korea Are Bitter," *New York Times*, June 2, 1976.

46. Daniel, "Mixed Race Children"; Paik, "Korean War 'Half-Breeds' Victims of Bias"; Halloran, "Now-Grown Children of G.I.'s in Korea are Bitter."

47. *Amerasian Immigration Proposals*, 13; Daniel, "Mixed Race Children."

48. Halloran, "Now-Grown Children of G.I.'s in Korea Are Bitter."

49. Betty Cuniberti, "Amerasian Children's Pied Piper," *Los Angeles Times*, June 7, 1982; Mike Winerip, "Priest Asks US to Take GI 'Love' Children," *Chicago Tribune*, August 3, 1980.

50. Meeky, "The Underside of the Rainbow," in *Mixed Korean: Our Stories, An Anthology*, ed. Cerissa Kim et al., 18–24 (Bloomfield, IN: Truepeny Publishing, 2018).

51. Ibid.

52. Field notes by author, March 9, 2023.

53. Ibid.

54. Meeky, "The Underside of the Rainbow."

55. Bernard Weinraub, "A Priest's Obsession: These Are Our Children,'" *New York Times*, April 9, 1982.

56. William Drozdiak, "Strangers in Their Own Lands," *Time*, December 14, 1981, entered on March 1, 1982, 97th Congress, 2nd sess., *Congressional Record* 128, pt. 2: 2667.

57. David Devoss, "The Warrior's Children," *GEO*, November 1980, entered on January 29, 1981, 97th Congress, 1st sess., *Congressional Record* 127, pt. 1: 1327.

58. Gordon Koestler, "Amerasians—A Stint in Korea Opened South Hill Family's Eyes," entered on July 23, 1982, 97th Congress, 2nd sess., *Congressional Record* 128, pt. 13: 17861.

(216)   *Notes to pages 148–151*

59. Robert J. Cornyn, "Half and Half, and Citizen Of?" entered on July 23, 1982, 97th Congress, 2nd sess., *Congressional Record* 128, pt. 13: 17861.
60. US Congress, *Immigration Reform*, 907.
61. John A. Shade, speech regarding "The Amerasian Children," on June 11, 1980, 96th Congress, 2nd sess., *Congressional Record* 126, pt. 11: 14046; Cornyn, "Half and Half, and Citizen Of?"; US Congress, *Immigration Reform*, 904.
62. For more testimony, see US Congress, *Amerasian Immigration Proposals*, 46–55; John Shade of the Pearl S. Buck Foundation estimated that more than 6,000 mixed race children were left behind in South Korea, 11,000 in Thailand, 30,000 in the Philippines, 5,000 in Taiwan, 3,000 in Okinawa, 50,000 in Japan, 25,000 in Vietnam, and 6,000 in Laos and Cambodia. By contrast, Father Keane estimated that there were 2,000 mixed race children in Korea, 1,500 in Japan, 1,000 in Taiwan, 5,000 in Thailand, 1,000 in Laos, 25,000 in Vietnam and the Philippine Islands. This discrepancy between Father Keane's figure (33,500) and Shade's figure (upwards of 136,000) reveals that even among Amerasian experts, there was no real sense of how large the population was: Shade, speech regarding "The Amerasian Children," 14046; US Congress, *Immigration Reform*, 901.
63. Ibid., 51–52.
64. Ibid., 48–49.
65. Senator Dale Bumpers, speaking on "Immigration of Vietnamese Amerasians," on August 6, 1987, 100th Congress, 1st sess., *Congressional Record* 133, pt. 16: 22923.
66. Kitry Krause, "Children of Vietnam," *Chicago Reader*, December 6, 1990.
67. US Congress, *Amerasian Immigration Proposals*, 26.
68. Intercountry adoption involving Vietnamese children would not really take off until the late 1980s, when the Vietnamese government invited US voluntary agencies back into the country. In 1969 only sixty children had been granted visas, 123 in 1970, less than 100 in 1971: Jones, *Vietnamese Adoption and Child Care*, 22.
69. US Congress, *Amerasian Immigration Proposals*, 78.
70. Ibid.
71. Ibid., 20.
72. Ibid.
73. Ibid., 25, 70.
74. Ibid., 65.
75. Ibid.
76. US Senate, *Immigration Reform*, 902.
77. US Congress, *Amerasian Immigration Proposals*, 65.
78. Representative William Lehman of Florida, speaking on "Amerasian Children—Meeting Our Responsibilities," on July 23, 1982, 97th Congress, 2nd sess., *Congressional Record* 128, pt. 13: 17860.
79. Ibid.
80. US Senate, *Immigration Reform*, 878.
81. Pearl S. Buck and Theodore F. Harris, *For Spacious Skies* (New York: John Day, 1966), 54.
82. US Senate, *Immigration Reform*, 901, 911.
83. Ibid., 901.
84. US Senate, *Amerasian Immigration Proposal*, 17–18.
85. Ibid., 17–18.
86. Ibid., 18.
87. Ibid.

Notes to pages 151–157 (217)

88. Ibid., 48.
89. *An Act to Amend the Immigration and Nationality Act to Provide Preferential Treatment in the Admission of Certain Children of United States Citizens*, Public Law 359, *US Statutes at Large* 96 (1982): 1716.
90. Ibid.
91. Ibid.
92. US Congress, *Amerasian Immigration Proposals*, 15.
93. Ibid., 14.
94. US Congress, *Immigration Reform*, 625.
95. Ibid.
96. Ibid., 925
97. Representative Stewart McKinney of Connecticut, speaking on "Strangers in Their Own Lands," on March 1, 1982, 97th Congress, 2nd sess., *Congressional Record* 128, pt. 2: 2667.
98. Representative McKinney, speaking on "Strangers in Their Own Lands."
99. Representative Lucien E. Blackwell of Pennsylvania, speaking on "Amendment to Immigration and Nationality Act to Extend Preferential Treatment in the Admission of Amerasian Children Born in the Philippines," on June 16, 1993, 103rd Congress, 1st sess., *Congressional Record* 139, pt. 9: 13105.
100. Senator Daniel Inouye, speaking on "The Amerasian Immigration Act Amendment of Act of 1997," on January 21, 1997, 105th Congress, 1st sess., *Congressional Record* 143, pt. 4: 855; Senator Inouye also introduced S. 56, "a bill to amend the Immigration and Nationality Act to facilitate the immigration to the United States of certain aliens born in the Philippines or Japan who were fathered by United States citizens" to the Committee on the Judiciary on January 22, 2001: 107th Congress, 1st sess., *Congressional Record* 147, pt. 7: S99.
101. Christopher M. Lapinig, "The Forgotten Amerasians," *New York Times*, May 27, 2013.
102. Representative Chris Smith of New Jersey, speaking on "Introduction of the Amerasian Relief Act," on March 21, 1985, 99th Congress, 1st sess., *Congressional Record* 131, pt. 5: 5978.
103. US Congress, *Amerasian Immigration Proposals*, 72–73.
104. *An Act to Amend the Immigration and Nationality Act to Provide Preferential Treatment in the Admission of Certain Children of United States' Citizens.*
105. Allison Varzally, *Children of Reunion: Vietnamese Adoptions and the Politics of Family Migrations* (Chapel Hill: University of North Carolina Press, 2017), 92.
106. US General Accounting Office, *Vietnamese Amerasian Resettlement: Education, Employment, and Family Outcomes in the United States*, GAO/PEMD-94-15, (Washington, DC, 1994), 4–5.
107. Ibid., 1; in 2002, *Time* magazine reported that some 23,000 Amerasians and 67,000 of their relatives entered the United States through the Amerasian Homecoming Act: Kay Johnson, "Children of the Dust," *Time*, May 13, 2002.

EPILOGUE

1. "Visit to Korea, June 23 to July 6, 1965," Box 35, Folder 2, ISS-USA Papers, SWHA.
2. "Asian Women Immigrants Admitted to US as Wives of American Citizens by Country of Origin and Year," US Commissioner of Immigration and Naturalization, Annual Reports, 1947–77, Table 6 (Washington, DC), reprinted in Bok-Lim Kim, *Women in Shadows: A Handbook for Service Providers Working*

with Asian Wives of US Military Personnel (La Jolla, CA: National Committee Concerned with Asian Wives of US Servicemen, 1981), 12.

3. Ibid.

4. While the marriages may have remained intact up until migration, scholars have estimated that 80 percent of the unions between American servicemen and military brides eventually ended in divorce once they arrived in the United States. My own parents divorced when I was three. J. T. Takagi and Hye Jung Park, *The Women Outside: Korean Women and the US Military* (New York: Third World Newsreel, 1995).

5. Margaret Simons, "'Do You Ever Think About Me?' The Children Sex Tourists Leave Behind," *The Guardian*, March 2, 2019.

6. I put the term "peacetime" in quotation marks because technically the Koreas remain at war.

7. Pearl S. Buck and Theodore F. Harris, *For Spacious Skies* (New York: John Day, 1966), 54.

8. The Cold War has been described by some scholars as "a competition over discourse, a 'struggle for the word.'" See Christian G. Appy, *Cold War Constructions: The Political Culture of United States Imperialism, 1945–1966* (Amherst: University of Massachusetts Press, 2000), 3.

9. Jinah Kim argues that because much of the death and destruction wrought by US waged wars in the Pacific has gone largely unresolved, Asian diasporic subjectivity exists in relation to afterlives. Similarly, much of the violence and trauma caused by the first Amerasian rescue remains unaddressed by the historical actors involved. This, too, has profoundly shaped mixed race Korean subjectivity and the lives of Korean birth mothers who lost their children. For more on "afterlives" see Jina Kim, *Postcolonial Grief: The Afterlives of the Pacific Wars in the Americas* (Durham, NC: Duke University Press, 2019).

10. Field notes by author, July 12, 2016.

11. Ibid.

12. Sunlit Sisters' Center, *Oral Histories of the Sunlit Sisters' Center's Grandmothers: Part III*, 38–39.

13. My translation of Sumin Pak's oral history inSunlit Sisters' Center, *Oral Histories of the Sunlit Sisters' Center's Grandmothers: Part IV* (Pyongtaek, KR: Sunlit Sisters' Center, 2013), 27.

14. My translation: Sunlit Sisters' Center, *Oral Histories of the Sunlit Sisters' Center's Grandmothers: Part III* (Pyongtaek, KR: Sunlit Sisters' Center, 2012), 74–75.

15. Korean American authors Heinz Insu Fenkl and Grace M. Cho have written extensively about the experience of camptowns, ghosts, and hauntings in their own families. See Heinz Insu Fenkl (New York: Dutton, 1996); Grace M. Cho, *Haunting the Korean Diaspora: Shame, Secrecy, and the Forgotten War* (Minneapolis, MN: University of Minnesota Press, 2008); Grace M. Cho, *Tastes Like War: A Memoir* (New York: Feminist Press, 2021).

16. Eleana Kim, *Adopted Territory: Transnational Korean Adoptees and the Politics of Belonging* (Durham, NC: Duke University Press, 2010), 110–114.

17. This delay is perhaps explained by the high percentage of older adoptees in the mixed race demographic. Comparatively, the individuals in Eleana Kim's study were generally of a younger generation that had come of age with the Internet and thus were willing to engage in online communities sooner.

18. Katherine Kim, interview by author.

19. The term "hapa" comes from the Hawai'ian language term meaning "of mixed blood." Mixed race Asians' usage of that term has been criticized by Pacific Islanders as cultural appropriation (and rightfully so). Nonetheless, "hapa" is often used by mixed race adoptees as a racial term to describe themselves. Notably, it is preferred over the word Amerasian. In fact, very few mixed race Koreans I have spoken with use or are familiar with Amerasian unless they were participants in the Amerasian immigration hearings of the 1980s. This underscores how the concept of Amerasian is not an expression of mixed race Korean identity and culture but rather a Cold War construction.

20. Eleana Kim, "Human Capital: Transnational Korean Adoptees and the Neoliberal Logic of Return," *Journal of Korean Studies* 17, no. 2 (Fall 2012): 309.

21. Katherine Kim, interview by author.

22. Cerissa Kim, "Koreans and Camptowns: Reflections of a Mixed-Race Korean," KoreanAmericanStory.org, http://koreanamericanstory.org/the-conference-that-introduced-me-to-the-legacy-of-being-a-mixed-race-korean.

23. Ibid.

24. Deann Borshay Liem has produced a number of critically acclaimed documentaries on intercountry adoption from Korea. Her first two films, *First Person Plural* (2000) and *In the Matter of Cha Jung Hee* (2010), document her own attempts to uncover her Korean past and origins. Her more recent documentary *Geographies of Kinship* (2019) highlights the stories of four Korean adoptees on their journeys to reconnect with their birth country and piece together their past.

25. Bella Siegel-Dalton, interview by author.

26. Ibid.

27. Ibid.

28. Katherine Kim, interview by author.

29. Ibid.

30. This number is based on the official numbers provided by the Ministry of Health and Welfare. For the full figures, see Table A.4 in the Appendix.

31. Katherine Kim, interview by author.

32. In some of these instances, the women were pressured to give up their children for adoption in order to improve their chances of marriage with an American GI. Women who had been abandoned by their first GI husbands or separated from them as the result of US military policies were often vulnerable to exploitation in the camptowns. Securing a second marriage later on was often one route out of these difficult circumstances.

33. Paul Lee Cannon, Katherine Kim, Nancy Lee Blackman, Cerrissa Kim, and Linda P. Rounds, *Together at Last: Stories of Adoption and Reunion in the Age of DNA* (Bloomington, IN: T and W Foundation, 2020).

34. The organization has been involved in several recent high-profile DNA cases involving adoptees of full-Korean parentage. On June 12, 2020, for instance, plaintiff Kara Bos made international news when the Seoul Family Court ruled her to be the biological daughter of an 85-year-old South Korean man. After 325KAMRA identified Bos's likely biological father through a DNA match to another relative, the court-ordered test confirmed a 99.9981% match. Bos's case represents a landmark decision for adoptees' legal rights to identity in South Korea. The ruling prevents her half-siblings from impeding future visits with her biological father and could even entitle her to an inheritance. Most important, however, as Bos explained to news outlets in 2020, she hopes that speaking with her Korean father will lead to her long-lost mother.

BIBLIOGRAPHY

PRIMARY SOURCES
Oral Histories
Thirty anonymous oral history interviews of mixed race Koreans born in the 1950s and 1960s. Conducted by author between the years 2016 and 2022.

Memoir and Interviews
Buck, Pearl S. and Theodore F. Harris. *For Spacious Skies*. New York: John Day, 1966.

Clement, Thomas Park. *Dust of the Streets: The Journey of a Biracial Orphan of the Korean War*. Bloomfield, IN: Truepeny Publishing, 2012.

Einhorn, Kim. "The Yellow Bus." In *Mixed Korean: Our Stories, An Anthology*, edited by Cerissa Kim, Katherine Kim, Sora Kim-Russell, and Mary Kim-Arnold. Bloomfield, IN: Truepeny Publishing, 2018.

Han, Hyun Sook. *Many Lives Intertwined*. St. Paul, MN: Yeong and Yeong, 2004.

Holt, Bertha. *Bring My Sons from Afar: The Unfolding of Harry Holt's Dream*. Eugene, OR: Holt International Children's Services, 1986.

Kim, Eugenia. "Cross-pollination: An Interview with the Honorable Judge Judy Preddy Draper." In *Mixed Korean: Our Stories, An Anthology*, edited by Cerissa Kim, Katherine Kim, Sora Kim-Russell, and Mary Kim-Arnold. Bloomfield, IN: Truepeny Publishing, 2018.

Kim, Jan. "Umma's Dreams Fulfilled." In *Mixed Korean: Our Stories, An Anthology*, edited by Cerissa Kim, Katherine Kim, Sora Kim-Russell, and Mary Kim-Arnold. Bloomfield, IN: Truepeny Publishing, 2018.

Kim, Jeong Ja. *The Hidden Truth of the US Military Comfort Women*. Seoul, KR: Hanul Academy, 2013.

Lee, Lily Lu. "Growing Up in Korea." In *Mixed Korean: Our Stories, An Anthology*, edited by Cerissa Kim, Katherine Kim, Sora Kim-Russell, and Mary Kim-Arnold. Bloomfield, IN: Truepeny Publishing, 2018.

Martin, Allison. "An Interview with Cherie Clark." *ComeUnity*, 2000. https://www.comeunity.com/apv/babylift-clark.htm.

Meeky. "The Underside of the Rainbow." In *Mixed Korean: Our Stories, An Anthology*, edited by Cerissa Kim, Katherine Kim, Sora Kim-Russell, and Mary Kim-Arnold. Bloomfield, IN: Truepeny Publishing, 2018.

Morey, Glenn and Julie Morey. "Side By Side Project." *Side By Side Project*, 2018. https://sidebysideproject.com.

Peterson, Joel. *Dreams of My Mothers: A Story of Love Transcendent*. Minneapolis: Huff Publishing, 2015.

(222)   *Bibliography*

Peterson, Joel. "Mom's Love in a Breakfast Bowl." In *Mixed Korean: Our Stories, An Anthology*, edited by Cerissa Kim, Katherine Kim, Sora Kim-Russell, and Mary Kim-Arnold. Bloomfield, IN: Truepeny Publishing, 2018.

Sams, Crawford F. *Medic: The Mission of an American Military Doctor in Occupied Japan and Wartorn Korea*. Armonk, NY: M. E. Sharpe, 1998.

Siegel-Dalton, Bella. "Chosun One." In *Mixed Korean: Our Stories, An Anthology*, edited by Cerissa Kim, Katherine Kim, Sora Kim-Russell, and Mary Kim-Arnold. Bloomfield, IN: Truepeny Publishing, 2018.

Sunlit Sisters' Center. *Oral Histories of the Sunlit Sisters' Center's Grandmothers: Part* I. Pyongtaek, KR: Sunlit Sisters' Center, 2008.

Sunlit Sisters' Center. *Oral Histories of the Sunlit Sisters' Center's Grandmothers: Part* II. Pyongtaek, KR: Sunlit Sisters' Center, 2011.

Sunlit Sisters' Center. *Oral Histories of the Sunlit Sisters' Center's Grandmothers: Part* III. Pyongtaek, KR: Sunlit Sisters' Center, 2012.

Sunlit Sisters' Center. *Oral Histories of the Sunlit Sisters' Center's Grandmothers: Part* IV. Pyongtaek, KR: Sunlit Sisters' Center, 2013.

Magazines, Newspapers, and Periodicals

Atlanta Daily World
Baltimore Afro-American
Baltimore Sun
Boston Globe
Chicago Daily Defender
Chicago Daily Tribune
Chicago Defender
Chicago Tribune
Chicago Reader
Chosŏn Ilbo
Daily Boston Globe
Ebony
GEO
Guardian
Guideposts Magazine
Korea Times
Life
Los Angeles Times
New York Herald Tribune
New York Times
New York Times Sunday Magazine
Oregonian
Philadelphia Tribune
Post Dispatch
Register Guard
Shindonga
Sun
The Record: Southwestern Union Conference of Seventh Day Adventist
Time
Tonga Ilbo
Washington Post
Washington Post and Times Herald

Bibliography *(223)*

Published Archival Collections

Headquarters of the Republic of Korea (ROK) Army. *War History on the Homefront, Volume on Personnel Affairs* Seoul, KR: Headquarters of the ROK Army, 1956.

Korean Child Welfare Committee. *Handicapped Children's Survey Report, Korea, 1961.* Seoul, KR: Ministry of Health and Social Affairs, 1961.

Unpublished Archival Collections

International Social Service, United States of America Branch Case Records. Social Welfare History Archives at the University of Minnesota, Minneapolis (SWHA).

International Social Service, United States of America Branch Papers. Social Welfare History Archives at the University of Minnesota, Minneapolis.

Leonard Mayo Papers. Social Welfare History Archives at the University of Minnesota, Minneapolis.

President's Speeches and Statements: Reading Copies. The Gerald R. Ford Presidential Library at the University of Michigan, Ann Arbor.

Records of General Headquarters, Far East Command, Supreme Commander of the Allied Powers, and United Nations Command (RG 554). United States National Archives and Records Administration, College Park.

Records of United States Army Operational, Tactical, and Support Organizations World War II and Thereafter (RG 338). United States National Archives and Records Administration, College Park.

Records of United States Army, Pacific (RG 550). United States National Archives and Records Administration, College Park.

Theodore C. Marrs Files. The Gerald R. Ford Presidential Library at the University of Michigan, Ann Arbor.

The War Department and the Army Records (RG 407). United States National Archives and Records Administration, College Park.

White House Press Releases. The Gerald R. Ford Presidential Library at the University of Michigan, Ann Arbor.

US Legislative Branch Documents

An Act for the Relief of Certain Korean War Orphans. Public Law 475. US Statutes at Large 69 (1955).

An Act to Amend the Act Approved December 28, 1945 (Public Law 271, Seventy-ninth Congress), entitled "An Act to expedite the Admission to the United States of Alien Spouses and Alien Minor Children of Citizen Members of the United States Armed Forces." Public Law 213. *US Statutes at Large* 61 (1947).

An Act to Amend the Immigration and Nationality Act to Provide Preferential Treatment in the Admission of Certain Children of United States Citizens. Public Law 359. *US Statutes at Large* 96 (1982).

An Act to Expedite the Admission to the United States of Alien Spouses and Alien Minor Children of Citizen Members of the United States Armed Forces. Public Law 271. *US Statutes at Large* 59 (1945).

An Act to Limit the Immigration of Aliens into the United States, and for Other Purposes. Public No. 139. *US Statutes at Large* 43 (1924).

An Act to Permit the Admission of Alien Spouses and Minor Children of Citizen Members of the United States Armed Forces. Public Law 717. *US Statutes at Large* 64 (1950).

(224)   Bibliography

An Act to Revise the Laws Relating to Immigration, Naturalization, and Nationality; and for Other Purposes. Public Law 414. *US Statutes at Large* 66 (1952).

Joint Resolution to Authorize the Completion of the Processing of Visa Cases, and Admission into the United States, of Certain Alien Fiancés, and Fiancées of Members, or of Former Members, of the Armed Forces of the United States, as was Provided in the so-called GI Fiancées Act (60 Stat. 339), as Amended. Public Law 51. *US Statutes at Large* 63 (1949).

US Congress. *Congressional Record.* 84th Cong., 1st sess., 1955. Vol. 101, pt. 10.

US Congress. *Congressional Record.* 84th Cong., 2nd sess., 1956. Vol. 102, pt. 10.

US Congress. *Congressional Record.* 84th Cong., 2nd sess., 1956. Vol. 102, pt. 11.

US Congress. *Congressional Record.* 85th Cong., 1st sess., 1957. Vol. 103, pt. 1.

US Congress. *Congressional Record.* 85th Cong., 1st sess., 1957. Vol. 103, pt. 9.

US Congress. *Congressional Record.* 86th Cong., 2nd sess., 1959. Vol. 105, pt. 11.

US Congress. *Congressional Record.* 96th Cong., 2nd sess., 1980. Vol. 126, pt. 11.

US Congress. *Congressional Record.* 97th Cong., 1st sess., 1981. Vol. 127, pt. 1.

US Congress. *Congressional Record.* 97th Cong., 2nd sess., 1982. Vol. 128, pt. 2.

US Congress. *Congressional Record.* 97th Cong., 2nd sess., 1982. Vol. 128, pt. 13.

US Congress. *Congressional Record.* 99th Cong., 1st sess., 1985. Vol. 131, pt. 5.

US Congress. *Congressional Record.* 100th Cong., 1st sess., 1987. Vol. 133, pt. 16.

US Congress. *Congressional Record.* 103rd Cong., 1st sess., 1993. Vol. 139, pt. 9.

US Congress. *Congressional Record.* 105th Cong., 1st sess., 1997. Vol. 143, pt. 94

US Congress. House. Committee on the Judiciary. *Immigration Reform: Hearing Before the Subcommittee on Immigration, Refugees and International Law.* 97th Cong., 1st sess., October 14, 15, 21, 26, 28, November 12, 17, and 19, 1982.

US Congress. House. Committee on Un-American Activities. *The Kremlin's Espionage and Terror Organizations (Testimony of Petr S. Deriabin Former Officer of the USSR's Committee of State Security (KGB): Hearing Before the Committee on Un-American Activities.* 86th Cong., 1st sess., March 17, 1959.

US Congress. Senate. Committee on Governmental Affairs. *Amerasian Immigration Proposals: Hearing Before the Subcommittee on Immigration and Refugee Policy of the Committee on the Judiciary.* 97th Cong., 2nd sess., June 21, 1983.

US Congress. Senate. Committee on the Judiciary. *Amending the Act to Expedite the Admission to the United States of Alien Spouses and Alien Minor Children of Citizen Members of the United States Armed Forces.* 80th Cong., 1st sess., July 11, 1947.

US Congress. Senate. Committee on the Judiciary. *Amendments to Refugee Relief Act 1953: Hearing Before the Subcommittee of the Committee on the Judiciary United States Senate Eighty-Fourth Congress Second Session on S. 3570, S. 3571, S. 3372, S. 3573. S. 3574, and S. 3606 Bills to Amend the Refugee Relief Act of 1953, So as to Increase the Number of Orphan Visas and Raise the Age; Extend the Life of the Act; Permit Issuance of Visas to Persons Afflicted with Tuberculosis; Permit the Giving of Assurances by Recognized Voluntary Agencies: Provide for the Reallocation of Visas, and Change the Conditions Under Which Visas May Be Issued to Refugees in the Far East.* 84th Cong., 2nd sess., May 3, 1956.

US Congress. Senate. Committee on the Judiciary. *Certain Korean War Orphans: Report to Accompany S. 2312.* 84th Cong., 1st sess., 1955, S. Rep. 1216.

US Congress. Senate. Committee on the Judiciary. *Final Report of the Administrator of the Refugee Relief Act of 1953, as Amended.* 85th Congress, 1st sess., November 15, 1957.

US Congress. Senate. Committee on the Judiciary. *Immigration Reform: Hearing Before the Subcommittee on Immigration, Refugees and International Law.* 97th Cong., 1st sess., October 14, 15, 21, 26, 28, November 12, 17, and 19, 1982.

US Congress. Senate. *Committee on the Judiciary. Indochina Evacuation and Refugee Problems (Part I: Operation Babylift & Humanitarian Needs): Hearing Before the Subcommittee to Investigate Problems Connected with Refugees and Escapees.* 94th Cong., 1st sess., April 8, 1975.

US Congress. Senate. Committee on the Judiciary. *Relating to Admission to United States of Alien Orphan Children: Hearing Held Before Subcommittee on Immigration and Naturalization of the Committee on the Judiciary—S. 1498, S. 1532, S. 1610, S. 2004.* 86th Congress, 1st sess., *vol.* 1, June 23, 1959.

US Congress. Senate. Committee on the Judiciary. *Relating to General Immigration Matters: Hearing Held Before Subcommittee on Immigration and Naturalization of the Committee on the Judiciary—S. 116, 504, 925, 952, 954, 1196, 1280, 1468, 1523, 1532, 1610, 1919, 1996, 1974.* 86th Cong., 1st sess., *vol.* 1, May 20, 1959.

US General Accounting Office. *Vietnamese Amerasian Resettlement: Education, Employment, and Family Outcomes in the United States.* GAO/PEMD-94-15. Washington, DC, 1994.

US Library of Congress. Congressional Research Service. *Vietnamese Adoption and Child Care,* by Jean Yavis Jones, *HV* 741 (1973).

SECONDARY SOURCES
Published Monographs, Books, and Essays

Alvah, Donna. *Unofficial Ambassadors: American Military Families Overseas and the Cold War 1946–1965.* New York: New York University Press, 2007.

Appy, Christian G. *Cold War Constructions: The Political Culture of United States Imperialism, 1945–1966.* Amherst: University of Massachusetts Press, 2000.

Appy, Christian G. *American Reckoning: The Vietnam War and Our National Identity.* New York: Penguin Books, 2016.

Bass, Thomas A. *Vietnamerica: The War Comes Home.* New York: Soho Press, 1996.

Briggs, Laura. *Somebody's Children: The Politics of Transnational and Transracial Adoption.* Durham, NC: Duke University Press, 2012.

Bu, Liping and Ka-Che Yip. *Public Health and National Reconstruction in Post-War Asia: International Influences, Local Transformations.* New York: Routledge, 2015.

Buck, Pearl S. *Children for Adoption.* New York: Random House, 1964.

Campomanes, Osar. "The New Empire's Forgetful and Forgotten Citizens: Unrepresentability and Unassimilability in Filipino-American Postcolonialities." *Critical Mass* 2, no. 2 (1995).

Ceniza Choy, Catherine. *Global Families: A History of Asian International Adoption in America.* New York: New York University Press, 2013.

Cheng, Cindy I-Fen. *Citizens of Asian America: Democracy and Race during the Cold War.* New York: New York University Press, 2013.

Cheng, Sealing. *On the Move for Love: Migrant Entertainers and the US Military in South Korea.* Philadelphia: University of Pennsylvania Press, 2013.

Cho, Grace M. *Haunting the Korean Diaspora: Shame, Secrecy, and the Forgotten War.* Minneapolis: University of Minnesota Press, 2008.

Cho, Grace M. *Tastes Like War: A Memoir.* New York: Feminist Press, 2021.

Choo, Hae Yeon. *Decentering Citizenship: Gender, Labor, and Migrant Rights in South Korea.* Stanford, CA: Stanford University Press, 2016.

Choo, Hae Yeon. "Selling Fantasies of Rescue: Intimate Labor, Filipina Migrant Hostesses, and US GIs in a Shifting Global Order." *positions* 24, no. 1 (2016).

Chung Simpson, Caroline. *An Absent Presence: Japanese Americans in Postwar American Culture, 1945–1960.* Durham, NC: Duke University Press, 2001.

(226) Bibliography

Chung, Soojin. *Adopting for God: The Mission to Change America through Transnational Adoption*. New York: New York University Press, 2021.

Cohen, Deborah. *Family Secrets: Shame and Privacy in Modern Britain*. New York: Oxford University Press, 2013.

Conn, Peter. *Pearl S. Buck: A Cultural Biography*. Cambridge: Cambridge University Press, 1996.

Coráñez Bolton, Sony. *Crip Colony: Mestizaje, US Imperialism, and the Queer Politics of Disability in the Philippines*. Durham, NC: Duke University Press, 2023.

Cumings, Bruce. *Korea's Place in the Sun: A Modern History*. New York: W. W. Norton, 2005.

Cumings, Bruce. *The Korean War: A History*. New York: Modern Library, 2011.

Cumings, Bruce. *North Korea: Another Country*. New York: New Press, 2003.

Cumings, Bruce. "Silent but Deadly: Sexual Subordination in the US-Korea Relationship." In *Let the Good Times Roll: Prostitution and the US Military in Asia*, edited by Saundra Pollack and Brenda Stoltzfus. New York: New Press, 1992.

Cumings, Bruce. *War and Television*. New York: Verso, 1992.

DeBonis, Steven. *Children of the Enemy: Oral Histories of Vietnamese Amerasians and Their Mothers*. Jefferson, NC: McFarland, 1995.

Doolan, Yuri. "The Camptown Origins of International Adoption and the Hypersexualization of Korean Children." *Journal of Asian American Studies* 24, no. 3 (October 2021).

Doolan, Yuri. "The Cold War Construction of the Amerasian, 1950–1982." *Diplomatic History* 46, no. 4 (September 2022).

Doolan, Yuri. "Transpacific Camptowns: Korean Women, US Army Bases, and Military Prostitution in America." *Journal of American Ethnic History* 38, no. 4 (Summer 2019).

Dorrow, Sarah K. *Transnational Adoption: A Cultural Economy of Race, Gender, and Kinship*. New York: New York University Press, 2006.

Dudziak, Mary. *Cold War, Civil Rights: Race and the Image of American Democracy*. Princeton, NJ: Princeton University Press, 2000.

Duncan, Patti. "Genealogies of Unbelonging: Amerasians and Transnational Adoptees as Legacies of U.S. Militarism in South Korea." In *Militarized Currents: Toward a Decolonized Future in Asia and the Pacific*, edited by Setsu Shigematsu and Keith L. Camacho. Minneapolis: University of Minnesota Press, 2010.

Eng, David. "Transnational Adoption and Queer Diasporas." *Social Text* 21, no. 3 (Fall 2003).

Espiritu, Yen Le. *Body Counts: The Vietnam War and Militarized Refugees*. Oakland: University of California Press, 2014.

Fehrenbach, Heide. *Race After Hitler: Black Occupation Children in Postwar Germany and America*. Princeton, NJ: Princeton University Press, 2005.

Gage, Sue-Je Lee. "The Amerasian Problem: Blood, Duty, and Race." *International Relations* 21, no. 1 (2007).

Gellhorn, Martha. *The Face of War*. New York: Atlantic Monthly Press, 1988.

Ghosh, Durba. *Sex and Family in Colonial India: The Making of Empire*. Cambridge: Cambridge University Press, 2006.

Go, Julian. *Patterns of Empire: The British and American Empires, 1688 to the Present*. Cambridge: Cambridge University Press, 2011.

Go, Julian and Anne F. Foster. *The American Colonial State in the Philippines: Global Perspectives*. Durham, NC: Duke University Press, 2003.

Green, Michael Cullen. *Black Yanks in the Pacific: Race in the Making of American Military Empire after World War II*. Ithaca, NY: Cornell University Press, 2010.

Graves, Kori. *A War Born Family: African American Adoption in the Wake of the Korean War*. New York: New York University Press, 2020.

Han, Won-sang. "The Japanese Armed Forces at War and their System of Sexual Slavery." In *Forced Prostitution in Times of War and Peace*, edited by Barbara Drinck and Chung-noh Gross. Bielefeld, DE: Kleine Verlag, 2007.

Hanley, Charles J., Martha Mendoza, and Sang-hun Choe. *The Bridge at No Gun Ri: A Hidden Nightmare from the Korean War*. New York: Henry Holt, 2001.

Höhn, Maria and Seungsook Moon. *Over There: Living with the US Military Empire from World War Two to Present*. Durham, NC: Duke University Press, 2010.

Hwang, W. Taejin. "The 'Amerasian' Knot: Transpacific Crossings of 'GI Babies' from Korea to the United States." In *Race and Racism in Modern East Asia*, vol. 3, *Interactions, Nationalism, Gender and Lineage*, edited by Rotem Kowner and Walter Demel. Leiden, NL: Brill, 2015.

Hwang, Taejin. "Militarized Landscapes of Yongsan: From Japanese Imperial to Little Americas in Early Cold War Korea." *Korea Journal* 58, no. 1 (Spring 2018).

Jeffords, Susan. *The Remasculinization of America: Gender and the Vietnam War*. Bloomington: Indiana University Press, 1989.

Kaplan, Amy. "Left Alone with America: The Absence of Empire in the Study of American Culture." In *Cultures of United States Imperialism*, edited by Amy Kaplan and Donald Pease. Durham, NC: Duke University Press.

Kelley, Patrick. *Military Preventative Medicine: Mobilization and Deployment*, vol. 1. Washington, DC: Office of the Surgeon General at TMM Publications, 2003.

Kerber, Linda. "The Stateless as the Citizen's Other: A View from the United States." *American Historical Review* 112, no. 1 (2007).

Kim, Bok-Lim. *Women in Shadows: A Handbook for Service Providers Working with Asian Wives of US Military Personnel*. La Jolla, CA: National Committee Concerned with Asian Wives of US Servicemen, 1981.

Kim, Cerissa, Katherine Kim, Sora Kim-Russell, and Mary Kim-Arnold. *Mixed Korean: Our Stories, An Anthology*. Bloomfield, IN: Truepeny Publishing, 2018.

Kim, Elaine and Chungmoo Choi. *Dangerous Women: Gender and Korean Nationalism*. New York: Routledge, 1998.

Kim, Eleana. *Adopted Territory: Transnational Korean Adoptees and the Politics of Belonging*. Durham, NC: Duke University Press, 2010.

Kim, Eleana. "Human Capital: Transnational Korean Adoptees and the Neoliberal Logic of Return." *Journal of Korean Studies* 17, no. 2 (Fall 2012).

Kim, Hosu. *Birth Mothers and Transnational Adoption Practice in South Korea: Virtual Mothering*. New York: Palgrave Macmillan, 2016.

Kim, Hosu and Grace M. Cho. "The Kinship of Violence." In *Mothering in East Asian Communities: Politics and Practices*, edited by Patty Duncan and Gina Wong. Bradford, ON: Demeter Press, 2014.

Kim, Jinah. *Postcolonial Grief: The Afterlives of the Pacific Wars in the Americas*. Durham, NC: Duke University Press, 2019.

Kim, Jodi. *Ends of Empire: Asian American Critique and the Cold War*. Minneapolis: University of Minnesota Press, 2010.

Kim, Nadia. *Imperial Citizens: Koreans and Race from Seoul to LA*. Stanford, CA: Stanford University Press, 2008.

Klein, Christina. *Cold War Orientalism: Asia in the Middlebrow Imagination, 1945–1961*. Berkeley: University of California Press, 2003.

(228)   *Bibliography*

Klein, Christina. "Family Ties and Political Obligation: The Discourse of Adoption and the Cold War Commitment to Asia." In *Cold War Constructions*, edited by Christian Appy. Amherst: University of Massachusetts Press, 2000.

Koshiro, Yukiko. *Trans-Pacific Racisms and the US Occupation of Japan*. New York: Columbia University Press, 1999.

Kowner, Rotem and Walter Demel. *Race and Racism in Modern East Asia*, vol. 2, *Interactions, Nationalism, Gender and Lineage*. Leiden, NL: Brill, 2015.

Kramer, Paul. *The Blood of Government: Race, Empire, the United States and the Philippines*. Chapel Hill: University of North Carolina Press, 2006.

Kramm, Robert. *Sanitized Sex: Regulating Prostitution, Venereal Disease, and Intimacy in Occupied Japan, 1945–1952*. Berkeley: University of California Press, 2017.

Lee, Mary. "Mixed Race Peoples in the Korean National Imaginary and Family." *Korean Studies* 32 (2008).

Lee, Na Young, "The Construction of Military Prostitution in South Korea during the US Military Rule, 1945–1948." *Feminist Studies* 33, no. 3 (Fall 2007).

Lee, Na Young. "Un/forgettable Histories of US Camptown Prostitution in South Korea: Women's Experiences of Sexual Labor and Government Policies." *Sexualities* 21, no. 5–6 (2018).

Leffler, Melvyn. *A Preponderance of Power: National Security, the Truman Administration, and the Cold War*. Stanford, CA: Stanford University Press, 1992.

Leong, Karen J. *The China Mystique: Pearl S. Buck, Anna May Wong, Mayling Soong, and the Transformation of American Orientalism*. Berkeley: University of California Press, 2005.

Lipman, Jana. "'The Face Is the Road Map': Vietnamese Amerasians in U.S. Political and Popular Culture, 1980–1988." *Journal of Asian American Studies* 14, no. 1 (2011).

Loren, Ralph. "The Historic Role of Military Preventative Medicine and Public Health in US Armies of Occupation and Military Government." In *Military Preventative Medicine: Mobilization and Deployment*, vol. 1, edited by Patrick Kelley. Washington, DC: Office of the Surgeon General at TMM Publications, 2003.

Luce, Henry. *The American Century*. New York: Farrar and Rinehart, 1941.

Maira, Sunaina Marr. *Missing: Youth, Citizenship, and Empire After 9/11*. Durham, NC: Duke University Press, 2009.

Man, Simeon. "Anti-Asian Violence and US Imperialism." *Race and Class* 62, no. 2 (2020).

May, Elaine Tyler. *Homeward Bound: American Families in the Cold War Era*. New York: Basic Books, 2008.

McAlister, Melani. *Epic Encounters: Culture, Media, and US Interests in the Middle East Since 1945*. Berkeley: University of California Press, 2005.

McKee, Kimberly D. *Disrupting Kinship: Transnational Politics of Korean Adoption in the United States*. Champaign: University of Illinois Press, 2019.

McKee, Kimberly D. "Monetary Flows and the Movements of Children: The Transnational Adoption Industrial Complex." *Journal of Korean Studies* 21, no. 1 (Spring 2016).

McNinch, Colonel Joseph H. "Venereal Disease Problems, US Army Forces, Far East 1950–53." *Medical Science Publication 4*, vol. 2 (April 1954).

Meade, Edward Grant. *American Military Government in Korea*. New York: King's Crown Press, 1951.

Millard, Ralph D. "Oriental Peregrinations." *Plastic and Reconstructive Surgery* 16, no. 5 (1955).

Mizutani, Satoshi. *The Meaning of White: Race, Class, and the 'Domiciled Community' in British India 1858–1930.* Oxford: Oxford University Press, 2011.

Molnar, Nicholas Trajano. *American Mestizos, the Philippines, and the Malleability of Race, 1898–1961.* Columbia: University of Missouri Press, 2017.

Moon, Katharine. *Sex Among Allies.* New York: Columbia University Press, 1997.

Moon, Seungsook. "Begetting the Nation: The Androcentric Discourse of National History and Tradition in South Korea." In *Dangerous Women: Gender and Korean Nationalism,* edited by Elaine Kim and Chungmoo Choi. New York: Routledge, 1998.

Moon, Seungsook. *Militarized Modernity and Gendered Citizenship in South Korea.* Durham, NC: Duke University Press, 2005.

Moon, Seungsook. "Regulating Desire, Managing Empire: US Military Prostitution in South Korea, 1945–1970." In *Over There: Living with the US Military Empire from World War Two to Present,* edited by Maria Höhn and Seungsook Moon. Durham, NC: Duke University Press, 2010.

Ngai, Mae. *Impossible Subjects: Illegal Aliens and the Making of Modern America.* Princeton, NJ: Princeton University Press, 2004.

Oh, Arissa. *To Save the Children of Korea: The Cold War Origins of International Adoption.* Stanford, CA: Stanford University Press, 2015.

Okazawa-Rey, Margo. "Amerasian Children of GI Town: A Legacy of US Militarism in South Korea." *Asian Journal of Women's Studies* 3 (1997).

Okihiro, Gary. *Third World Studies: Theorizing Liberation.* Durham, NC: Duke University Press, 2016.

Palumbo-Liu, David. *Asian/American: Historical Crossings of a Racial Frontier.* Stanford, CA: Stanford University Press, 1999.

Park, Jeong-Mi. "A Historical Sociology of the Korean Government's Policies on Military Prostitution in US Camptowns, 1953–1995: Biopolitics, State of Exception, and the Paradox of Sovereignty under the Cold War." *Korean Journal of Sociology* 49, no. 2 (April 2014).

Park, Jeong-Mi. "Liberation or Purification? Prostitution, Women's Movement and Nation Building in South Korea Under US Military Occupation, 1945–1948." *Sexualities* 22, no. 7-8 (2019).

Park Nelson, Kim. *Invisible Asians: Korean American Adoptees, Asian American Experiences, and Racial Exceptionalism.* New Brunswick, NJ: Rutgers University Press, 2016.

Pascoe, Peggy. *What Comes Naturally: Miscegenation Law and the Making of Race in America.* New York: Oxford University Press, 2009.

Pate, Soojin. *From Orphan to Adoptee: US Empire and Genealogies of Korean Adoption.* Minneapolis: University of Minnesota Press, 2014.

Petiss, Susan T. "Effect of Adoption of Foreign Children on US Adoption Standards and Practices." *Child Welfare* 37 (1958).

Pollack, Saundra and Brenda Stoltzfus. *Let the Good Times Roll: Prostitution and the US Military in Asia.* New York: New Press, 1992.

Pomfret, David. *Youth and Empire: Trans-Colonial Childhoods in British and French Asia.* Stanford, CA: Stanford University Press, 2015.

Sachs, Dana. *The Life We Were Given: Operation Babylift, International Adoption, and the Children of War in Vietnam.* Boston, MA: Beacon Press, 2010.

Said, Edward. *Orientalism.* New York: Random House, 1978.

Shibusawa, Naoko. *America's Geisha Ally: Reimagining the Japanese Enemy.* Cambridge, MA: Harvard University Press, 2006.

Shimizu, Celine Parreñas. *The Hypersexuality of Race: Performing Asian/American Women on Screen and Scene*. Durham, NC: Duke University Press, 2007.

Shin, Dong-Myeon. *Social and Economic Policies in Korea: Ideas, Networks and Linkages*. London: Routledge Curzon, 2003.

Shin, Dong-Won. "Public Health and People's Health: Contrasting the Paths of Healthcare Systems in South and North Korea, 1945–60." In *Public Health and National Reconstruction in Post-War Asia: International Influences, Local Transformations*, edited by Liping Bu and Ka-Che Yip. New York: Routledge, 2015.

Shin, Gi-Wook. *Ethnic Nationalism in Korea: Genealogy, Politics, and Legacy*. Stanford, CA: Stanford University Press, 2006.

Soh, C. Sarah. *The Comfort Women: Sexual Violence and Postcolonial Memory in Korea and Japan*. Chicago: University of Chicago Press, 2008.

Stoler, Ann. *Carnal Knowledge and Imperial Power: Race and the Intimate in Colonial Rule*. Berkeley: University of California Press, 2002.

Stoler, Ann. "Sexual Affronts and Racial Frontiers: European Identities and the Cultural Politics of Exclusion in Colonial Southeast Asia." *Comparative Studies in Society and History* 34, no. 3 (July 1992).

Takeuchi, Michiko. "'Pan-Pan Girls' Performing and Resisting Neocolonialism(s) in the Pacific Theater: US Military Prostitution in Occupied Japan, 1945–1952." In *Over There: Living with the US Military Empire from World War Two to Present*, edited by Maria Höhn and Seungsook Moon. Durham, NC: Duke University Press, 2010.

Tchen, John Kuo Wei. *New York Before Chinatown: Orientalism and the Shaping of American Culture, 1776–1882*. Baltimore: Johns Hopkins University Press, 2001.

Teng, Emma Jinha. *Eurasians: Mixed Identities in the United States, China, and Hong Kong, 1842–1943*. Berkeley: University of California Press, 2013.

Thomas, Sabrina. "Blood Politics: Reproducing the Children of 'Others' in the 1982 Amerasian Immigration Act." *Journal of American-East Asian Relations* 26, no.1 (2019).

Thomas, Sabrina. *Scars of War: The Politics of Paternity and Responsibility for the Amerasians of Vietnam*. Lincoln: University of Nebraska Press, 2021.

Valverde, Kieu-Lin Caroline. "From Dust to Gold: The Vietnamese Amerasian Experience." In *Racially Mixed People in America*, edited by Maria P. Root. Newbury Park, CA: Sage Publications, 1992.

Varzally, Allison. *Children of Reunion: Vietnamese Adoptions and the Politics of Family Migrations*. Chapel Hill: University of North Carolina Press, 2017.

Virden, Jenel. *Good-bye, Piccadilly: British War Brides in America*. Urbana: University of Illinois Press, 1995.

Von Eschen, Penny. *Race Against Empire: Black Americans and Anticolonialism, 1937–1957*. Ithaca, NY: Cornell University Press, 1997.

Von Eschen, Penny. "Who's the Real Ambassador? Exploding Cold War Racial Ideology." In *Cold War Constructions*, edited by Christian Appy. Amherst: University of Massachusetts Press, 2000.

Woo, Susie. *Framed by War: Korean Children and Women at the Crossroads of US Empire*. New York: New York University Press, 2019.

Wu, Judy Tzu-Chun. *Radicals on the Road: Internationalism, Orientalism, and Feminism during the Vietnam Era*. Ithaca, NY: Cornell University Press, 2013.

Yarborough, Trin. *Surviving Twice: Amerasian Children of the Vietnam War*. Washington, DC: Potomac Books, 2005.

Yoshiaki, Yoshimi. *Comfort Women: Sexual Slavery in the Japanese Military During World War II*. New York: Columbia University Press, 2002.

Yoshihara, Mary. *Embracing the East: White Women and American Orientalism*. New York: Oxford University Press, 2003.

Yuh, Ji-Yeon. *Beyond the Shadow of Camptown: Korean Military Brides in America*. New York: New York University Press, 2002.

Zeiger, Susan. *Entangling Alliances: Foreign War Brides and American Soldiers in the Twentieth Century*. New York: New York University Press, 2010.

Television and Film

Dead Men on Furlough. Directed by John O'Dea. Portland, OR: World Vision, 1954.

First Person Plural. Directed by Deann Borshay Liem. San Francisco, CA: Center for Asian American Media, 2000.

Geographies of Kinship. Directed by Deann Borshay Liem. Berkeley, CA: Mu Films, 2019.

In the Matter of Cha Jung Hee. Directed by Deann Borshay Liem. Harriman, NY: New Day Films, 2010.

The Loretta Young Show. "Dateline Korea." Episode no. 5430. National Broadcasting Company, March 13, 1955.

The Other Sheep. Director unknown. Portland, OR: World Vision, undated 1950s.

Precious Cargo. Directed by Janet P. Gardner. San Francisco, CA: Independent Television Service, 2001.

The Women Outside: Korean Women and the US Military. Directed by J. T. Takagi and Hye Jung Park. New York: Third World Newsreel, 1995.

Unpublished Dissertations and Theses

Doolan, Yuri. "Being Amerasian in South Korea: Purebloodness, Multiculturalism, and Living Alongside the US Military Empire." Honors thesis, Ohio State University, 2012.

Fish, Robert A. "The Heiress and the Love Children: Sawada Miki and the Elizabeth Saunders Home for Mixed-Blood Orphans in Postwar Japan." PhD diss., University of Hawai'i, 2002.

Gage, Sue-Je Lee. "Pure Mixed Blood: The Multiple Identities of Amerasians in South Korea." PhD diss., Indiana University, 2007.

Graves, Kori. "Domesticating Foreign Affairs: The African-American Family, Korean War Orphans, and Cold War Civil Rights." PhD diss., University of Wisconsin Madison, 2011.

Lee, Na Young. "The Construction of US Camptown Prostitution in South Korea: Trans/formation and Resistance." PhD diss., University of Maryland, College Park, 2006.

Lipman, Jana. "Mixed Voices, Mixed Policy: Vietnamese Amerasians in Vietnam and the United States." Senior thesis, Brown University, 1997.

Nakamura, Masako. "Families Precede Nation and Race? Marriage, Migration, and Integration of Japanese War Brides after World War II." PhD diss., University of Minnesota, 2010.

Thomas, Sabrina. "The Value of Dust: Policy, Citizenship and Vietnam's Amerasian Children." PhD diss., Arizona State University, 2015.

Welty, Lily Ann Yumi. "Advantage Through Crisis: Multiracial American Japanese in Post-World War II Japan, Okinawa and America 1945–1972." PhD diss., University of California Santa Barbara, 2012.

Woo, Susie. "A New American Comes 'Home'": Race, Nation, and the Immigration of Korean War Adoptees, 'GI Babies,' and Brides." PhD diss., Yale University, 2010.

INDEX

For the benefit of digital users, indexed terms that span two pages (e.g., 52–53) may, on occasion, appear on only one of those pages.

abandonment
  of children by mothers, 49–51, 55–56
  of Korean wives/children, 48–50, 84, 87–88, 194n.24
abuse/neglect, 128–32
Adoptee Citizenship Act of 2021, 133
adoption. *see also* Holt, Harry/Holt adoption programs; International Social Services (ISS)
  abandonment of Korean wives/ children, 82
  adjustment period, 181–82n.47, 214–15n.38
  adverse views of, 83–85, 99
  advocates' narratives, 60–63, 73– 76, 92–93, 198n.90, 198n.98, 202n.169, 204n.21
  age limits, 56–57, 62–63, 204n.27
  applications statistics, 51, 197n.71
  background checks/parent vetting, 63–64, 127, 181–82n.47
  of Black Korean children, 61–62, 63–64, 93, 103–4, 103f, 104f, 112– 13, 142, 148–49, 198–99n.108, 199n.110, 201n.153
  Buck on, 61–62, 73–74, 198–99n.108, 199n.110, 202n.172
  coercive/deceptive tactics, 66–72, 72f, 89–90, 93–94, 96, 119–20, 160–62, 201n.153, 219n.32
  critical adoption studies, 181n.44, 181n.45
  documentaries discussing, 167f, 168– 69, 219n.24
  eligible orphan criteria, 195–96n.48

  expansion of, 9–10
  financial requirements of, 66, 199n.110, 200n.136
  follow up by social workers, 181–82n.47
  of full Korean children, 112–13, 210n.17
  GI baby mortality statistics, 60–61, 198n.90, 198n.98
  home visits, 63–64, 74, 125, 181–82n.47
  immigration quotas, 56–57
  institutional barriers to, 40–42, 48– 49, 74–75, 194n.24
  international organizations 1961, 205n.51
  Korean social workers in, 8–9, 85, 91, 94, 99
  legislation generally, 46–47, 53, 56– 57, 62–63, 74, 75–76, 78, 139
  legislative reform, 216n.62, 216n.68
  media coverage of, 47–48, 50–51, 55, 60, 61, 93–94, 194–95n.36, 204n.21
  of mixed race Koreans generally, 3–6, 7–10, 42–43, 47–48, 66–72, 178n.16, 180n.35, 201n.153
  mixed race Vietnamese *vs.* Koreans, 10–11, 15, 149, 216n.68
  motivations, 112–13, 142–43, 161–62
  placement by proxy, 8, 46, 53, 63–64, 74–76, 80, 92, 113, 125, 181–82n.47, 199n.116, 202n.179
  quotas, 56–57, 58–59, 62–63
  special counseling, 63–64
  sponsorships, 97–98, 101–2
  statistics, 9–10, 113, 135, 174t
  testimonies, 56–58

Index

adoption (*cont.*)
US narratives regarding, 8–9, 13, 42–43, 45, 46–47, 51–53, 58–60, 182n.50, 194–95n.36, 195n.38
whiteness preference in, 10, 61–62, 69, 93, 103–4, 109–11, 112–14, 114*f*, 198–99n.108, 209n.3, 209–10nn.10–11
Amerasian Homecoming Act of 1987, 155–56, 177–78n.11
Amerasian Immigration Act of 1982, 1–2, 7–8, 10–11, 137–38, 137*f*, 147–56, 158, 177n.7, 177–78n.11, 216n.62, 216n.68
Amerasians
concepts, definitions, 1–2, 7–8, 151, 159–60, 176n.3, 176n.4, 176n.6, 177n.9, 180n.35, 218n.9, 219n.19
Eurasians as resembling, 4–5
immigration statistics, 177–78n.11
legacy of, 160–61
legal definition of, 153
terminology, 4–5, 159, 180n.35
American exceptionalism, 2, 9–10, 177n.10
American Friends Service Committee, 142
American Soul Clinic, 205n.51
anti-Asian violence
abuse/neglect, 124–25
Asian women ban/immigration, 6–7, 31–36, 38–39, 48, 175n.2, 179–80nn.29–31, 191n.142
childhood sexual abuse, 129–32, 145–46, 212n.95
depression/mental illness, 125–26
discouraging of marriages, 40–42, 48–49, 157, 194n.24
ethnic nationalism/racism in Korea, 69, 73–74, 79, 106, 203n.10, 203n.11
Korean heritage erasure, 114–16, 119–21, 124, 127–28, 161–62, 211n.58
perceptions of Korean women, 16–17, 18–19, 19*f*, 20*f*, 21–22, 25, 36–38, 40–41, 68–69, 192n.170
prejudicial behavior towards in Korea, 82–83, 88–89, 104–6, 144–45
procurement of children by Holt, 66–72, 72*f*, 201n.153
separation trauma, 117–19, 119*f*
social isolation of adoptees, 111–12, 121–22, 209–10nn.10–11

socialization in abuse of children, 131
stigmatization, 128–32
as US imperialism, 4, 14–15, 76, 110–11, 178n.16, 209n.3
Appy, Christian G., 177n.9, 213n.3
Arthur Murray Dance Studios, 92
assimilation
abuse/neglect, 124–25, 128–32
behaviors/memories, 116–20, 118*f*, 124, 125, 126, 132
Black children/Black adoptive families, 121–24, 123*f*
celebratory narratives of, 134–35, 134*f*, 209–10n.11
childhood sexual abuse, 129–32, 145–46, 212n.95
depression/mental illness, 125–26
development/sense of self, 124–25
disillusionment with America, 127
education in US, 121–22, 123*f*, 124, 134–35, 151, 152*f*
English language acquisition, 114–15, 119–20, 124
erasure of Korean heritage, 114–16, 119–21, 124, 127–28, 161–62, 211n.58
of Eurasians, 61
failure to bond with adoptive parents, 119–20
familial relations/colonial policy, 5–7, 18–19, 179–80nn.29–31
follow up by social workers, 120–21, 125, 181–82n.47
food assimilation, 115–16, 120–21, 210n.32, 211n.58
integrationist movement, 99–103, 101*f*, 208n.143, 208n.151
lived experiences, 8, 10, 14–15, 55–56, 56*f*, 60–61, 79–80, 109–11, 136, 181n.44, 181n.45, 181–82n.47, 198n.98, 209n.3
maladaptive coping, 125–26
marriage prospects, 121–22, 148–49
overview, 14–15
plastic reconstructive surgery, 110, 209n.3
positive coping, 126
prejudicial behaviors towards mixed race Koreans, 121–24, 123*f*
re-homing of, 119–20

Index (235)

re-naming of, 114–15, 115*f*
rural placement of, 111–12, 121–22, 209–10nn.10–11
separation trauma, 117–19, 119*f*
social isolation of adoptees, 111–12, 121–22, 209–10nn.10–11
stigmatization, 128–32
US citizenship, 133
US social workers' role, 119–22, 133
"Association with Korean Women" (Circular No. 9), 17–18

Baltimore Afro-American, 61–62
birth family search, 161–69, 219n.19, 219n.24
Black Korean children
adoption of, 61–62, 63–64, 93, 103–4, 103*f*, 104*f*, 112–13, 142, 148–49, 198–99n.108, 199n.110, 201n.153
assimilation of, 121–24, 123*f*
ethnic nationalism/racism in Korea, 47
whiteness preference in adoption, 10, 61–62, 69, 93, 103–4, 109–11, 112–14, 114*f*, 198–99n.108, 209n.3, 209–10nn.10–11
Blackwell, Lucien, 153–54
Bos, Kara, 219n.34
Buck, Pearl S., 7–8, 61–62, 73–74, 92–99, 159, 198–99n.108, 199n.110, 202n.172

camptowns/camptown women. *see also* interracial intimacy
acceptance of children of, 49–50, 60–61, 69, 77
access to American goods by, 82, 83, 204n.27
adoption of children of (*see* adoption)
American-oriented culture in, 99–102, 101*f*, 102*f*, 103*f*, 208n.143
comfort women systems, xvii, 16, 17–18, 39–41, 191n.147
laundries as meeting places, 23
living conditions in, 80–83, 93, 102–6, 204n.21, 204n.27, 204n.29
living conditions ISS assessment, 80–81, 83–85
motivations, 49–50, 83–85, 89–90, 105
perceptions of by military, 12–13

portrayals/perceptions of, 12–13, 128–32
prejudicial behavior towards, 82–83, 88–89, 104–6, 144–45
as privileged class, 82, 83, 204n.27
prostitution encouraged, 6–7, 17–18, 21–22
prostitution outlawed, 22–23, 186n.51
regulation of contacts with, 185n.18, 186n.51
as ruined, xvii, 16, 18–19, 49, 175n.5
stigmatization of, 18–19, 19*f*, 49–50, 68–69, 81, 128–32
warnings against pickups, 25, 187n.72
Caritas, 141–42
Catholic Maryknoll, 208n.151
Cericole, Victor, 38
Chicago Defender, 16–17
Child Citizenship Act of 1983, 133
childhood sexual abuse, 129–32, 145–46, 212n.95
Cho, Grace M., 11
Christian Children's Fund, 195n.38
Chung, Jonny, 151
Circular No. 9 ("Association with Korean Women"), 17–18
citizenship
Asian naturalization ban, xvii, 175n.2
Asian *vs.* European wives, 31–34
birthright, xvii–xviii, 175n.2, 177n.7
birthright in Korea, 48, 205–6n.67
children of foreign women/ US servicemen, xvii–xviii, 42, 176n.7, 177n.7
by marriage, xvii, 31–34, 175n.3
nationality determinations, xvii–xviii, 33–34, 175–76n.6
by naturalization, 133
Clay, Phillip, 133
Clement, Thomas Park, 164, 166, 168–69
colonial concubinage, 6–7, 18–19
color line placement criterion, 10, 61–62, 69, 93, 103–4, 109–11, 112–14, 114*f*, 198–99n.108, 209n.3, 209–10nn.10–11
comfort women systems, xvii, 16, 17–18, 39–41, 191n.147
communist propaganda, 61–62, 74, 140–42, 150, 178–79n.17

(236) Index

Congressional Record, 56–59, 153–54
cosmetic surgery, 110, 209n.3
Cumings, Bruce, 11, 183n.61, 215n.39

Davison, Anne, 68–69, 81
DNA testing, 164–69, 219n.34
Doolan, Yuri, 157–58, 160
Driscoll, Natasha, 81–82, 204n.21
Dulles, John Foster, 60

Espiritu, Yen Le, 138
Eurasian Children Living as Indigenous
    Residents (ECLAIR), 13–14, 78, 88–
    92, 94, 96–99, 106, 205n.66
Eurasians. *see also* Amerasians
    Anglo-Indians, 5–6, 7–8, 150–51
    assimilation of, 61
    colonial concubinage, 6–7, 18–19
    colonial policy towards, 4–8, 150–51
    in immigration reform, 150–51
    Indos/Dutch Empire, 5–6, 150–51
    Métis of Indochina, 5–6, 150–51
    as priviledged class, 82
    terminology, 159, 180n.35

Facebook, 162–163–164–63
Filipino Amerasians, 153–54, 158
For Spacious Skies (Buck), 159
forced assimilation. *see* assimilation
Ford, Gerald, 140–41
France, 5–6, 150–51

Gellhorn, Martha, 215n.39
GEO magazine, 147–48
GI babies. *see* camptowns/
    camptown women
Gi-Wook Shin, 203n.10
Gonzaga University, 151, 152f
Great Britain, 5–6, 176n.7
Guardian, 158

hapa, 162–63, 219n.19
Hapa homeland tour, 163–64
Hefner, Hugh, 140
Hirai, Kowashi, 35–36
Hodge, John R., 17–18, 30–31
Holt, Harry/Holt adoption programs
    adoptee mortality in transit, 66, 67f,
        200n.137
    adoption advocates narratives, 60–63,
        198n.90, 198n.98

adoption statistics, 57–58, 97–98,
    201n.153
Buck's support of, 61–62, 73–74, 198–
    99n.108, 199n.110
child abuse/neglect among
    placements, 63–64
failed adoption rate, 63–64
financial support by, 66, 199n.110,
    200n.136
institutional care provided by, 99, 101f
ISS opposition to, 64–69, 80, 109–10,
    200n.137
legislative support of, 56–58, 62–63
media coverage of, 53–56, 56f,
    196n.58, 200n.137
motivations, 51–53, 52f, 54f, 80, 113–
    14, 161–62, 195n.38, 195–96n.48
overview, 46
parent testimonials, 57–58, 59f
placement by proxy, 53, 63–64, 113–
    14, 199n.116
procedures, 55, 63–64, 66,
    181–82n.47
procurement of children by, 66–72,
    72f, 201n.153
public support of, 55–58, 197n.71
re-homing of children, 119–20
reunion statistics, 166–67
years in operation, 205n.51
HR 808, 137–38

ilguk, ilminju, 79
immigration
    adopted children/American citizens,
        195–96n.48
    Amerasians legal definition, 153
    Asian women admitted as wives by
        origin/year, 172t
    Asian women ban/racial restrictions,
        6–7, 31–36, 38–39, 48, 175n.2,
        179–80nn.29–31, 191n.142
    Filipino Amerasians, 153–54, 158
    fourth preference status, 195–96n.48
    Japanese *vs.* Korean brides statistics,
        6–7, 33–35, 38–39, 180n.32,
        192n.170
    Korean military/war brides, 31–38,
        190n.131
    legislation governing, 6–7, 31–34,
        171t, 173t, 177n.7, 177–78n.11,
        179n.30

Index

legislative reform, 139, 145, 147–49, 157–58

by marriage, 157, 219n.32

Nisei military brides, 35–38, 191n.142

non-quota status, 31–33, 38–39, 151–53, 180n.31

of pregnant women, 36

sponsorships, 151–53

spouses of US citizens, 180n.31

statistics, 179n.30, 180n.32

Immigration and Nationality Act of 1924, 31–33, 47, 171*t*

Immigration and Nationality Act of 1965, xvii, 137–38, 175n.2, 209n.10

Indiana Department of Public Welfare, 64

integrationist movement. *see also* International Social Services (ISS)

American-oriented culture effects on, 99–102, 101*f*, 102*f*, 103*f*, 208n.143

assimilation, 99–103, 101*f*, 208n.143, 208n.151

ECLAIR in, 13–14, 78, 88–92, 94, 96–99, 106, 205n.66

education of mixed race Koreans, 86, 88–91, 89*f*, 94, 99, 105, 205n.66

Foster Care Family program, 87

ISS in, 85–87, 95–96, 205n.47, 205n.51

KAVA Resolution on Children with Racially Mixed Parentage, 87–88

Korean Association of Voluntary Agencies (KAVA), 86, 87–88, 92–93, 205n.51

motivations, 90–91

Nixon Doctrine effects on, 102–5

Pearl S. Buck Foundation, 61, 92–99, 113–14, 147–48, 208n.140

prejudicial behavior effects, 104–6

International Korean Adoptee Association (IKAA), 162–63

International Social Services (ISS)

adoption advocacy by, 71–73

adoption case files, 12

adoption motivations, 112–13

adoption procedure, 109–10

adoption statistics, 113

assessment of camptowns by, 80–82, 83–85

ECLAIR, 13–14, 78, 88–92, 94, 96–99, 106, 205n.66

Foster Care Family program, 87

in immigration policy reform, 78

in integrationist movement, 85–87, 95–96, 205n.47, 205n.51

motivations, 113–14

opposition to Holt program, 64–69, 80, 109–10, 200n.137

opposition to Pearl S. Buck Foundation, 94, 95–97

placement of full Korean children, 112–13

public acceptance/mixed race Koreans, 87–88, 94

interracial adoption. *see* adoption

interracial intimacy. *see also* camptowns/ camptown women

authorized marriages, 34–38, 157, 190n.130, 190n.131

authorized marriages/pregnant women, 36, 190n.130

on base, 25–27, 27*f*, 28*f*, 29*f*

casual dating vilification, 25, 26*f*

comfort women systems, 39

contact tracing, 23, 25, 187n.72

culture of acceptance, 25–27

discouraging of marriages, 40–42, 48–49, 157, 194n.24

impacts on children of, 42

military housing/garrisoning, 30–31, 32*f*

off-base housing, 34–35

penalties for violations, 23–25, 27

perceptions of Japanese women, 31–36, 37*f*

perceptions of Korean women, 16–17, 18–19, 19*f*, 20*f*, 21–22, 25, 36–38, 40–41, 68–69, 192n.170

reassignment policy, 35, 41, 48–49, 165

regulations governing, 6–7, 17–18, 22–23, 179–80nn.29–31

unauthorized marriages, xvii–xviii, 36–38, 40, 48–49, 175n.1

by unit commanders, 25–27

VD colored *vs.* white rates of, 30–31

VD control regime, 12–13, 21–30, 24*f*

VD education, 23–27, 187n.72

VD screening, 21–23, 40, 192n.160

VD statistics, 21–22, 23–25, 27, 30, 40

intimacy. *see* interracial intimacy

intimate Cold War, 12

(238) Index

Japan. *see* Occupied Japan
Japanese American Citizens League, 31–33, 191n.142
Ji-Yeon Yuh, 208n.143
Joint Legislative Committee on Matrimonial and Family Laws, 73–74
Judiciary Committee report, 58

Keane, Alfred V., 136, 139, 145–48, 151, 208n.151, 216n.62
Keller, David, 41, 42f
Keller, John, 137–38, 147–48
Kim, George, 36–38
Kim, Jaisook, 38
Kim, Jeong Ja, 60–61, 84
Kim, Jina, 218n.9
Kim, Katherine, 162–64, 165–69
Kim, Minyoung, 163–64
Kim, Soon Ja, 48–49
kimchi, 120–21, 211n.58
kŏmdungi, 82–83, 204n.29
Korea
  adoption of children by foreigners, 51
  authorized marriages/pregnant women, 36, 190n.130
  birthright citizenship in, 48, 205–6n.67
  Child Placement Service (CPS), 51, 91, 92–93, 95–102, 205n.51
  Christianity narratives regarding, 61, 195n.38
  DNA testing in, 164–69, 219n.34
  education of mixed race Koreans in, 86, 88–91, 89f, 94, 99, 105, 205n.66
  enmity against American soldiers, 18–19
  ethnic nationalism/racism in, 47, 69, 73–74, 79, 106, 203n.10, 203n.11
  familial relations/colonial policy, 5–7, 18–19, 179–80nn.29–31
  foreign aid reliance, 85–86, 96–97, 205n.47
  government inauguration 1948, 27
  grade school exclusion policies, 205n.66
  institutional care in, 88–89, 88f, 99, 101f, 141–42
  integrationist movement, 13–14, 78–79, 85–106, 208n.140

KAVA Resolution on Children with Racially Mixed Parentage, 87–88
Korean Association of Voluntary Agencies (KAVA), 86, 87–88, 92–93, 205n.51
Korean Social Service (KSS), 95–96
Ministry of Health and Social Affairs, 51, 73–74, 91, 96–97, 106, 210n.17
mixed race Koreans statistics, 80–81, 93–94, 98–99, 144, 149, 216n.62, 216n.68
motivations, 27–30
public acceptance/mixed race Koreans, 47, 69, 73–74, 77, 87, 94, 104–6, 141–42
social welfare budget, 85–86, 96–98, 205n.47
South Korean Economic Planning Board, 96–97
as US capitalism model, 30
as US democracy model, 61–62, 194–95n.36
US dollar donation requests, 194–95n.36, 195n.38
US military presence in, 1, 17–18, 27–30, 39, 176n.3, 185n.18
USAMGIK rule of, 18–31, 185n.18
Korean adoptee (KAD) networks, 162–64, 219n.19
Korean War
  Amerasian portrayal, 3–4
  anti-Asian violence as US imperialism, 4, 14–15, 76, 110–11, 178n.16, 209n.3
  armistice agreement, 41
  atrocities, 11, 178–79n.17, 183–84n.62
  as forgotten/never known war, 11, 183–84nn.61–62
  legacy of, 11–12, 184n.64
  statistics, 178–79n.17
"Koreans and Camptowns" conference, 164, 219n.24
"Koreans and Camptowns" page, 162–64
Koronel, Hilda, 153–54
Koshiro, Yukiko, 176n.7

lactose intolerance, 115–16, 119–20
Lea, Patricia, 50–51
Lee Chun Ja, 44–46
Lehman, William, 150–51

Index

Levittown (Occupied Japan), 31
Liem, Deann Borshay, 164, 167*f*, 209n.3,
219n.24
Life magazine, 53–55
Los Angeles Times, 47–48, 50–51
Luce, Henry, 7–8

MacArthur, Douglas, 178–79n.17
maladaptive coping, 125–26, 160
Mang Chung Hi, xvii–xviii, 38
Martindale, Walter, 149
Mayo, Leonard, 194–95n.36
McCain, John, 155–56
McCarran-Walter Act (Immigration and
Nationality Act of 1952), A1T1*t*,
38–39, 48, 180n.31, 191n.142,
195–96n.48, 209n.10
McKinney, Stewart B., 149
milk sensitivity, 115–16
miscegenation laws, 5–6, 33–34, 121–22
Miss Saigon, 215n.40
Mixed Korean: Our Stories (Kim et al),
168–69, 168*f*
mixed race Koreans. *see also* Amerasians;
assimilation; Eurasians
adoption of generally, 3–6, 7–10,
42–43, 47–48, 66–72, 178n.16,
180n.35, 201n.153
birth family search, 161–69, 219n.19,
219n.24
diasporic subjectivity, 159–60, 218n.9
education of in Korea, 86, 88–91, 89*f*,
94, 99, 105, 205n.66
in Korea, statistics, 80–81, 93–94, 98–
99, 144, 149, 216n.62, 216n.68
lived experiences, 8, 10, 14–15, 55–56,
56*f*, 60–61, 79–80, 109–11, 136,
181n.44, 181n.45, 181–82n.47,
198n.98, 209n.3
portrayal of by communists, 4–5
portrayal of by US, 2–6, 177–78n.11
prejudicial behaviors towards, 121–24,
123*f*, 136, 142–43, 144–45, 147–48
problem of the mixed blood child, 44–
45, 138–39, 193n.5
public acceptance of, 47, 69, 73–74,
77, 87, 94, 104–6, 141–42, 149–50
as refugees, 177–78n.11
reunions, 166–67
socialization in abuse of, 131

South Korean narratives, 60–61
Vietnamese *vs*. Koreans, 10–11, 15,
149, 216n.68
Moon, Seungsook, 175–76n.6
Morinaka, Masaru Mac, 36–38
Morse, Wayne, 56–57
Mrazek, Robert, 155–56

National Catholic Welfare Committee,
205n.51
National Venereal Disease Center, 21–22
Nelson, Kim Park, 209–10n.11
Neuberger, Richard, 56–57, 60, 73–74,
202n.169
New York Times, 61, 73–74
Nixon Doctrine, 102–3
No Gun Ri massacre, 11, 178–79n.17,
183–84n.62

oatmeal, 116, 210n.32
Occupied Germany, 176n.7
Occupied Japan
adoption of children from, 9, 64–65
authorized marriages in, 34–36,
190n.130
citizenship, children of foreign
women/US servicemen, 42, 176n.7
comfort stations in, 17–18, 30
military housing/garrisoning,
30–31, 33*f*
perceptions of Japanese
women, 31–36
pregnant women removal from, 36
prostitution outlawed in, 186n.51
as US capitalism model, 30
VD control regime, 21
VD rates in, 30
Operation Babylift, 15, 53–55, 138–44,
149, 196n.58, 214–15nn.37–38,
215nn.39–40
Opportunity Center, 99
Orderly Departure Program (ODP), 149,
155–56, 177–78n.11, 216n.68
Ordinance No. 72, 21
Orientalism, 8–9, 182n.50
Oropesa, Elizabeth, 153–54
Other Sheep, 51–53
Ott, Wendy Kay, 64

Pacific Stars and Stripes, 95

Palms, William, 36
pass privileges, 23–25, 24f
Pearl S. Buck Foundation, 61, 92–99,
113–14, 147–48, 208n.140, 216n.62
Philippine Heritage Federation, 153
Pierce, Robert, 51–53
plastic reconstructive surgery,
110, 209n.3
portrayals/perceptions
adoption advocates narratives, 60–
63, 73–76, 92–93, 159, 198n.90,
198n.98, 202n.169, 204n.21
of camptowns/camptown women, 12–
13, 128–32
of Filipino Amerasians, 154
of Japanese women, 31–36, 37f
of Korean mothers, 44–46, 71–72, 81
during Korean War, 3–4
Korean women, 16–17, 18–19, 19f,
20f, 21–22, 25, 36–38, 40–41, 68–
69, 192n.170
media coverage in, 47–48, 50–51, 55,
60, 61, 93–94, 95, 144–45, 147–48,
194–95n.36, 204n.21
of mixed race Koreans, 60–63, 73–76,
77–79, 93–94, 144–45, 159–60,
198n.90, 198n.98, 202n.169,
204n.21, 218n.9
Operation Babylift, 138–44, 149–50,
213n.3, 215nn.39–40
public acceptance/mixed race Koreans,
47, 69, 73–74, 77, 87, 94, 104–6,
141–42, 149–50
Private Law 475 of 1955, 53
Public Act No. 7, 22–23
Public Law
13, 22–23
213 of 1947, 31–36, 171t, 175n.3,
179n.30
253 of 1959, 74, 173t
301 of 1961, 75–76, 78, 80, 173t
316 of 1957, 62–63, 73, 74, 173t
648 of 1960, 74, 173t
717 of 1950, 38–39, 171t, 180n.31,
191n.142
Pullman, James L., 97–98

Quakers, 142

Raynor, Paul, 47–48
Reagan, Ronald, 137–38, 137f

Refugee Relief Act of 1953, 46–47,
53–59, 73, 173t, 177–78n.11, 195–
96n.48, 202n.172
Rhee, Syngman, 73–74, 79, 185n.18,
202n.172, 203n.10
Ridge, Thomas, 155–56
Robson, Irene, 50–51
Rossow, Nicholas, xvii–xviii, 38,
175n.1
Rounds, Linda Papi, 168–69

S. 3198, 137–38
Said, Edward, 182n.50
Sams, Crawford F., 16
Sasebo Replacement Depot, 40
Sato, Etsuko, 36
Schroeder, Pat, 150–51
Seoul Sanitarium and Hospital
Orphanage, 49, 50–51
Seventh Day Adventist Mission, 49, 97–
98, 121–22, 205n.51
Shade, John, 147–48, 216n.62
Siegel-Dalton, Bella, 164–66
Smith, Milton A., 16–17
Smolan, Nick, 204n.21
Somewhere Between, 162–63
Sook Kyung Ko, 41, 42f
South Korea. see Korea
sponsorships, 97–98, 101–2, 151–53
St. Joseph County Department of
Welfare, 64
St. Vincent's Home for Amerasians, 145–
48, 147f, 151, 208n.151
Subcommittee on Immigration and
Naturalization, 74
sugar sensitivity, 115–16, 119–20

Tahk, Youn Taek, 97–98
tanil minjok, 79
325KARMA, 165–69, 219n.32
Time magazine, 53–55, 93, 147–48
Together at Last: Stories of Adoption and
Reunion in the Age of DNA, 168–69
Tonga Ilbo, 60–61
transnational adoption. see adoption

United Presbyterian Mission, 77–78, 91
United States
abandonment of Korean wives/
children, 48–49, 82, 84, 87–88,
194n.24

anti-Asian violence as US imperialism, 4, 14–15, 76, 110–11, 159–60, 178n.16, 209n.3, 218n.9
  foreign policy impacts, 79–80, 84–85, 102–4
  identity/ideologies in, 138–41, 149–51, 213n.3
  motivations, 2, 18, 23, 27–30, 58, 177n.10
  prejudicial behaviors in, 121–24

Venereal Disease Control Council, 23
Venereal Disease Rehabilitation Center, 23–25, 27–30
venereal disease (VD). *see also* camptowns/camptown women; interracial intimacy
  colored *vs.* white rates of, 30–31

control regime, 12–13, 21–30, 24*f*
  education, 23–27, 187n.72
  screening, 21–23, 40, 192n.160
  statistics, 21–22, 23–25, 27, 30, 40
Vietnam War, 3–4, 7–8, 10–11, 15, 102–3, 137–39, 144–45, 213n.3, 215nn.39–40

War Brides Act of 1945, 31–36, 171*t*, 175n.3, 179n.30, 180n.31
Welcome House, 61, 92–99, 113–14
World Vision, 51–55
World Vision Reception Center, 53, 200n.136

yanggongju/yanggalbo, 18–19, 19*f*
Yongsan Garrison, 17–18
You Chan Yang, 73–74

The manufacturer's authorised representative in the EU for product safety is Oxford University Press España S.A. of El Parque Empresarial San Fernando de Henares, Avenida de Castilla, 2 – 28830 Madrid (www.oup.es/en or product.safety@oup.com). OUP España S.A. also acts as importer into Spain of products made by the manufacturer.

Printed in the USA/Agawam, MA
April 4, 2025

885391.008